Michael Matthews spent more than 20 years as a police officer in London. He is a keen traveller, writer and photographer and has had articles and photographs published in numerous books, newspapers and magazines. He has appeared on radio and television in the UK, USA and Canada commenting on crime and issues around policing. *The Riots* is his second book. His first, *We Are The Cops*, was a collection of real-life stories from US police officers and was a Kindle Non-Fiction number 1 bestseller. He has vast knowledge of American policing and continues to spend time working with US police departments. Michael likes eating lobster and watching ballet (yes, ballet). He now lives in Canada.

GW00480583

THE RIOTS

Michael Matthews

SILVERTAIL BOOKS • *London*

First published in Great Britain by Silvertail Books in 2016
www.silvertailbooks.com
Copyright © Michael Matthews

1

The right of Michael Matthews to be identified as the author
of this work has been asserted in accordance
with the Copyright, Design and Patents Act 1988

ISBN 978-1-909269-51-4

To my father Robert, PC 248H/548Q/CO678,
who held the line more than once in the 1960s

'We always win, don't we? We always win because we're the Old Bill and we've got good on our side. But during those nights, I remember thinking: Fuck me, there's potential for this to go very, very wrong. We've lost control. We could actually lose this.'

Metropolitan Police riot officer

Introduction to the 2021 edition: Ten Years Later

This new edition of *The Riots* marks ten years since nationwide rioting brought fire, destruction and death to the streets of cities and towns across England, following the police shooting in London of Mark Duggan. Those six appalling days and night ended livelihoods, careers and, most tragically of all, the lives of five people. In addition, many were injured, including almost two hundred police officers.

Since 2011, parts of the UK have suffered further riots. These more recent disturbances have occurred for often all too familiar reasons but also for reasons that on the surface seem to have little – if anything – to do with the UK.

Though many thousands of miles away, killings of black Americans by US police – Eric Garner in New York, George Floyd in Minneapolis, Michael Brown in Ferguson, to name just three – have dominated headlines for several years. One of the reactions to these deaths was the emergence of movements such as Black Lives Matter, which quickly took the lead in demonstrations against alleged police brutality. Black Lives Matter – the call, as well as the organisation – quickly spread from America, to around the world, including the UK.

Police shootings on the streets of the UK are extremely rare but the shootings and killings in America – and the response to them – became our own. Demonstrations were held in solidarity with those in America, and the events in the US became a reason to protest against police in the UK.

George Floyd's murder by Minneapolis police officer Derek Chauvin led to protests in London and elsewhere in the UK, and some turned violent. Never mind that his murder happened on a street corner in a mid-west American city.

It seems that now more than ever police are viewed as being the same everywhere, no matter which country or department you are in. But this isn't correct, and I should know. I spent over 20 years with the Metropolitan Police in London and worked during the 2011 riots. I have also spent the past 20 years regularly working and patrolling with police departments all across the United States (as well as other countries). I'll concede that the nature of policing, no matter where you are, can be comparable (the job and role often dictates it as such), but it's also accurate to state that policing in the UK and US can be very different. Though common ground is often found, the culture and attitudes between these nations can sometimes be as wide as the Atlantic. Take police shootings. Officers in the United States kill around 1,000 people a year – mostly in what is classified as 'Justifiable Homicides'. By comparison, the number of people shot and killed annually by police in the UK is in the low single figures. In fact, there are entire years where no one is shot and kill by the police in the UK – something that we as a nation should recognise and applaud.

That there is racism and inequality in society is without doubt. People often counter 'Black Lives Matter' with 'All Lives Matter', but you only need to spend a small amount of time in poor neighbourhoods – particularly in parts of America – to see that some lives clearly matter less than others. But – and this, for me, is a key point – not to the police (notwithstanding the actions of some individual officers). Judging by my own decades of experience, there can be few in public service who work as closely and as uniquely with communities as the police. I often see officers caring far more for the people they have sworn to protect, than many other public servants. That officers can and do get it wrong at times – whether for criminal, accidental or negligent reasons – shouldn't be ignored, but it also shouldn't completely distract from the huge positives that policing brings.

There have been calls to defund – and even *disband* – the police. The arguments are easily understood, and, on paper at least, seem worthy; take money away from police departments and give it to community and social programs, which will hopefully lead to improved conditions, better lives, less crime, and thereby less need for police, and fewer negative encounters.

I absolutely agree that more funds need to be directed to schools, neighbourhoods, social programs, employment and housing. I've spent years in some of the worst, most deprived, dangerous and hopeless areas in the US, including Detroit, Chicago, Baltimore and L.A., and I worked in inner city neighbourhoods in London – so I understand the argument. But the 'defund' message to me seems back-to-front. If you take money from police departments (as has actually happened recently to the LAPD and NYPD, as well as others), they will have fewer resources to combat crime. Crime, including homicides, will naturally rise – in fact we are already seeing this, with crime and homicides up substantially in many cities in America as well as the UK. By the time the positives of that transferring of funds to social programs begins to take effect (and it could take years), crime will have already gotten far worse, meaning that everyone is now playing catch-up. What do you do? Defund the police further? The thing to do it to fund those programs with money from elsewhere – not with police budgets. Only then, once – and if – crime starts to drop, and peoples lives start to get better, can you think about defunding the police. As an illustration of where things could be heading, a man in Minneapolis recently sued the city for inadequate policing.

But of course for some the plan and goal is simply to attack the police. Some of those who claim that *defund the police* doesn't mean *disband the police* are not being honest. There are those who simply hate the police, and nothing is ever going to change that. It may start with defunding but for some, ultimately the goal is to disband police completely and also to shut down prisons (I've seen these plans and objectives in written 'manifestoes'). Personally, I cannot imagine a utopia where no police or prisons would be a workable solution to the complicated world we live in, though I would happy to be proven wrong.

There must never be room for bad policing or bad cops but the fact is, most people want police; they want *good* police, of course, but they still want police. In some of the most deprived neighbourhoods and dangerous cities that I've visited in the US, locals have told me repeatedly that they want more police, not less. If you lived surrounded by gangs, crime and gunfire, wouldn't you? These are the people we should be listening to – the ones who live with crime and its terrible consequences every day.

Calls for police reforms are all very well and I'm sure most if not all police officers would support improvements to the service they provide, but I don't believe police reforms alone will change much. Policing is policing. What officers' face in their day-to-day can often be unexpected and violent, and this sometimes leads to tragic outcomes. We can – and should – work to minimise these outcomes but I doubt we'll ever eradicate them completely.

Reforms are needed but if we truly want change I believe these should be social and political reforms. The police are the end of the line. What happens before things reach the police, and addressing those issues – poverty, education, racism, inequality, jobs, hope – is key. But it is not the job of the police to make these changes, and they don't have the ability to make them happen anyway. Yes, there will always be crime, there will always be criminals and there will always be people who want to throw bricks and bottles at the police; but politicians need to seriously address these social issues, because repeatedly pushing the police forward to deal with their failures is not a solution.

Equally important, the agenda-driven lies, half-truths and fact twisting of some politicians, groups, individuals and media outlets, against law enforcement, needs to cease; the very real social damage it causes has caused lives to be lost.

Ten years ago, things were different here. Despite being legally sound, the shooting of Mark Duggan in 2011 led to six days of rioting. But that was it. When it was done, it was pretty much done. There was little noise afterwards. Nothing really changed.

The more recent media spotlights on police killings in America have altered that. The next time we see a 'controversial' police shooting or death in the UK, what will the response from the public, the police, politicians and protest groups be? I'd say look towards America for the answer. Look towards America for the new normal.

Michael Matthews
June 2021

Introduction

On Thursday 4th August 2011, Mark Duggan, a 29-year-old from Tottenham, north London, went to Leyton in east London to collect a gun from drug dealer called Kevin Hutchinson-Foster. The gun was a BBM Bruni Model 92 – a blank-firing replica of a Beretta 92. But this replica had been converted and was now capable of firing live rounds.

Just after 6pm, minutes after collecting the gun, Duggan was travelling in a mini cab along Ferry Lane in Tottenham Hale, north London. Unknown to Duggan, police had been carrying out surveillance on him, and the cab, a silver Toyota Estima people carrier, was being followed by members of SCD11 – Operation Trident, the Metropolitan Police's Specialist Crime Directorate's gang and gun crime unit. They were supported by officers from the Met's Specialist Firearms Command, CO19, and all travelled in unmarked cars.

Knowing Duggan was now armed, the police vehicles put in a 'hard stop' on the cab, surrounding it and forcing it to come to a halt. As they did so, Duggan, who was sitting in the back of the cab, opened the door and got out. An officer from CO19, believing that Duggan was holding the gun and fearing for his own life and those of his colleagues, opened fire with a Heckler and Koch MP5 semi-automatic carbine, the type of weapon you sometimes see officers carrying at Heathrow Airport or outside Downing Street. The officer fired two bullets. One hit Duggan in the arm, the other in the chest.

Duggan was obviously seriously injured and police officers immediately started carrying out first aid on him. Paramedics from the London Ambulance Service along with medical staff and crew from the Helicopter Emergency Medical Service – HEMS

– arrived to help, but his injuries were too serious for him to be saved, and at 6.41pm Mark Duggan was pronounced dead.

The reasons for Mark Duggan having the gun are a matter of dispute. It has been alleged that Duggan was a drug dealer and gang member and that he intended to carry out a shooting in revenge for the murder of his 23-year-old cousin, Kelvin Easton, who was stabbed to death at an east London nightclub in Mile End a few months previously. But this has never been proved.

Following a protest outside Tottenham police station on 6th August 2011 – two days after Mark Duggan was shot – a crowd turned on the police, attacking them and setting two police cars on fire. This was the start of what would become five days of the worst rioting that the country had seen in many years. Across England, hundreds of police officers were injured, thousands of people were arrested and five died – all just a year before the 2012 London Olympics. During the rioting, police resources were so dangerously stretched that there were genuine fears that the country would be lost, with some even calling for the army to be deployed.

Shootings by police are, thankfully, a very rare event in the UK. Entire years can pass without a single death from police firearms (compare this with the United States, where cops kill hundreds of people every year). Although the shooting of Mark Duggan is often cited as the reason for the rioting, other commentators have laid the blame on the police, stating that the relations between police and the young had deteriorated for reasons such as excessive use of 'stop and search' – something that has been a contentious issues for decades. Others have blamed social issues, and commented on a lack of opportunities, unemployment and poverty. Perhaps all these reasons played a part or, as others have claimed, perhaps it was simply bad people wanting to do bad things and hoping they would get away with it.

Regardless of what caused the troubles, it is significant that they began in Tottenham. This is an area that has seen tension between the police and the local community for decades. Broadwater Farm, also known as 'The Farm', is a large, late 1960s housing estate in Tottenham with close to 4,000 residents, and it was the site of the dreadful riots of October 1985, which with the 2011 riots were inevitably compared. The *Independent* newspaper even ran a cartoon, depicting police riot officers standing by a burning number '1985' double decker bus, showing the destination 'Broadwater Farm' and with the movie title 'Back to the Future' emblazoned across the advertising panel on its side.

The fact that the riots started in Tottenham added an element of anxiety for all involved in dealing with the violence, especially the police, because of the horrific murder of PC Keith Blakelock on 6th October 1985. While trying to protect fire fighters who were under attack from rioters in Broadwater Farm, PC Blakelock was hacked to death by a mob of rioters in a stairwell on the estate. Every police officer knows Keith Blakelock's name, and they know every detail of his murder.

I spent a number of years as a Level 2 public order trained officer and worked at many major events and demonstrations, including a few that went sideways. Things can change very quickly from standing around chatting with seemingly friendly demonstrators to suddenly having to raise your riot shield to protect yourself from falling missiles. It can be a frightening experience, especially when you remember that you have to follow the rules and act within the law whereas those attacking you have no such restrictions or concerns. No police officer is ever looking to kill a rioter, but some rioters look to kill police officers.

Whenever I found myself fully kitted up with my protective riot uniform and equipment and entering a violent situation,

Keith Blakelock's name was always at the front of my mind. His death will always stand as a reminder of just how dangerous being a police officer in a riot can be. It didn't change my attitude to the role of being a public order officer but it was something I was always conscious of whenever I pulled on my riot helmet. And I was not alone with those thoughts. Many other officers, including some who appear in this book, felt the same.

Remarkably, even though it was 26 years later, some officers on the streets during the 2011 riots were also on duty during the Broadwater Farm disturbances. One officer told me how he heard the news of Keith Blakelock's murder in 1985 on his car radio while driving home after his shift. He pulled over and wept. Years later he saw PC Blakelock's bloodied overalls at the Black Museum (now called the Crime Museum, and only open to serving police officers and staff) at New Scotland Yard.

One chief inspector working at Tottenham during the 2011 riots was a young constable during the riots of 1985. A few hours before Keith Blakelock was killed, he remembered how the situation had become so bad that he was worried an officer would be murdered. During the first night of the 2011 riots, he felt those same fears.

So it was against that terrible history that rioting in Tottenham broke out once more. The events might have been separated by more than a quarter of a century, but the 1985 Broadwater Farm riots were a constant reminder to every police officer of just how bad things could get.

1700 hrs

Tottenham

Two days had passed since Mark Duggan was shot dead by police on the streets of Tottenham, and outside the area's police station a demonstration had started. Duggan's family and around 120 protestors were calling for 'answers' and 'justice'. A line of police officers had been deployed outside the police station to protect the building. The situation was calm but as officers spoke with demonstrators, the mood changed. No one knows exactly why. It has been alleged that the cause was an incident involving a 16-year-old girl. Some say she threw something at the police. Others claim the police attacked her first. Either way, the crowd suddenly turned, and what was a vocal but peaceful demonstration and vigil quickly deteriorated into violence. There was pushing and shoving, and people started throwing bottles at officers in regular beat uniform. Then several marked police cars parked in the road nearby were rolled away and set alight, creating burning barriers across the street.

Just like that, the riots had begun.

Alan had been on duty when Mark Duggan was shot, and he was aware that a protest would be going ahead at Tottenham on the Saturday. As a constable with eight years experience, two of which were with the Territorial Support Group (TSG), he understood the potential for trouble that the shooting presented. He also had a dentist's appointment on Monday and figured that if things did turn violent he would be suffering with toothache a little longer.

Early that evening, Alan and the rest of his TSG unit – a total of 21 officers, made up of one inspector, three sergeants and 18 PCs, travelling in three vans – were called out to Merton in south

London to search for a knife used in a recent stabbing. At 8pm, however, they were told to redeploy to Tottenham. As they made their way, they heard over the police radio that an IRV – a police car – was on fire. They were told to ensure that they were 'kitted up' – dressed in their full riot equipment of flameproof overalls, riot helmets, gloves and armour – before arriving.

While Alan's unit was in Clapham, another was already in north London. This second TSG unit had been called in urgently to help local officers with the disturbance outside Tottenham police station, where things were starting to get dangerously out of hand. Local officers and the TSG unit were outnumbered and under sustained attack as they fought to defend the police station. Alan's unit were told to make their way to Tottenham 'on the hurry-up'.

As they drove, the carrier's driver tuned the police radio to the local channel so that they could listen to the local officers. The first words they heard made the officers' blood run cold.

'URGENT ASSISTANCE! URGENT ASSISTANCE! WE ARE UNDER ATTACK!'

Every police officer knows what it means to call 'Urgent Assistance' over a radio: your life or those of others is in danger. In an entire career a police officer may only hear those two words on a handful of occasions, sometimes never, even if they stay in the job for 30 years. And no police officer ever cries wolf with 'Urgent Assistance'. For that reason, Alan and the other officers in his TSG knew how serious the situation was. The noises coming from the radio were chilling: officers who truly believed they were in danger of being killed or seriously hurt were desperately calling for help as shouts and screams could be heard in the background.

Some newer officers on the carrier questioned whether it was really necessary to get fully kitted up in their riot gear, wondering if they should just put on the overalls and leave the rest – their helmets and shields – in the van. Alan and the other more experienced officers told them in no uncertain terms that if police cars are burning in the streets then full kit was their only option.

As they continued on their way to Tottenham, another unusual order came through – one that Alan had never heard given before: 'Grills down on the carriers! Come in with your grills down!'

'Dropping the grills' meant that they were to enter Tottenham with the heavy, black, latticed metal grill dropped down over the front windscreen, a protective measure reserved for serious disorder. The driver reached up and pulled the lever above his head. There was a screeching sound and followed by the noise of metal sliding down and clanging into position. The grills now covered and protected the windscreen and the mood in the carrier immediately changed. The officers became quieter, more serious.

Their rendezvous point (RVP) had been given as Tottenham police station but as the carriers arrived Alan saw a mass of some 600 or 700 people further up Tottenham High Road, many of whom had scarves pulled over their faces and hoods on their heads. The other TSG unit had already placed a cordon across the street but they were just a handful of officers in riot gear stretched out across the road. A Level 2 unit had joined them, but they still looked hopelessly outnumbered – 40 or so officers facing hundreds of demonstrators.

Alan's unit stepped out of their carrier to form up, with each of the three carrier-loads of officers creating a line across the road. The PSU inspector stood at the front of the first line, along with that carrier's sergeant. The second line of officers stood behind the first, with the third line at the rear, each with their own sergeant. They were well organised, well trained, professional and committed police officers with the best equipment available. But they were also just three lines of seven officers facing hundreds of people who clearly meant them harm.

Almost immediately they came under missile attack from the crowd. Bottles, bricks and rocks began to rain down on them, and the officers moved quickly to bolster the other TSG unit to ensure that the cordon was held across the street which would prevent the crowd reaching the police station. But the mob was becoming increasingly brazen and started to push towards the line of officers, who were at serious risk of being overwhelmed. It quickly became obvious that their only option was to go on the offensive. Alan's unit were told that they would be taking a junction on their right while, at the same time, the other unit would be pushing the crowd backwards along Tottenham High Road.

The order to go was given and both units simultaneously began to move on the crowd, which fell back slightly. The barrage of missiles continued to rain down on the officers, but they kept pushing forward against the mass of people.

Alan and his small unit turned into the junction to the right and began to clear it of protestors, forcing them further away from the area. But at the same time, another large crowd began to make their way towards the officers. During the original push, one officer from Alan's unit had managed to get himself separated from the rest of the group. He was at the end of a row and went only a couple of yards further forward than he should have, along the building line. Alan saw the separated officer and he and another officer from his unit immediately jumped forwards to bring him back to their line. But by moving forward so quickly, they opened up a small gap between themselves and the rest of their unit. This gap allowed some of the mob to creep in behind Alan and the two officers he was with. Now they were completely cut off.

Then Alan heard a noise behind him and as he turned around, he found himself facing three men, all dressed in dark clothes and partly hidden by the evening shadows. The men stared back at him. They looked nervous and agitated, angry and dangerous. As they stepped forward out of the shadows and into some light, Alan noticed they were each holding something in their hands. He recoiled in horror; the men were armed with machetes. Small knives would have been bad enough, but these huge bladed weapons were altogether different, not least because of what they represented: the murderous intent of the men carrying them. The men lifted the machetes, hacking at the air menacingly. Then they stepped closer, to attack the three officers.

Alan jumped back and raised his shield, drawing it against his body. The other officers had seen the machetes and they too brought their shields up to defend themselves. The three officers looked about desperately, for help or an escape route. But they were trapped. The men lunged forward and began to take quick, forceful swings with the blades, hacking down at the officers' small, round shields, bodies and helmets. The officers, now fighting for their lives, parried the blows with their shields, before moving to make themselves harder to strike. This wasn't protesting, this wasn't demonstrating, this wasn't even rioting – this was the attempted murder of three police officers.

They're trying to kill us, Alan thought. *They're actually trying to kill us.*

Then one of the officers pushed forward, holding up his personal issue fire extinguisher. He sprayed a burst of Halon gas at the faces of the armed men, who immediately retreated a couple of paces. Alan and the other officer, sensing an opportunity to gain the initiative, moved forward, holding their shields in front of their bodies and raising their batons above their heads, as if ready to strike down with them. With that, the three machete-wielding men turned and ran.

Alan's unit inspector stormed over to the three officers. 'If you lot don't fucking switch on, you'll end up as another Keith Blakelock!' he shouted.

By now, the other unit, only a few hundred metres away from Alan, was being overrun. They were in desperate need of more officers. Their inspector made the 'Urgent Assistance' call over the radio – it was something officers would hear time and time again today and for the next few days. Alan and his unit ran back to Tottenham High Road and bolstered their colleagues' line, which was stretched dangerously thin across the street. The level and intensity of missiles had increased dramatically and Alan found himself in the middle of a fully blown battle.

The ferocity of the attack was like nothing these officers had ever faced before and their line was in serious danger of breaking. If the rioting mob got through, the police station would be theirs. With a station full of civilian staff, equipment and even prisoners, the possible consequences were horrendous. There was little doubt that if they were given a chance, the rioters would set the place alight. Officers were beginning to wonder if baton rounds should be deployed, as a last resort. Although they had been used in Northern Ireland since 1973, baton rounds – sometimes called plastic or rubber bullets – had never been used on mainland Britain. Using them would change the police response to the disorder dramatically, raising it to a new level of violence that could, in turn, bring more violence in reply. In fact, as the trouble grew, and as a contingency, the Met would make them available, but they would never be used.

And so, for now, Alan and his colleagues carried on fighting with what they had. They were literally the front – and last – line of defence. If they were overwhelmed, no one would be coming to save them, and they all knew it.

Inspector Walpole arrived early for his shift at Hounslow police station. He was still buzzing from the previous evening, when he went with some friends to see Iron Maiden perform at the O2 Arena in London. He took the previous night off especially for the concert and had no idea what was going on in Tottenham. He was the night duty inspector, and now that he was back at work he needed to do the handover with the late turn inspector, to catch up on the day's events and take over any incidents that were still running or crime scenes that needed guarding. He gathered some paperwork and headed into the borough control room – the 'Grip and Pace' room. Trawling through the calls for police assistance that had come in during the day, he could see for himself how busy the earlier shifts had been. And there were, as always, calls that were still outstanding and unanswered.

As he went through the list on the computer screen, he briefly looked up at the large TV on the wall. As usual they were set to the rolling, 24-hour news channels. He saw that something was happening in Tottenham; people were gathered outside the police station, a demonstration, perhaps, but he thought nothing more of it – there was always something going on somewhere – and he returned to completing the handover with the previous team, keen to have it done before his own officers arrived for the start of the night shift. Being a Saturday night, they could expect a busy one, and no sooner had the handover been completed than Inspector Walpole had to rush out. There was a firearms call – a serious incident by anyone's standards – and he needed to get to it.

But Inspector Walpole's shift was about to go seriously sideways. Officers in the control room got the message first – the order for an immediate 'service mobilisation' from the IBO – the Integrated Borough Operations office, which deals with duties, shifts and resources, and to where requests from outside the borough were sent. Looking up at the TV screens, it was obvious what was happening. A 'service mobilisation' request was a huge indication of just how serious things had become in Tottenham. It meant that they needed to know how many Level 2 inspectors, sergeants and PCs the borough had available and ready to deploy.

With three levels of public order training, Level 2 officers were the most common and the most used. Level 1s were the TSG – considered the elite riot trained officers. Then came the Level 2s, like Inspector Walpole and his officers. These were usually regular officers who had volunteered for extra, enhanced riot training, and who had been issued with their own riot equipment. And then there was the Level 3s. They were the ones with the basic level of training that all officers received when they joined the police. Level 3s weren't issued any extra kit or equipment.

For Hounslow, the request for sergeants and PCs was normal but the request for inspectors wasn't. This was a further indication of how far things had gotten out of hand. The call had gone out: they were after everyone that they could get.

The IBO contacted Inspector Walpole, who was already at the scene of the firearms incident, and gave him his orders. First, he, along with a sergeant and seven PCs, needed to make their way to Feltham to collect their riot kit. Then they needed get over to Tottenham. Inspector Walpole had a choice: he could either ask for volunteers or he could pick the officers himself. He knew that he would have no problem finding volunteers but he also knew that if he made that request, his officers would start asking questions, and there wasn't time for that. So one sergeant and seven PCs were quickly chosen and all were ordered to make their way to Feltham.

Inspector Walpole was the last to arrive. He'd had a number of things to sort out with the rest of his shift before he could go, such as who he would be leaving behind to continue the regular policing in Hounslow. As he pulled into the station yard at Feltham, his sergeant and PCs were already standing around, getting their kit ready. He joined them and they boarded their carrier. After looking round to check everyone was strapped in, the driver switched on the blue lights, turned on the sirens and they made their way to north London, to the riots.

Inspector Walpole turned to look at his group of officers. Most were still young in service with little experience of serious public disorder, and there was anticipation and excitement among them. Their only fear was of not doing their job properly, even though they already knew about the 'Urgent Assistance' calls, and how dangerous it would be.

'This is real,' Inspector Walpole warned them. 'We'll be on the rioters' territory, so be careful.'

2300 hrs
Tottenham
The crowd ahead of Alan was getting more and more worked up. Missiles were raining down and masked thugs were jumping about in a frenzy. At the top of the street Alan could see a marked police car abandoned and burning out of control. The windows and paintwork were all gone and it was now nothing more than a metallic wreck with flames flaring in all directions.

The officers had been defending the police station for a good couple of hours, fighting almost continually in warm weather and in full riot kit. They were drained and dehydrated. Their physical condition was getting serious: they needed drinks or they would collapse.

One of the carrier drivers was called over by the unit inspector. 'I don't care what you do,' the driver was told. 'Get in that nick and get water, drinks, whatever you can.'

'Leave it with me Guv,' the officer said, and he jogged away, towards the police station.

A few minutes later he returned with arms full of Lucozade bottles and other drinks. The inspector stared at the booty and then looked at the officer in wonder.

'You don't want to know,' the officer said.

A decision was made that Alan's unit and the other unit would stay together and move up Tottenham High Road as one. Sending up just half of them wouldn't be enough.

The officers lined up and the order was given to begin moving forward, against the swelling numbers of the crowd. The frequency of missiles landing on them increased as the crowd responded to the advancing line of shields. The crowd was throwing anything they could get their hands on – bricks, bottles, drinks cans. At one point an enormous frozen fish had been flung through the air towards the officers, and it now lay half splattered on the charred tarmac, an icy eye popping out of its socket and its mouth wide open as if in shock. It was ridiculous.

Alan's line was ordered to continue moving. He lifted his round plastic shield above his head, covering himself from the hail of bricks and bottles, and took a step forward, and then another and another, building up the pace, forcing his way through the barrage. He felt good, as though his side was gaining momentum. Then, to his left, one of his colleagues – a female officer from his unit – fell to the ground, hit on the head by a litre-sized plastic bottle full of liquid. Alan watched in horror as the unconscious officer started to fit. A sergeant and two police medics quickly dragged her back from the frontline and did what they could to stabilise her, checking her neck and getting her into a more comfortable position. Rioters, seeing the fallen officer, roared and rushed towards her but a line of shields and batons appeared, blocking their path and forcing them back.

All around them were broken piles of glass and smashed bricks. Even with an injured officer on the ground and medics working to save her, the torrent of missiles continued to cascade down on them. Alan felt sick and angry at the sight of one of his own unit wounded on the ground, his anger magnified by the rioters' attempts to continue attacking her, their sheer savagery at the sight of an injured police officer. She was already being helped so Alan's best option was to keep moving and do his job. For all Alan knew she could be dying, and the rioters couldn't seem to care less. In fact they seemed to want to finish her off. It was sickening.

Alan knew these rioters were going to keep attacking, so he pushed forward once again, leaving the medics to do whatever they could for his injured colleague. All he could do for her was provide as much protection as he could, and hope she was okay.

As Inspector Walpole's small collection of officers drew closer to Tottenham, they found that more and more of the roads were blocked off. Tottenham High Road was ablaze – smoke and fire had consumed the area, and masked, hooded youths roamed the streets throwing objects at anything that moved. They had been using a satnav but in these streets it quickly became obsolete as it continually directed them into increasingly dangerous areas. In the end the officers were forced to find a way through the quieter back streets to get to where they needed to be.

No sooner would they reach the assigned RVP, than it would suddenly change again because of the activity of the rioters, and they would be forced to negotiate yet more streets, desperate to avoid the violence while at the same time trying to find a new meeting point. Finally they reached one, on a side street just off Tottenham High Road itself. The officers sat in their carrier waiting for other PSUs and their Bronze Commander, a chief inspector, to arrive. As they waited, there was a dull thump as something heavy hit the metal body of the carrier. Then there was another, and another. Inside, the officers realised what had happened: being so close to Tottenham High Road meant that they were close to the trouble, and a few of the rioters had stumbled upon the lone vehicle. They were now taking pot-shots at it.

Then another carrier arrived. It was the chief inspector with his 'runner' – an officer who was acting as his messenger, log-keeper and general assistant. There was no one else with them, just the two officers in a carrier. No one else arrived.

Despite the missiles that were starting to come down in increasing numbers, the chief inspector and his runner approached Inspector Walpole's carrier.

'No one else here?' the chief inspector asked.

Something hit the carrier: THUMP.

'No, just us,' Inspector Walpole told him.

The chief inspector nodded his head as if it were the answer he had been expecting to hear.

THUMP... THUMP... THUMP.

The chief inspector turned around and looked towards the junction. More rioters had spotted them and bottles, bricks and lumps of wood were all being thrown at the officers. Then the missiles stopped. The officers looked over and saw that the rioters were now charging towards them. The chief inspector and his runner leapt aboard Inspector Walpole's bus and the driver started the engine. But before they could drive away, the rioters surrounded them. The situation had developed rapidly from a few youths lobbing stuff at a police riot carrier, to a large mob intent on causing serious harm to officers trapped inside.

The driver had no choice – he revved the engine hard and then drove through the crowd, watching them move out of the way. The chief inspector's own vehicle was abandoned, left to the mercy of the rioters. The carrier was quickly set on fire and when it was found the next day, it was nothing more than a burnt out shell.

As they drove out of the junction, the Hounslow carrier was quickly caught in heavy traffic. Incredibly, despite the anarchy that had descended upon Tottenham, regular cars and buses were still on the streets. Perhaps they were people trying to get away or, more likely, they were people just going about their normal business with no idea of just how serious the situation around them had become. And as Inspector Walpole had seen for himself, it could develop even further with frightening speed – a quiet, untouched street could become the scene of intense rioting in moments.

As the carrier driver forced his way through the lines of cars and traffic, the chief inspector managed to contact other units and arranged for a new RVP. They needed to get there quickly, before that too was overrun.

Alan continued to move forward against the mob, forcing them further back. As they advanced, the junctions they were passing were quickly filled with Level 2 officers, who were moving in to try to stop the rioters from getting behind the frontline and cutting them off. The police had no intention of giving up the ground that they had taken.

Then things became even more serious, and lives of people other than police officers were put at risk. Ahead of Alan, he and the other officers watched as groups from within the rioters began to set fire to shops along the street. Above the shops were flats and, to Alan's horror, it quickly became apparent that they were still occupied. People began hanging out of windows screaming for help, terrified that they would be burnt alive in their own homes. But the rioters didn't seem to care. They gave no thought to the danger their arson was creating. Men, women and children were all screaming at the officers, begging to be rescued. With smoke and fire taking hold of the buildings, and rocks and bottles continuing to rain down on the officers, the situation was utterly desperate.

Alan turned to look for fire engines, and felt a surge of relief when he saw some behind their lines, their blue emergency lights bleeding into the smoke and flames that had engulfed the street. They needed to get the engines through immediately but the rioters were making it impossible. Unless the mob was pushed far enough back, the fire brigade wouldn't be able to reach the fires and they would only come under attack themselves.

The officers surged forward with fresh urgency, charging towards the crowds, with their shields held in front of them or above them, in a desperate bid to protect themselves from the volley of missiles so they could gain enough ground to let the fire engines through. Alan felt the impact of a rock or brick hitting his shield. Then he felt another slam into his legs. But he didn't slow down – pain was being countered by adrenaline. Then there was another and another. He looked up at the grey, smoky sky – it was filled with a rolling cascade of missiles tumbling down towards him and his fellow officers. A bottle smashed into his arm, and a rock hit his shoulder. The bombardment was continuous. He could feel missiles slamming into his body just as much as he could feel them landing against his shield. But he kept moving. Every hit sapped a little bit more energy from him, but he did not stop.

The officers took the next junction, the crowd running backwards, away from the advancing line. Then the officers dropped back a few steps as they were trained to do, before charging forward again as the crowd began to tentatively step forward, picking up previously thrown bricks and lumps of wood. They were pushed back to the next junction and the next, while the people in the flats continued screaming for help, screaming to be saved from the burning buildings. Eventually the crowd was pushed back far enough for the fire engines to advance and tackle the blaze and rescue the trapped residents. Even as they did this, missiles continued to fall down on them.

By now some of the crowd had managed to get into the side streets behind Alan's line but the Level 2 officers who had taken the junctions were able to deal with them, doing all they could to hold them back and prevent them from entering Tottenham High Road.

Ahead of him, Alan could see some of the rioters overrunning a small Turkish grocery shop, looting whatever they could take. The officers moved forward and the looters ran off further up the road, where they joined other rioters. Alan's unit stopped briefly and their inspector approached the shop owner, telling him that he needed to close up the shop. He told him that they – the police – would soon be moving forward again, against the looters and rioters, which meant that there would be no one to protect his business. But the owner explained that there was little he could do. There was no door on the premises, just shutters. It was a 24/7 shop, with large stalls of fruit and veg placed outside. It would all need clearing away before he could get the shutters down but clearing it all would be impossible without bringing in a van and there was no chance of that happening now. And so the man stood by his shop in an attempt to protect it himself. Before they left, he handed out some chocolate and very welcome bottles of water to the thirsty officers, thanking them all the same and wishing them luck.

The officers continued on. Ahead of them, further up on Tottenham High Road, a double-decker bus was fully ablaze. It was an enormous fireball – an inferno in a world which was otherwise darkness. Flames and smoke were billowing into the sky, rising far above the roofs of the three-storey buildings around it. The bus had been abandoned and was burning out of control, well on its way to being no more than a metal skeleton. The flames had forced their way out of the wretched vehicle, and into the surrounding space – the windows had long been shattered by the rioters or by the heat and power of the fire. Even the road below the bus was on fire and burning as, eerily, the bus's headlights continued to shine. Loud, aggressive popping sounds, explosions, hissing and metallic sounding screams erupted from it. The officers had to get past it quickly in case they were caught in a larger, more lethal explosion. They did and saw two police cars a little further on which had already been burnt out.

As well as the main crowd of rioters ahead of them, they also had to contend with others who suddenly appeared from small passages and alleys at their sides. Yet more rioters were darting out of shops and houses along the road, throwing missiles and attacking the police lines before disappearing again into the buildings. Alan kept pushing on with the rest of his unit, further up the High Road, forcing the rioters back, or else chasing them off into the side streets.

Eventually the officers reached Bruce Grove, where they were ordered to stop and hold their line. With the crowd pushed back, the continuous assault by missiles had started to lessen; it was now just the occasional brick or bottle, until eventually it stopped altogether. There was a welcome lull in the violence but Alan stood with his shield still held up ready, just in case. Around them and ahead of them was a thick bank of smoke, some of which had wrapped itself around their bodies, drifting creepily before settling in between the lines of officers.

There was a silence of sorts, although noise from other streets still travelled around, bouncing off the buildings. The gentle crackling and spitting of the fires was also evident but it was a slow sound which was calming, in a strange way. Then the moment of peace was over. Alan heard the distinct noise of a motorbike engine. Then there was another. Two motorbikes were roaring and revving behind the screen of smoke. The revs were deep – the sounds of high-powered engines – and then they came closer. The bikes were moving left to right, right to left, going back and forth through the bank of smoke, hidden behind its veil, not clearly seen but clearly heard. It was as though they were taunting the officers. Then the officers began to be able to make out the silhouettes of the bikes as they came closer to the edge of the smoke. The riders continued to rev their engines, moving back and forth across the street, intimidating the line of officers who were watching them intensely, wondering why they were there and what they were going to do.

'I think these boys could start shooting,' the officer standing next to Alan said.

Alan knew exactly what he meant. The bikes had no reason to be there. He stood perfectly still, listening to them closely, expecting them to open fire and expecting to get shot. It wasn't just paranoia; guns on these streets were a reality and hitmen often used motorbikes. It would be simple for the bikers to open fire, hidden behind the curtain of thick smoke, easily able to get away.

'Be ready,' a sergeant said. 'Something bad could be about to happen.'

The bikers revved their engines harder and harder but then, just like that, the bikes moved away and disappeared.

It was a moment of relief. Alan had already wondered how many people – members of the public and police officers – had been killed in the rioting. There had been so many injuries, so many fires, so much screaming for 'Urgent Assistance' over the radio, that he felt certain people must have died.

As the officers stood around, word reached them that Mounted Branch was to be deployed to bolster and support the foot officers. This was good news – everyone knew how effective police horses were – but as they waited, there was no sign of them and the officers were eventually ordered to move north, up the High Road, alone.

They continued past Bruce Grove rail station, turning right at the fork in the road, moving further up the High Road. There was fire and destruction the entire way up; the rioters had gone berserk. Ahead of them they could see a small Aldi supermarket on fire. Flames were rising up through the single storey building and out through the roof, which had partially collapsed. With the scale and ferocity of the fire forcing even the rioters to move away, Alan felt sure that things would now start to die down. The rioters had done enough damage now, surely?

But as his unit stepped closer towards the inferno, he quickly realised how wrong his assessment was. Far from becoming quieter, things now started to kick off even more intensely than before. He would later find out that BBC and Sky News crews had already come under attack and been pulled out by their organisations for their own safety.

The short shield advances that the officers had been repeatedly performing up the High Road with some success had, unfortunately, given the rioters a measure of the police. They had seen their numbers, their tactics and techniques, their abilities, and now they were more ready than ever to take them on with new strategies of their own. A line of Aldi shopping trolleys had been dragged across the road, creating a barrier. The rioters stood defiantly behind their barricade, goading the officers, throwing the usual assortment of bottles, bricks, paving slabs and abuse. Some waved sticks, knives, hammers and other weapons, mocking the officers and daring them to approach.

Alan looked at the scene ahead of him. What they needed, he thought, were horses to charge the rioters and go through the barricade, but there were none to be seen. Everyone was being stretched to the limit and Mounted Branch were no doubt already being run into the ground somewhere else.

Instead, the order came through that the officers were to charge the barricades themselves. Alan tightened his grip on the shield he was holding, pulled at the visor on his helmet to ensure it was fully down, and stared dead ahead at the masked mob waving their weapons menacingly at the officers. The police helicopter circled above, its rotor-blades hammering out a constant thumping of noise as a huge spotlight – its 'Nightsun' – shone down, flooding the scene and illuminating the missiles as they were flung through the air towards the lines of police.

'How's that dodgy tooth of yours?' Alan's sergeant suddenly asked, as they waited to advance.

'Painful,' Alan told him.

'Well, with a bit of luck you'll get a brick thrown at your face and that will sort it out for you.'

Alan looked at him, but before he had time for a witty retort of his own, the command was given to 'GO! GO! GO!'

Alan sprinted forward, listening to the reassuring shouts and urgent, encouraging screams from the officers around him who were also storming the barricade. They were determined but broken house bricks and other missiles pummelled them. The ferocity of the onslaught was too much and it quickly forced the officers back. As the police line began to retreat, the rioters moved forward to pick up the same bricks, to use and throw again. Then the officers charged forward once more, but again they received a heavy pounding. Bricks, bottles and lumps of broken concrete slammed into the officers, smashing against their bodies and legs. Alan was in pain all over and had lost count of how many times he had been hit. Waves of missiles came crashing through the air at them all at once and it was impossible to avoid every one. They weren't just running towards the barricade, they were also running towards hundreds of flying bricks. And then, on reaching the barricade of trolleys, more bricks were thrown at the officers at point blank range, over and over and over. The intensity was unlike anything Alan had ever experienced.

Alan's right shoulder exploded in pain. A huge chunk of masonry had been flung through the air and had hit him at full force. The impact made Alan drop to one knee. He reached down with his left hand and shield, touching the ground so as not to collapse completely. His shoulder was agony.

'Are you all right?' his sergeant asked, looking down at him, concerned.

'FUCK OFF!' Alan shouted at him instinctively. His adrenaline had taken over and he didn't want anyone to see that he was injured. He didn't want anyone telling him to leave the line. 'I'm fine!'

Alan got back on his feet. He lifted his shield with his left arm and battered away some more missiles. In truth, though, he knew that he had been hurt badly and he wondered just how much damage had been done. He was right handed, so his shield was held on his left arm but he held his baton in his right hand. He tried to lift it, but intense, almost electric pain shot through his arm and chest and back. If he needed to use his baton to defend himself or strike anyone he wouldn't be able to. He was effectively one-armed now. The shield on his left arm was the only defence – and only weapon – that he had.

Then the officers retreated once more, bombarded by yet more bricks. The continued assaults on the rioters' defences were beginning to feel pointless. Where were the horses? Where were the dogs, even? Something more was needed.

Peering over the rim of his shield, Alan watched the masked mob stepping up once more, throwing their bricks and bottles before scampering back behind their own lines to collect more objects to throw. Ahead of Alan were three pairs of officers holding long shields, with Alan and the rest of the short shield officers behind them. Looking towards the crowd, he noticed one man moving through the mob, some of who had separated to give him space. The man was carrying a large, glass bottle with a rag dangling from the neck – a petrol bomb.

Alan called it out, warning the other officers so they were prepared, and he watched as the man used a lighter to ignite the rag. But as the lighter sparked, the man panicked and the bottle slipped from his hands, smashing on the ground by his own feet. The rag hadn't lit and a pool of petrol spewed out, soaking into the debris littered ground. The man looked down at the mess and then slunk back into the crowd, embarrassed. Alan managed a smile at the man's failure, but psyched himself up once more, knowing that probably wasn't the last petrol bomb he'd see tonight, knowing he would be charging the rioters again at any moment, and knowing that he would be doing nothing more than running into a flying wall of bricks. *How long can we keep taking this battering for?* he wondered.

'GO!' came the order.

Alan ran. The black, smoky sky was immediately filled with another barrage of missiles. He took the usual pounding as brick after brick slammed into his body, and as he and his unit retreated once more, he received another heavy hit as a brick smashed into his back. It was crazy. He was being hit all the time.

'In a way, it's kind of funny,' he said to the officer next to him. 'You take a pasting as you go forward and then you take another pasting as you go back.'

'I fail to see the humour,' the officer replied, batting away another falling brick.

The amount of bricks and masonry that was being thrown was astonishing. It was as though the rioters had an unlimited supply of weaponry. But in a way, they had. Just by the Aldi store was a new property development, still in the process of being built. The building site provided the rioters with a practical wish list and an almost never-ending supply of missiles. They could keep throwing bricks and immediately re-arm themselves all night.

As Aldi blazed and the officers repeatedly stormed the rioter barricade, they saw an old house nearby had been set alight. Even worse, there were people still inside. As Alan blocked more bricks, he watched as other officers rushed over to the house, forcing their way in through the front door and bringing out the residents.

The police had to act because it was once again impossible for the fire brigade to reach them, thanks to the ferocity of the rioters' attacks. And this was happening elsewhere too. The officers had even heard that burning cars had been placed across the entrances to fire stations in an attempt to stop fire engines from coming out. Alan knew that until the barricade was taken and the rioters pushed back, Aldi, the house, nearby flats, offices and other commercial premises would be left to burn.

The officers were struggling to break through the barricade. As they retreated, rioters were reaching out, clawing at the officers' overalls, in an attempt to drag them back, away from their colleagues and into their own murderous number. The result, if they had succeeded, didn't bear thinking about.

It seemed to Alan that everyone around him had been injured in some way. No one had avoided being hit by the flying bricks. As he silently questioned once more the futility of their task, Mounted Branch finally arrived. Officers wearing riot helmets rode up towards them on huge police horses. The horses were wearing protective riot gear too – shin and leg guards and clear visors across their eyes. Cantering in pairs towards Alan's unit, they were an awesome sight.

The ground was covered in bricks and broken glass. Fires raged all around and up ahead, masked rioters were still lobbing missiles towards the police. But the horses and their riders were used to the sounds and the fires and the missiles – they too attended riot training sessions at the Metropolitan Police's riot training facility, where wooden blocks and tennis balls were thrown towards them as fires and petrol bombs burned in the gutters, while other officers, acting as rioters, shouted and screamed at the horses, so that they became accustomed to the noise. The only difference here in Tottenham was the level of violence, which was much more than anything they ever witnessed in training, Even so, they were ready to advance on the barricade, and the presence of the horses changed everything.

The horses created a line across the street and stood steady. Some chomped at their bits, others stamped their hoofs, moving a step or two backwards and forwards in anticipation. One rider leaned down, patting his horse with his gloved hand as it breathed heavily through its nostrils. Then the order came. The lines of foot officers broke, creating a gap that the horses could ride through. They charged past the exhausted officers and rode towards the barricade amid a storm of bricks and bottles. There was a hellish noise of hoofs, glass, screaming and shouting. The horses leapt over the top of the barricade and disappeared into the twirling mist of black, acrid smoke and dim, grey light. The police helicopter circled above, its huge spotlight glaring down onto the street. Shadows and silhouettes of horses and men, a sky filled with deadly missiles, all blurred together until the noise lessened and the smashes and thuds of bottles and bricks hitting the ground around Alan stopped.

Up ahead, the horses and their mounted riders were now coming under their own bombardment of missiles. Bricks and rocks, fireworks and thunderflashes were all aimed at them and the horses were struck repeatedly in the chest and legs. But the horses rode on undeterred, forcing the rioters further back.

'FORWARD!'

Alan's unit moved back towards the barricade. It was still there but the rioters weren't. Up ahead, the horses were pushing the rioters away and the officers on foot now had to move up quickly to take the ground ahead of the barricade. Now it was the rioters who were on the back foot. The horses had done their job.

'GO!'

The officers ran across the barricade, swarming over the top and taking the ground. They created a line of shields and the rioters fell back further, although the bricks continued.

Now, finally, the fire brigade could reach the burning buildings. Fires raged from the blackened skeletons of shops and homes. The fire fighters crouched down, supporting huge hoses as thick jets of water shot upwards into the openings where windows had once been, and disappeared into the flames. So much of what Alan had seen had reminded him of scenes from the Blitz.

Shielded officers remained with the fire fighters, protecting them from attack. The arsonists and rioters wanted these buildings to burn; they certainly didn't regard the fire brigade as being there to help them or their communities. Fire fighters would also be attacked during the riots and many fire engines damaged. Windscreens were targeted with missiles and fire fighters were injured by flying glass. Others were attacked and hurt either going into or coming from their place of work – which was often within the riot zones anyway. No one was safe; it seemed everyone was a target for the rioters.

The London Fire Brigade was being severely tested. On just this one small stretch of Tottenham High Road they were now dealing with a dozen serious fires. The heat from the flames and the falling embers were impacting on properties on either side, and the fires were growing. Council buildings, betting shops, a bus, multiple cars, an entire shopping parade, a local police office, solicitors, homes and supermarkets; all burnt wildly out of control and were beyond saving. But with the area going up in flames around them, the rioters continued to attack and fight the police and other emergency services.

Alan's attacking line of officers stopped briefly. To their right, Aldi was crumbling into itself.

'Bloody idiots,' the officer to Alan 's left said. 'I mean, that's probably the store where their mums shop. Where are they supposed to go now?'

Alan agreed – their behaviour was madness. Why burn down your own town?

Just three hundred yards further to the north, the plan for Inspector Walpole's collection of officers had been to reach Lansdowne Road at the junction with Tottenham High Road, close to the riot's epicentre. To Inspector Walpole's amazement, there were four other carriers there. Three of them had a full complement of officers, and one, for some reason or other, only had half the officers it should have. But with the way things had gone, he figured that any number of extra officers was a bonus.

Everyone debussed and quickly formed up, creating a cordon across Tottenham High Road, just south of Lansdowne Road. It was Inspector Walpole's first opportunity to really take in what was happening on Tottenham High Road, and ahead of him was a scene of utter horror. The whole of the High Road appeared to be on fire. A menacing, grey fog of acrid smoke had settled along the street, below a glowing shroud of orange and red – the fires were so powerful the light they gave off seemed to be coating the old brick buildings lining the road.

There were no 'normal' people out; anyone on the street now was a rioter. All the shop windows were smashed and the ground was almost lost under a carpet of shattered glass. Then Inspector Walpole saw a double-decker bus; it was completely consumed by flames. And among it all, close to the bus, crowds of threatening, faceless rioters were jumping around in crazed joy and excitement. It was a scene of pure anarchy.

'Right, here's what we're going to do,' the chief inspector barked to the line of officers, a jolt of authority that snapped the coppers' attention from the scene ahead of them and back into the job at hand. 'We're going to move forward on foot,' he continued. 'Short shield advances, push the rioters back and take the junction with Lansdowne.'

'VISORS DOWN!' a sergeant yelled.

Each officer pulled down the protective visor that was attached to the front of his or her riot helmet. Then they pulled their arms tighter into the metal arm-rings on the back of the shields. They drew their batons and turned to face the rioters, ready to move forward.

As they did, they immediately came under a barrage of missiles – bricks, bottles, pieces of street furniture – anything and everything. With hundreds of rioters ahead of them the bombardment was constant.

Then the order came for the first wave of short shield officers to push forward. 'GO!'

Twenty officers surged forward, all repeating the order as they sprinted towards the rioters.

Missiles thundered down on them, glass bottles smashed at their feet, bricks slammed into their shields, other items were striking their helmets and bodies but the mob still retreated until the line of riot officers came to a halt, having gained a small amount of ground. They held their line, reaching up with their shields, to protect themselves from the next volley of bricks and bottles. Everywhere Inspector Walpole looked there were piles of bricks that had been gouged out and torn from walls and buildings.

A second line of officers stepped up, stopping just behind the first.

'To the next junction, GO!'

Twenty voices in unison – including Inspector Walpole's – repeated the order, 'GO!'

The second wave of riot officers rushed past the first and ran straight into a hail of rocks and bottles, pieces of masonry, wood and traffic cones; anything that could be lifted and hurled was directed at them as they charged.

As he ran with his line of officers, Inspector Walpole could see the blur of missiles dropping down all around him. Then he felt himself being hit. A falling brick slammed into his body. He didn't see it coming down, but a sudden rush of pain shot out from his shoulder as the brick struck him. Inspector Walpole was wearing most of his riot kit but he hadn't bothered with the shoulder pads as he found them a pain to fit around his stab vest. As he shouted out in pain, it was something he now regretted.

'Guv, you okay?' his sergeant asked, concerned.

Inspector Walpole nodded and looked up in time to block more falling bricks with his shield. His shoulder hurt but he was only walking-wounded and kept moving forward with his unit.

'HALT!' the sergeant ordered.

The officers came to a stop at the next junction and stood for a few seconds, blocking the missiles. Moments later, from behind them, they heard the familiar order being shouted once again.

'To the next junction, GO!'

As the first wave of riot police stampeded past them, a couple of officers suddenly dropped to the ground. In the rushed blur of moving bodies and tumbling missiles, it was impossible to see if they had been struck by something or had tripped over a piece of debris. To the relief of everyone around them, both officers quickly got back onto their feet and caught up with their colleagues at the next junction. The intensity of missiles had increased.

Inspector Walpole felt someone grab hold of his overalls.

'Governor, watch out,' one of his sergeant said, pulling him to the side.

Inspector Walpole turned around. A dozen mounted riot officers, riding huge horses, cantered past, nearly knocking several unsuspecting officers out of the way.

'Mounted Branch!' Inspector Walpole said out loud, with a smile.

The officers, unaware of what had happened at Aldi further down the High Road, watched in awe as the enormous beasts stormed forward, crunching broken glass under their hooves. They reached the junction where the frontline of officers hastily moved out of their way. The mounted officers and horses came to a halt, standing in a line, facing the rioters ahead of them. The constant assault of missiles suddenly came to a stop as the rioters looked on in trepidation, unsure as to what was about to happen. But the relief was only temporary, and quickly a few brave souls stepped forward again and lobbed rocks and bottles towards the line of horses.

One of the mounted officers raised his gloved hand in the air and then pointed forward, towards the mob and for a brief moment, everything stopped. The horses chomped at their bits and pulled on their reins in anticipation, and then, just a moment later, the entire line surged up the road.

Volley after volley of bottles and bricks came down on the horses and their riders, but they continued to charge forward. It was an impressive and invigorating sight, and the foot officers quickly followed up behind them. The effect of the charging horses was immediate and their benefit was unquestionable. The crowd retreated in panic, individuals darting off in all directions, terrified of being trampled. It took three or four pushes from the mounted officers but with their help, Inspector Walpole's unit eventually made it to Lansdowne Road. But there, they would be faced by another horrifying sight. On the corner of Lansdowne Road and Tottenham High Road, the three-storey, 1930s art deco building that now housed the Carpet Right store was fully ablaze.

Above the carpet shop itself, the upper floors had been sold to the Metropolitan Housing Trust – a charity – and turned into a couple of dozen affordable homes and flats. The fire had taken hold of the entire building, and huge flames together with swells of black smoke billowed from every window and every doorway. The heat was intense and forced back anyone who came too close. Inspector Walpole looked around hopefully, but there were no fire engines to be seen.

A plan was quickly put together. Units were to push up Tottenham High Road, forcing the rioters further back. Inspector Walpole's section was to push right, into Lansdowne Road, while a couple of other sections were to push left, into Lordship Lane. Once everyone was in place, they were ordered to hold their lines regardless of the level of attack they came under. The sterile area in the centre of the junction had to be defended to allow the fire brigade in to fight the fire. It was now out of control and the building was long past saving. But other buildings were also on fire, and the fire brigade needed to get in to stop the flames from spreading any further. Inspector Walpole had a momentary flashback to the Iron Maiden concert he had been at the previous evening. The wild crowds, the deafening noise, the blinding lights.

'Okay, on me! On me!' Inspector Walpole called out to his unit.

The officers created a line and pushed into Lansdowne Road. Immediately bottles, bricks, scaffold poles and anything else that could be picked up and thrown appeared out of the smoke, flew through the air and slammed into the officers' shields and bodies. They kept moving, knowing that they had to get past the fire as quickly as possible. Officers on Lordship Lane and Tottenham High Road were coming under their own assaults of missiles, but each section pushed into their respective roads and police carriers moved in behind them to block the High Road off and claim that sterile area.

Inspector Walpole's officers came to a stop. They were just east of the carpet store fire, which was burning wildly behind them and to their left. On their right was another fire and ahead of them were 20 or 30 rioters. Inspector Walpole stood there, holding the line with just seven others – one sergeant and six of his PCs. Despite their numbers, the group felt they could hold off 20 or 30 rioters, especially with the fire raging behind them. The rioters seemed to understand that the fire was now so out of control as to be potentially deadly to get close to. But Inspector Walpole knew that should the rioters be joined by some of the hundreds that were still battling police lines on Tottenham High Road, the mob might be crazy enough to charge anyway. If that happened, he and his small section of officers would have no chance.

Then Inspector Walpole heard something above the noise of the fire and the rioting. He turned around to look into Tottenham High Road. The heavy vibration of diesel engines punched through the crackling noises of the fire and he watched as three dark blue armoured police 'Jankels' slowly moved up the road, towards the main group of rioters. The weighty vehicles, with their armoured, boxy, American truck look, were usually only used in firearms situations, but these were highly unusual circumstances. With the heavy grills pulled down over their windscreens, the Jankels made for a far more robust riot van than the regular carriers and looked far more intimidating. In military terms it was the difference between a Jeep and a tank. Most of the rioters had never seen anything like them before.

On Lansdowne Road the most intense bombardment of bottles and bricks was over but the occasional missile still hurtled through the air and officers had to be ready to raise their shields and block them. Despite the fire, it was dark and the smoke made it difficult to see the various objects that were flung their way. But then Inspector Walpole heard a monstrous noise. A screeching, cracking, slow explosion of a sound, that grew louder and louder behind him and the other officers. Inspector Walpole twisted around to see. The Carpet Right building was collapsing. Interior walls crumbled and sections of the eighty-year-old building crashed to the ground, finally defeated by the fire.

The officers instinctively stepped forward, and the line of rioters backwards, both heading away from the flying embers and the officers staying in formation to ensure the fire brigade were protected from the rioters.

Shortly before 5am a new unit of police officers arrived to relieve Inspector Walpole and his exhausted section from the junction they had been holding. They were ordered to meet further up Tottenham High Road, close to White Hart Lane, and as they moved along the now eerily quiet roads in the early morning light they saw the total devastation that had befallen Tottenham. Everything was in ruins. It seemed as though every single inch of ground was coated in smouldering rocks or broken, blackened glass. Shops looked as though bombs had exploded in them – their fronts had been blasted away and lay scattered among the rest of the debris that carpeted the street. To add to the surreal atmosphere of the moment, there were a handful of bewildered looking people milling around. The rioters had all gone.

Inspector Walpole was amazed by what had happened over the previous few hours. At the start of the night, he should have had an entire PSU – himself, three sergeants and 21 PCs – but the other two carriers hadn't shown up, so he had ended up with just his own carrier – one third of the number of officers he should have had. The other units on the High Road and Lordship Lane also seemed to be fighting with fewer officers than they should have. Yet somehow, between them all, they had managed to secure and clear that whole end of Tottenham. It was a small miracle.

Alan's unit were heading back to Tottenham police station, where the inspector needed to complete his handover to the next shift. The station was still surrounded by police but the nick had been saved. This area was now sterile and any fears that the building would be razed to the ground were now, thankfully, past.

As the inspector was going to complete the handover, he walked into the station canteen to grab a drink. In the corner of the room, the drinks vending machine had been completely smashed up and wrapped in crime scene tape. Not a single bottle was left inside. Throughout the station, lying across the tables and floors, spent officers were sleeping.

As the inspector did his thing, the officers themselves took a few minutes to use the toilets and generally sort themselves out. Alan carefully unzipped his flame proof overall and pulled down the top to reveal his right shoulder. It was a mess of black, blue and red. He checked the rest of his body and saw that he was covered in more bruises and various swellings. Every other officer from his unit was in a similar state. They really had taken a battering at Aldi, and now looked as though they'd been beaten with baseball bats. As the adrenaline wore off, sharp pain and aching stiffness followed but there was no time to recuperate. Before they could go home, they had to head back to their base and write up their notes and evidence about what had happened that night. And then they would be back on duty a few hours later, when there would be more rioters to fight.

The officers stood outside the police station. They were shattered and they had pulled the top halves of their overalls down and tied them around their waists, in an effort to get cool. They looked like what they were – knackered police officers who had been working hard all night fighting to defend Tottenham, even as they lost their own colleagues to serious injury.

At that moment, a chief inspector from Tottenham police station walked out and stared at the injured, dirty, exhausted riot officers gathered outside the station. 'That doesn't look very professional, does it?' he barked at them.

The officers couldn't believe what they were hearing. For the sake of that chief inspector's health, it was probably a good thing that they were already exhausted.

Once the handover was completed, the officers boarded their carriers with what was left of their unit. Everyone was shattered. They all knew that they had been involved in the largest incident of public disorder that the TSG had seen since the Tottenham riots of the 1980s and in a way they were pleased to have been a part of it. It was, after all, what they trained for.

The carrier driver started the engine. He peered round at the officers who sat scattered around on the seats behind. They all looked utterly finished. He dropped the handbrake and began to move, finally leaving Tottenham. Driving over the debris of bricks, bottles and frozen fish, the carrier rocked back and forth like a 4x4 on a rocky mountain road. The bouncing around aggravated the injuries that the officers were all now carrying and it was a final reminder of intensity of what they'd faced during the previous night.

As Inspector Walpole and his officers trudged up Tottenham High Road, no one spoke. The only sounds they heard were glass crunching loudly beneath their boots, and the crackling of fires that continued to burn defiantly in the gutters and the ruined buildings.

As they walked, the officers approached a group of dog handlers, who were standing in the road, tending to the bleeding feet of their animals.

'Why don't you put some kind of boot on their feet?' one of the officers asked.

The dog handlers looked up, still holding up the paws of their dogs. 'We tried,' one of them replied. 'But it doesn't work; the dogs just keep trying to take them off.'

'Best thing you can do is just let them go,' another handler said. 'The dogs will carry on regardless and then we just have to treat their injuries afterwards.'

Cut paw pads weren't the only injury to be suffered by police dogs on that night. Another dog – three- year-old Linpol Luke, known as 'Obi' to the handlers – had been seriously hurt during the rioting. While under a heavy bombardment of bottles, masonry and petrol bombs, Obi was struck in the head with a brick, just above his left eye. Obi had been in shock but his handler gave him a quick check for injuries and Obi seemed okay. Unaware of how badly Obi was hurt, the pair continued on into the riots for a further two hours. It was only after seeing blood coming from Obi's nose that PC Wells realised that there was a bigger problem. After leaving the riot, Obi was taken to see a vet who had him transferred to the Royal Veterinary School in Cambridge where a CT scan would show he had a serious fracture to his skull. Obi would go on to make a full recovery.

At 8am Inspector Walpole and his officers boarded their carrier and set off for home. Inspector Walpole wouldn't have any involvement in the riots for another three days, where he would finally have a full PSU of officers and an entirely different – and surprising – situation to deal with.

'Okay, let's go,' he told the driver.

As they drove out of the epicentre of the nights rioting, they watched as PSU after PSU streamed into Tottenham.

1400 hrs
Enfield
Messages had been circulating on BlackBerry Messenger among criminals and rioters all day. They were to gather in Enfield town centre at 4pm for 'a repeat of what happened last night' in Tottenham.

Unaware of this, officers started arriving at Enfield for their regular Sunday late-turn shift. Some were immediately required to collect their riot kit and join PSUs to be ready for deployment to other areas of London, while other officers who either weren't trained or didn't have any kit were to remain on regular duties.

By the late afternoon groups of youths were beginning to gather in the town centre and soon reports began to filter in of shops being attacked. Officers manning the borough control room were searching through the numerous CCTV screens to get a better understanding of what was happening and they soon spotted the gangs attacking shops on Church Street.

Enfield's 'Area Car' – a BMW and the biggest and fastest car on the fleet – was told to get down there to see what was happening. The car's driver, Louise – tall, blonde, sporty and active – had just returned to work after a three-week trekking holiday in Peru and she was telling her young operator, Dale, all about it. But as they drove along Church Street, they were forced to stop both their car and their conversation. A barricade had been placed across the street. Traffic cones, bins, street furniture – anything that could be lifted or taken had been piled up in the road. With traffic now jamming up behind them on the one-way street, the officers had no option but to get out of their car and start dismantling the barrier.

Members of the public began approaching them, demanding to know what they were going to do about the trouble that was beginning to grow in Enfield.

'Where are all the police?' they wanted to know. 'Why aren't they stopping it?'

Louise and Dale did their best to try and calm the people down while simultaneously pulling apart the barricade. More traffic had joined the growing line of jammed cars and they needed to get it all moving again.

As they continued to try to explain themselves to an increasingly irate and demanding public, Louise noticed the station van driving towards them from the opposite direction – against the one-way system – on the other side of the barricade. The van came to a stop and the officers stepped out. Louise continued to calm people and throw various pieces of the obstruction out of the road. But then she noticed the officers from the van suddenly jumping back into their vehicle. The van reversed, u-turned and then made off at speed, away from Louise and the barricade. She wasn't sure why, and had enough to concentrate on with taking the barrier apart and dealing with the demands and pointing fingers of the public. But then she heard a commotion behind her. She turned around and in an instant she realised exactly why the van had driven off. Dozens of masked and hooded youths were coming towards them.

'Get back in the car!' Louise told Dale.

Before they knew it, the mob was aiming rocks and bottles at them. Louise's recent holiday suddenly seemed like a long time ago. She tried to start the BMW but in her panicked state, she couldn't get the engine going. Missiles were now striking the car and the mob was moving closer and closer towards them.

She looked over her shoulder. The line of cars was still there, blocking them in. With most of the barricade still stretched across the road, there was nowhere for them to go. She and Dale were trapped.

Louise and Dale stared at their attackers. More rocks and bottles together with any other item the mob could get hold of were being pelted at the car. Then a lump of concrete – a paving slab – smashed down on the windscreen. The glass immediately gave way under the weight of the solid block. A huge hole was punctured into the windscreen, sending a shower of shattered glass towards Louise and Dale.

Louise and Dale realised what danger they were in. They had one option and took it: they opened their doors, jumped out of the BMW and ran. Tiny fragments of glass poured off their clothing and tumbled to the ground like jewels. Bottles, rocks and other missiles continued to fall down on them as they sprinted away. Louise could only hope that the crowd didn't chase after them.

As the officers ran, Louise looked back to see if they were being followed. But to her relief the crowd had stayed at the car, celebrating like hunters gathered around a slain animal. She watched them smashing it up and then one rioter removed the petrol cap in an apparent attempt to set the car alight.

Leaving the mob with their prize, Louise and Dale sprinted up Church Street towards Windmill Hill. They didn't know it, but everything had been witnessed by the staff in the control room, who were watching on CCTV. They had seen the mob arriving and had been shouting over the radio for the officers to get away. Seeing the pair now running along Church Street, they directed another police unit to sweep in and pick them up before another mob found them. A police car quickly made its way to Windmill Hill and the two officers jumped in, thankful to have made it out alive.

As Louise's car was being attacked, four PSUs were already being directed to the borough. But they wouldn't arrive until nearly an hour later, by which time serious disorder was underway.

Edmonton

The previous evening, Darren had been swinging his wife around on a hotel dance floor in Southampton. The food, the music, the drinking – his friend's wedding had been a great success. Darren had been having the time of his life, and, best of all, he didn't have to drive home – he and his wife were staying overnight at the hotel. It also meant that he didn't have to work in the morning, which was even better. Without a care in the world, he had grabbed his fair share of pints of Guinness, totally unaware that the phone in his jacket, which was slung over a chair, had been ringing and buzzing so much the battery was close to running out.

A few hours later, Darren slid under the covers of the hotel bed, exhausted but satisfied by his night of food, booze and dancing.

He woke up to sunlight piercing the curtains. Darren's vision was an early-morning, watery blur and his head was a fog of arching pain. As his senses began to form, he heard a low purr coming from his jacket pocket – the final plea of his phone, before the battery died completely. Without looking, he reached over, grabbed his jacket and took out the phone. He rubbed his raw eyes and moved the phone backwards and forwards, trying to adjust his vision to the screen. There were dozens of text messages and missed calls. Some of the numbers were withheld, and he knew what that meant: work. Then he had a vague memory of someone at the wedding reception talking about trouble in London but he could barely remember what it was all about.

Darren called his borough headquarters at Lewisham. The phone was answered immediately and Darren gave the person on the other end his name.

'I had a few missed calls from you,' he said.

'We need you in work this afternoon,' he was told.

Darren lifted himself up and sat on the edge of the bed. He groaned as he rubbed his forehead. He picked up the controls and turned the TV on.

'Shit,' he said softly, staring at the news.

His wife woke up and looked over at him. 'Everything all right?'

By 2pm, having rushed to get back to London, Darren was standing in his uniform in the parade room at Lewisham police station. He was a Level 2 public order trained officer and after stopping briefly to collect his riot gear from Catford police station, where he was usually based, he was now with five other officers waiting to hear from the sergeant about what was going on and what they would be doing. His head was pounding.

'Okay everyone, thanks for coming in on such short notice,' the sergeant said. 'I'm sure you've all seen the news and know why you're here. We're being deployed to Edmonton tonight, so get your kit together, make sure you have all your riot equipment and get to the carriers, ready to go.'

'Where's the rest of the PSU?' Darren asked.

'This is it. Just us,' the sergeant told him.

'Just one and six?' Darren questioned, referring to them being just one sergeant and six PCs.

'Just one and six, although I am sure we will meet up with other units when we get to Edmonton.'

The sergeant explained that Edmonton was seeing an increase in violence, and disorder was breaking out on a large scale. CCTV had initially picked up groups of youths gathering in the housing estates around Joyce Avenue. These groups had then moved onto nearby Fore Street – the A1010 – a major thoroughfare and local shopping street. Here the gangs had begun to attack businesses. The Ipek furniture store had its windows smashed and a nearby pawnshop had also been attacked.

Soon the rioters' attention switched from looking for places to loot to the police. Officers who attended the area came under attack from bottles and other missiles, thrown by the growing groups of troublemakers. The officers charged at the rioters but there was a real danger that with so few of them they would soon find themselves dangerously separated from one another so they stayed close together.

The whole situation had become grave for the officers on the ground, who were now dangerously outnumbered, and there was an urgent need for more units, which was why Darren and the other six officers were now on their way.

The driver hit the carrier's sirens and blue lights and they hurried from Lewisham in south London towards Edmonton in north London – a journey of around 15 miles – through heavy traffic.

As they arrived on Fore Street, the officers noticed a burnt out police car that had been abandoned outside a McDonalds restaurant. A scaffold pole had been thrown through the windscreen. Bricks and bottles crunched under the carrier's tyres. There was silence from the officers, who were all staring out at the destruction in the otherwise deserted street.

'Where the hell is everyone?' an officer at the rear of the carrier asked. 'It's like a ghost town out there.'

They continued slowly on. Further up the street they could see smoke billowing from somewhere – a shop perhaps? Another police car set alight? They didn't know what it was. They could only see the black, acrid smoke. On the police radio they could hear other units being deployed all over the area and they waited for their own orders. Eventually they came through.

'Okay, everyone de-bus,' the sergeant said. 'They want us to guard the high street.'

'Guard against what?' someone asked. 'There's no one here.'

The officers stepped off the carrier, joining other police units, and they began patrolling the high street. They were fully kitted up in their riot gear and carrying shields, the only problem was, there appeared to be no riot – at least not any more, not here on the high street.

The main streets were washed in blue lights and heavy with the blaring sound of sirens as convoys of police riot carriers rushed past. Other police vehicles were passing each other, heading in different directions, going to different – new – scenes of disorder. More carriers remained at traffic junctions, engines running, waiting for a deployment.

Darren could only watch as the carriers disappeared, and he trudged slowly along the road, passing smashed-in shop fronts where the alarms were still ringing. Nearby, a Royal Mail van had been pushed into the middle of the road and a little further up another car burned out of control. A TV camera crew walked around with bodyguards and Darren listened on the radio as elsewhere a youth had been stabbed and police medics were doing what they could to fix him up. He heard friends of the stabbed youth arguing with the officers, and then shouting abuse when the police asked for information about who had stabbed him.

Darren remained standing by a pile of broken glass outside a Carphone Warehouse, and listened almost with envy as other units were reporting disorder and rioting a short distance away. Then he and his colleagues heard the distressing voices of officers calling for help, 'URGENT ASSISTANCE!'

Knowing what that call meant, they desperately wanted to respond but were ordered to remain on the high street. Frustrated, they stood in the near-empty street. As they grumbled, Darren saw a couple of people approaching. They weren't hooded youths, they were older and smarter looking. They were local residents.

'What are you doing standing here?' they asked Darren. 'They're setting our cars on fire down those streets and you're standing here guarding shops!'

'I'm sorry,' Darren said. 'We're just doing what we're told to.'

The residents looked bewildered. Darren *was* bewildered. Cars were being attacked and set alight, other officers were in serious danger, and yet here they were protecting shops that had already been attacked. The residents pleaded with the officers but Darren and his colleagues could do nothing to help. Darren felt terrible. As a police officer, it was in his nature to help people – and these were decent people, decent locals – but all he could say to them was, 'Sorry, we're just following orders.' Residents were having their property attacked and burnt and they – the police, the very people the residents relied on – were doing nothing about it.

The despondent locals walked away and were soon replaced by handfuls of hooded youths. The youths started to move towards the officers, as if trying to bait them to do something but no sooner did the officers start to walk towards the yobs than they would run off.

Darren returned to walking the high street and took another look at the damaged police car, which had now been sectioned off with police crime scene tape. A sure sign, if ever there was one, that the area they were in was now safe.

1600 hrs
Brixton

In south London, the annual Brixton Splash event was underway. The Splash, like a smaller version of the Notting Hill Carnival, was a street festival, a celebration of the area's African and Caribbean cultural history and heritage, and a promotion of its diversity. It attracted just a fraction of the many thousands that attended Notting Hill, but by summer 2011, the Splash had built quite a reputation. With many food stalls, music stages and reach-out programs for local kids, it was regarded as a success.

However, it suffered from some of the same problems faced by the organisers of Notting Hill and other large-scale events, one of which was crime. Most people enjoyed a trouble-free, fun day out but there were always criminals and gangs looking to take advantage of the large crowds or cause trouble. So although it was nowhere near as busy or as well known as Notting Hill, local criminal gangs would attend and sometimes, usually later in the evening, they would come together and fight.

The police kept a strategically low and friendly profile, and although the trouble in Tottenham wasn't being ignored, it was a long way from Brixton. Everyone connected to the event hoped that the rioting wouldn't spread to south London, but they knew the potential if it did. Like Tottenham, Brixton had suffered with its own difficult history and riots. Race riots had broken out a couple of times in the 1980s – once in 1981 and again in 1985, just a week before the Broadwater Farm riots – and there was more rioting in 1995.

With problems either brewing or already erupting elsewhere in London, by the early evening people in Brixton were tense. Peckham and Enfield were already seeing trouble and so were other places. In Waltham Cross, just north of Enfield and the M25, but actually located in Hertfordshire, jewellers and police cars were attacked and damaged. It was the first time that the rioting had spread beyond London. Hertfordshire Constabulary, backed up by Bedfordshire's police, had moved in to contain the violence.

In Wood Green, two miles west of Tottenham, Turkish and Kurdish shop owners were out in force around Green Lanes and Turnpike Lane, creating gangs of their own to protect their businesses and livelihoods from those who had already attacked and looted shops along Wood Green High Road.

There was some minor disorder and skirmishes between police and youths on the Edward Woods Estate, just behind the large Westfield shopping centre in Shepherds Bush. A little further south, in Fulham, police came under fire from missiles on Lillie Road and shops were attacked on North End Road, just below smart Kensington.

Just to the south of Brixton, Streatham would soon see looters attacking sports and phone shops, with one shop owner beaten so badly around the head that he would require hospital treatment.

The Hackney One Festival, a similar event to the Splash in

Brixton, had already been cancelled. Other areas were also reporting trouble and the rioting was now spreading far beyond Tottenham. Many wondered if Brixton could somehow avoid the trouble – praying that it would but perhaps knowing that it wouldn't.

All was going well at the Splash now, though. It was a nice day and families were enjoying the Caribbean food and booming beats from various sound systems set up along the streets. James had been a Brixton constable for a number of years and he always enjoyed the Splash. He loved the music, the food, the culture and even having a boogie with some of the revellers; he had been seen on the news more than once, over the years, dancing away. But he also knew that if there were to be any trouble, it would come later in the evening, when the gang members started to show up, puffing out their chests and looking to antagonise one another. That was how it always was – things would start to bubble and there would probably be a bit of fighting as the gangs clashed, but for now, all was good and the Splash only required a small police presence.

By early evening, as predicted, more and more gangs started to appear on the streets of Brixton. They were out looking for each other and looking for trouble. That was normal practice though, and nothing to do with the rioting that was going on elsewhere across London. But it would still require a police presence and officers moved in quickly to prevent any disorder or fighting between the rival groups. But something was different this time. Rather than run off when the police arrived, as was their usual habit, the gangs suddenly began to turn on them, throwing missiles as they approached. Police vehicles were also targeted, with objects being thrown and windows smashed as they drove through the streets.

James and his small band of officers were deployed towards Coldharbour Lane, near the crossroads with Atlantic Road. A Merton serial was already there, so they joined up with them, instantly creating a more dominant presence. The youths had now gathered across a large grass area in front of the Somerleyton Estate. In the confusion of the disorder, rival gangs had become mixed, and a youth from one of the gangs had been stabbed. Even with everything else that was happening – even though they had joined together to fight the police – the gangs still found an opportunity to fight each other. Then some other youths began running around, openly brandishing their knives and threatening each other. They didn't seem to care at all that the police were there.

The boy that had been stabbed was lying in the gutter, and officers were trying desperately to reach him. They could see that he was alive and conscious but stab wounds are notorious for not showing the full picture of someone's injuries. It was impossible to see if he had any other stab wounds or if the knife had penetrated a major organ or artery, which could mean he was bleeding to death. Officers needed to reach the boy as quickly as possible but as they moved forward there was an immediate and dramatic increase in the number of bottles and bricks that came flying through the air towards them. The officers pushed forward regardless. They weren't wearing protective riot equipment – no flameproof overalls, no padded gloves, no helmets and no shields – just their beat duty uniform. James moved up, stepping closer to the mob in an effort to push them back as more bottles and bricks rained down. Most smashed and splintered on the tarmac but others landed with painful force against officers' bodies and legs.

Then a female officer from the Merton serial, who had been

standing next to James, suddenly fell backwards and dropped to the ground. A bottle had struck her directly in the head. James looked down, horrified. The officer lay on the floor, injured and unconscious as bricks and bottles continued to crash down all around them, shattering into tiny, jagged fragments of glass and stone. James noticed the small, metal Metropolitan Police badge on the front of the downed officer's hat. It was bent and twisted into a 'V' shape and was a clear indication of the force with which the bottle had struck her. As James did his best to protect her from the falling missiles, a pair of police medics rushed over. At the same time, the lines of officers also surged forward, charging through the barrage of missiles, pushing the rioters further back until eventually they had pushed them far enough away that the missiles no longer reached the injured officer. The space that had been created also gave officers a chance to reach the boy who had been stabbed. Other officers stood firm, creating a protective line and not allowing the rioters to draw them any further into the estate. The priorities now were the injured officer and the stabbed kid.

With the police holding their ground rather than advancing, the mob began to move towards the police line again, picking up previously thrown missiles and lobbing them at the officers once more. With the rioters approaching, the boy was quickly taken from the area and the female officer was dragged away by the medics, to get her out of the range of this new attack.

The line of officers rushed forward again. They charged towards the youths, some of whom were again showing off their knives. But as the officers moved towards them, the youths scattered, unwilling to fight hand-to-hand with the police. The officers halted their advance and held the ground, batons in hand. Knives or no knives, the police were ready to take them on.

With the youths unwilling to fight the police directly, and with the police showing no sign that they were going to back down, things quickly became calm. It was a chance for some officers to take a break and get some food – perhaps their first bite to eat in hours. Other officers came out to relieve them so that there was a continual police presence on the streets. The lull was welcomed but it wouldn't last.

As James remained in the street, holding the area, further police units began to arrive to support the Brixton officers. Riot carriers together with unprotected VW minibuses full of police officers streamed into the area. Some officers looked fresh and clean but others had either already been in the thick of the action elsewhere or else they had come under attack on their way to or through Brixton. James watched as one particular minibus drove towards them and parked up along the street. The windows of the vehicle had all been smashed in.

'Bloody hell, look at the state of those poor fuckers,' someone said.

The occupants of the wrecked minibus stepped out, onto the pavement. Every single officer was bleeding from tiny cuts that covered their skin and face, caused, no doubt, by the hundreds of shards of glass spraying them when the windows were smashed in. They all seemed to be in shock. It looked to James as though the officers had reacted to the showering of glass by reaching up and rubbing their faces, a natural reaction but one that would only cause more harm, as the tiny splinters were rubbed deeper into their skin.

James noticed that the officers had their riot kit bags stacked at the back of their bus. The bags were still full and the bleeding coppers stood in the street in their regular beat uniform. Whatever had happened to them, they clearly hadn't had time to kit up, and

James assumed they'd been ambushed somewhere. But they wouldn't have much time to recover. They were in Brixton now and they had a whole new fight ahead of them, regardless of their cut faces and smashed vehicle.

Watching their screens closely, CCTV operators in Brixton started to pick up various large groups gathering again around the Somerleyton Estate. Once more, the yobs were armed with bricks and bottles and some had started to set fire to large commercial bins. James and his unit were finally ordered to get their public order equipment on. There would be no more fighting rioters in beat uniform; this time they would be prepared, and their objective was to keep the rioters away from the town centre, where the main concentration of shops and businesses were.

A short time later, James was back standing on the crossroads of Coldharbour Lane and Atlantic Road, but now fully kitted up in his riot uniform. He stood just under the railway bridge, on a tight, almost claustrophobic junction that felt hemmed in by the Victorian brick buildings and local shops.

Ahead of them was a mob of 200 people. The officers' orders were to stop them from heading into the town centre, so James's unit began to move against the crowd, pushing them east. The police advance was met with an immediate barrage of missiles. Rocks, bottles and bricks cascaded down from the sky. The officers lifted their shields to protect themselves as they continued to march forward. Taking advantage of the raised shields, some rioters stepped up and aimed missiles directly at the officers' unprotected bodies. As they did, an orange glow appeared behind the rioters, creating tall, black silhouettes, and casting menacing shadows against the buildings' facades. Then some of the crowd parted and a handful of rioters worked together, rolling a huge, burning bin towards the police line. With giant fingers of flames flicking out, the blazing bin rolled forward a few feet but quickly came to a stop – too heavy and cumbersome to move any great distance unaided. The rioters, perhaps hoping for more, realised that the bin was going to do little to stop the police, and they began to skip backwards in anticipation of a full-on assault from the officers.

Then the charge came. Lines of riot police ran forward. The rioters, seeing the lines of shielded officers sprinting towards them, turned and ran until the police line came to a halt. Then the rioters regrouped, ready for a counter-attack. There were more bricks, more bottles, traffic bollards, blocks of wood, chairs. The rioters were throwing anything they could get their hands on. An order to charge the rioters came once more and the officers ran towards them again. The rioters dropped back, flinging their missiles as they turned. Another order to charge. James ran forward once more, pushing the rioters even further back. The charges were having an effect and the rioters' numbers started to thin out as some broke away and disappeared down surrounding streets.

The officers returned to the crossroads of Coldharbour Land and Atlantic Road and waited for the mobs to return. But, for now at least, the constant barrage of missiles, the shouting and the fighting seemed to have ceased.

With the situation at the junction calming down, James and the other officers were redeployed further along Coldharbour Lane, this time by the junction with Brixton Road. Over the radio, James could hear other officers saying groups of rioters were starting to join together again. The gangs were moving through the area and the calls over the radio were beginning to sound increasingly chaotic, with officers chasing groups away through the streets only for them to quickly reappear somewhere else. It was standard cat-and-mouse stuff but James was beginning to question why they were being held at Coldharbour Lane when it seemed to him that the rioters had already moved on.

Finally they were told to move into Brixton Road. The officers prepared themselves for more bottles and more bricks. They checked their helmet straps, tightened their grips on their shields, and drew their batons. But as they swept round into Brixton Road, the officers faced something altogether unexpected – traffic. Lots of it. Cars, taxies, busses, were all travelling along the road like it was any other day. The officers had been ordered to create a cordon across the street but to James it seemed like an insane idea. As they tried to form up, the traffic was driving through them, with drivers trying to negotiate their cars through pairs of shield-carrying police officers. The officers couldn't understand what they were doing – why on earth were they putting a shield cordon across a regular, busy road? Someone, somewhere, realising the mistake, called it in over the radio and the officers were ordered back to Coldharbour Lane.

The officers then heard that looters were attacking nearby shops. They looked to their inspector for direction.

'We're to remain here,' he told them. 'We're to hold this junction.'

'But they're just around the corner, we could take them,' an officer pleaded.

'We've been ordered to stay here and hold this junction,' the inspector said.

The officers were left confused once again. Just thirty yards away, looters and rioters were attacking shops. Windows were being put in, clothing and mobile phones stolen but the officers were ordered to remain where they were.

The rioters were no longer interested in attacking the police lines and instead, with increasingly frustrated officers standing by and watching, they concentrated with their looting instead.

James lifted up the visor on his helmet, allowing some air to wash over his hot, sticky face. Tesco and Currys were now also being attacked and other officers were attempting to restore some order and prevent more looting. James was desperate to do something somewhere to stop the looters, but orders had come from above and they were to remain where they were. All James could do was stand there, listening to other officers making increasingly desperate radio calls as they repeatedly came under attack every time they tried to fight off groups of rioters or looters. He shook his head in frustration.

1700 hrs
Enfield

As Louise and Dale were recovering from their lucky escape, Richard, a TSG sergeant, pulled into Enfield with his PSU of Level 1 officers and stopped outside Enfield Town railway station. Someone pulled opened the large, sliding door at the side of the carrier and the officers jumped out. There were people milling around but so far things seemed fairly low key and normal. Quiet, even. There was no sign of the kind of trouble Louise and Dale experienced earlier.

Richard was glad to be back at work. He had been off for almost a year to the day, thanks to a bone infection in one of his feet. He still carried a slight limp, which became more pronounced the longer the day went on, to the extent that his 75-year-old mother would later turn on the TV and identify her son on a news report by the way he was walking.

Richard was working with a different TSG unit from his own that day, as the other unit was low on sergeants. There was a positive side to this, however, as it meant they called him by his real name rather than the nickname he had picked up with his own group. Richard was tall and stocky and when he drove the riot carriers, he would hunch over the wheel – 'all shoulders and arms' – and due to this unique style of driving he had been named 'Donkey Kong'. This other unit only knew him as 'Richard', though, and he was happy with that.

Richard had originally been assigned to lead a group of six PCs at the Manchester City versus Manchester United match at Wembley but other events had taken priority, and instead they had been sent here to Enfield. His day was now going in a completely different direction to the one he had been expecting.

'Grab your shields and form up by the station,' the PSU inspector ordered.

Richard took hold of one of the round plastic shields, and slipped his arm through the metal ring on the back. Then he joined the other officers, close to the entrance of the single storey brick building that was Enfield Town station. Around the station, it was very much a typical north London town centre – a narrow main road leading through some two and three storey brick built buildings containing local shops and flats. It was still bright outside and with handfuls of commuters coming from the station, standing in the sun wasn't unpleasant, which made it all feel a bit odd because Richard was holding a riot shield and waiting for trouble. He had been a sergeant on the TSG for several years and knew the Met didn't deploy officers with shields without a good reason, so the fact that they had been deployed with them immediately today was a tell tale sign that something was up.

As he watched the commuters coming out of the station, Richard began to notice a few other people who looked as though they were there for other reasons. They weren't smartly dressed and skulked about either watching the coppers closely or staring into their phones. Richard wasn't the only one to notice them, either. As he stood outside the station, members of the public began to approach him.

'Something's going on here,' they said, whispering into the side of his riot helmet. 'You need to know, there are people here who aren't from Enfield.'

Unknown to Richard, groups of troublemakers were pouring into the area from all over London. The rioters and looters had been using BlackBerry Messenger to communicate and organise themselves and the crowd in front of him was becoming intimidatingly large. As the numbers grew, they became increasingly noisy, and the energy among them felt more aggressive. The officers could sense their rising belligerence.

Then, with no obvious trigger, the crowd turned and faced Richard's PSU. Seconds later, bottles and bricks were coming down on the line of officers. To Richard, watching the mob turn had been like watching a flock of starlings in the sky – one moment they were flying one way and then suddenly, in a split-second, they all veered off in a different direction, as one. Richard's unit responded by lifting their shields to meet the falling missiles but the sheer number meant that some managed to get through, striking officers' legs and feet. Richard noticed a few officers hopping backwards or lifting a boot in pain but all of them were quick to return to their position, standing side-by-side with their colleagues.

Richard's PSU remained at the station while a second PSU held the high street, just to the left. A plan was quickly put in place to get officers behind the rioters, to try and surround them and to stop them from getting any more ammunition to throw; the rioters had knocked down a wall and had been smashing the bricks into smaller chunks, which would be easier to throw. But no sooner had the plan been made than the rioters took off, running down the high street. By now the crowd was committed to causing destruction and the throwing of missiles at the police lines were just a precursor of what was to come. As the rioters charged past Richard's PSU and along the high street, there was the unmistakeable sound of shop windows being smashed. One after another, shops were being attacked. There were shouts from within the crowd to attack the small, family owned jewellers, G Mantella. Mobs of hooded youths set about kicking in the protective metal shutters, and then trying to yank them away from the building. Eventually the shutters buckled, allowing access to the glass windows and displays. They were quickly smashed and watches worth thousands of pounds were looted in a matter of seconds by youths who escaped by foot or on bicycles.

By now other police units were cordoning off the bottom end of the street but the mob headed off in another direction, where there were no police to stop them. Richard began to wonder if there was any plan at all for handling the rioters. From where he was standing, getting bricks thrown at his head, there seemed to be no real coordination between the different police units. He considered suggesting that their PSU just did their own thing and move their own lines against rioters, but he also knew that if there were any plans in place – or if they were in the process of creating plans – doing their own thing could ruin it all. And, as they chased after another group, dodging the falling bricks and bottles, Richard wondered if they would ever be able to regain any kind of control.

Having survived the attack on her car, Louise was ready to head back out. Other cars had returned to the patrol base at Lincoln Road, and Louise jumped into the front passenger seat of one of the IRVs. Gangs of rioters were swarming around Enfield, and calls for assistance were coming out fast.

The officers set out in a convoy of four police cars, racing towards Southgate on blues-and-twos, where rioters and looters were reportedly smashing the place up. The convoy entered a roundabout but the driver had taken the wrong side of the road, to avoid some traffic. As Louise turned to look around, to check for oncoming vehicles – SMASH! The sound of the crunching, screeching metal, the force of the impact, the jerking of her body – she knew in that slow-motion instant what had happened. As they had travelled around the roundabout another car had come across and t-boned them. The sickening sound of the impact disappeared for the briefest of moments and was followed by a rapid *whoosh*. Louise was hit full on by the passenger airbag as it exploded into her.

Great, she thought to herself, in disbelief. *I am having a brilliant day!*

Tottenham

A group of officers from Croydon arrived in Tottenham. All were Level 2 public order trained, and although some had worked on previous public order events, none had seen anything like this. This was a real riot – the type they always trained for but never actually ended up dealing with. The evidence of that first night of rioting in Tottenham was everywhere – the looted shops, the burnt out buildings and vehicles, weary officers dragging their shattered shields and bruised bodies along the scarred streets. The streets themselves were blackened by the fires, and covered in smashed glass, rocks, bricks, pieces of wood – everything and anything. In that single night of violence, there had already been over fifty arrests, and nearly thirty police officers had been injured.

The Croydon officers were directed towards the local Aldi supermarket that had been set ablaze during the night, and which was still on fire. It was clear to the officers that the store couldn't be saved. It was just a blackened shell with a fierce orange glow inside; the final act of what had clearly been a huge blaze. The officers were told to guard the area, so they created a cordon around what was left of the building, allowing the fire fighters to do what they could to contain the flames and finally put it out.

Tom took his place in the line, across the street, holding his riot shield in front of his body and feeling the heat of the fire against his back. Everything was new to him. He was just a few months out of his probation and had only completed his Level 2 public order training at Gravesend three weeks before. It was the first time that he had every put his riot kit on in a real situation. And being 6' 4", he already knew from his training that he would be getting hit by flying objects more often than others. But he was young and single, no one would be worrying about him and he was excited to be a part of what was going on. There were very few people on the streets now and the orgy of violence from the previous night had shrunk back to just the odd person coming for a look. But Tom had been told they could expect things to get bad again as it started to get dark.

After a few hours, the fire was finally put out, and the officers were moved to Tottenham police station. They hoped that there would be a chance for a rest, along with some food and some water but this wasn't the case. There was a vending machine in the canteen, but it was empty and for some reason it had been cordoned off with crime scene tape.

'What the fuck happened to that?' someone asked.

'Don't know,' Tom said. 'It looks like someone killed it.'

The officers were tired, hungry and thirsty but there was

nothing for them. Instead, they were told to create another cordon outside the police station itself, because there were fears it would come under attack again.

'Perhaps we can get something to eat from one of the local shops,' an officer said.

'Where?' Tom replied. 'Everything is either closed, boarded up or burning down.'

It was true. It seemed that any shop that had remained open had been looted and attacked. The wise shopkeepers – or the ones that could – closed their shutters and waited out the troubles somewhere else, hoping their businesses wouldn't be destroyed. The officers remained hungry.

The afternoon turned to evening and the officers surrounding the police station were beginning to have missiles thrown at them from the groups that had started to gather again. Nearby, another line of officers, already defending themselves against the flying bottles and bricks, had suddenly heard the roar of a car engine. Rioters leapt out of the way, laughing and jumping in crazed excitement as a car was driven at the police line. So, as predicted, with darkness came the beginnings of another night of trouble.

Though not to the same level as the first night, the trouble in Tottenham was the most violent rioting that Tom and the other Croydon officers had ever faced. They were bombarded with missiles, fought hand to hand several times, but finally, in the early hours, there was a lull. The rioters ran off to cause trouble elsewhere and the barrage of abuse and missiles stopped.

The officers had been on their feet for hours fighting off sporadic attacks and they were looking forward to standing down and getting home for some food and sleep. They had been told that they would be relieved by a night duty serial but as the hours went by, there was no sign of their relief. The officers started to become antsy. *Where was the night duty? Where was their relief?* In fact there weren't enough officers to spare and soon Tom and the late turn Croydon officers began to realise that they wouldn't be going home to their families after all. They would be staying on through the night. They had been the late shift and now they had become the night shift too. But they were assured that they would be relieved by the early turn officers, who, they were told, had already been warned to come in and take over from them in the morning.

'There's been a Force Mobilisation,' they were informed. 'You'll be out of here by 7am.'

Tom scoffed. 'No chance,' he said to the officers around him.

'What do you mean?'

'Mate, the early turn will be coming *on* at 7am, not *relieving* us at 7am. They will need to get their briefing and get sorted out with their kit beforehand. And who even knows where they are coming from? We won't get relieved at 7am, believe me.'

The officers still hadn't had anything to eat or drink and they were all feeling hungry, dehydrated and fatigued, which affected their mood as well as their performance. A few of the officers disappeared to try and find some food. Some distance away they found a lone corner shop that was still open. They bought whatever they could, which was mostly just chocolate bars. But it was better than nothing at all.

Despite the lull, the officers still had to contend with the occasional clown testing their line and throwing a brick or bottle. It was a wearisome interference to what they had hoped would be a quiet period of the night.

In Brixton, the looters had taken full advantage of the shortage of police. Hooded, masked men and women descended on Brixton Road and went straight for the shops. As a woman shouted, 'Cover you faces! Cover your faces!' the horde began their attack. Using bins, bricks, rocks, even their feet, they began to smash in the windows and pull and yank at metal security shutters. The glass doors of the large H&M store were smashed open and people poured in, running out moments later with arms full of clothing. At the same time the glass door of the T-Mobile store, next door to H&M, was also smashed. A hooded man climbed through the broken glass and immediately began to lift up the security shutters on the inside. Others, seeing him, started to gather outside, waiting for the shutters to be raised. As soon as they were, the group stormed through, grabbing anything they could get their hands on before running back out with their stolen boxes of phones. Shop alarms rang out all around but no one cared; they just took what they wanted. At Foot Locker, a few doors further north, things had taken a darker turn. Having already been broken into and looted, someone had started a fire that quickly took hold, and engulfed the building.

Police finally moved in, and the rioters and looters were pushed back so that the London Fire Brigade could reach the shop. The fire had grown so great that it took six engines to deal with it. The fire engines came under attack even as they fought the blaze.

A short distance to the south, along Effra Road, other groups of looters were helping themselves to the contents of the large Currys and Halfords stores.

Having returned home at about 10am that morning, after working all night in Tottenham, Alan's unit was back on again and this time they were sent to Brixton. He still ached from the countless cuts and bruises that covered his arms and legs and body. He rubbed his right shoulder, where the brick had struck him with particular force as he had been advancing on the crowds at Aldi. Ordinarily, injuries like this would mean taking time off, recovering, seeing a doctor to ensure there were no fractures – but times weren't ordinary.

The rioting and looting in Brixton had been underway for several hours and the entire area looked as though it was on fire. Alan's unit were sent to Effra Road. Ahead of them they could see countless rocks and bottles flying through the sky, and falling on other TSG officers, who were running short shield advances against their attackers, close to Currys. Gangs of looters had targeted the store, forcing up the shutters and smashing their way in through the glass doors. Other officers had earlier attempted to deal with the thieves but they had come under heavy bombardment. Three police vans had to reverse and escape as hundreds of masked men aimed rocks and scaffold poles and paving slabs at the vehicles, smashing windscreens and almost overrunning the police. The TSG had then moved in and were now in the process of taking the area back.

As another unit was already taking on the rioters, Alan's unit was ordered to hang back and make a cordon across the street to prevent anyone else from joining in the trouble. Being held back from the main fighting and advances came as a relief as they were still exhausted from their night at Tottenham.

The police helicopter circled above, illuminating the scene below. Alan watched as bricks and other missiles dropped through the air, landing on and around the other unit. If this had been the first night, he may have been more shocked, but he had already spent a night fighting for his and other people's lives, and this now seemed minor in comparison. He had no fears that the other unit wouldn't be able to handle the trouble on their own. Sending a TSG unit in behind another TSG unit wouldn't have made any difference, other than having a bunch more officers standing in the street. Besides, the trouble was contained in a small area and there were only so many officers that could be sent in. Had they needed support, Alan's unit was there, but the advances that they were making were having the right effect, and the looters were falling back.

Word then came through that Alan's unit were required elsewhere. A couple of streets to the west, off Acre Lane, the large Tesco supermarket had been attacked, and officers were rapidly being redeployed there.

They arrived at the same time as some dog handlers and their angry sounding German Shepherds. Glass and stolen goods were scattered all across the car park. Not knowing if any looters were still inside, the officers entered the Tesco store through various entrances and exits, ensuring that anyone still inside couldn't escape, but only one person was found and it was clear that the others had made off before the officers had arrived.

By the early hours, as fire crews doused the flames and officers held cordons, things in Brixton finally began to calm down. Heavy rain had replaced the missiles, and as was often the case when the weather turned, rioters, looters and other criminals disappeared, not wanting to get wet.

The streets had been retaken and the fight, at least for tonight, was over.

Monday 8th August 2011

0100 hrs
Enfield

Richard and his TSG unit had been chasing looters all over Enfield. He lost count of how many people he had seen running off with stolen televisions and other such items. Now he was back on his carrier, doing 'roving patrols', dealing with anything they stumbled upon or were sent to. In the early hours they were called to attend one location after a chief inspector's carrier had been attacked.

Pulling up in a dark side street, Richard saw the carrier parked along the kerb. Standing with it were the chief inspector and a sergeant. Also with them was an ARV unit; two armed police officers were looking at the side of the riot carrier and appeared to be inspecting something.

'Everything alright guv?' Richard asked.

'I think we've been shot at,' the chief inspector told him.

'What? Seriously?'

'Yep,' said one of the ARV officers. 'Looks like a shotgun.'

Richard peered at the bodywork at the side of the carrier by the large sliding door, where the sergeant would have been sat. It was peppered with numerous small dents and holes.

Richard looked over at the sergeant, who stood ashen-faced.

'Have you called it in?' Richard asked.

'Yeah,' he was told. 'But control are suggesting that it may have been a firework rather than a firearm. Doesn't look like a firework to me, though.'

'No, it doesn't,' Richard agreed.

'We were just driving along and there was a flash from an alley that we were passing,' the sergeant said. 'We heard a massive bang on the side on the carrier but thought nothing more of it and just blue-lighted it away. After we pulled over a little further down, to take a look, we saw the damage.'

Richard and his unit left the sergeant and chief inspector with the ARV officers, and went for a drive, to see if they could find anyone who may have been responsible for firing at the carrier. What they would do if they did find anyone, he didn't know, but they were going to hunt around all the same. But the streets were becoming quieter and their search would prove fruitless.

0500 hrs
Cambridge
Up in Cambridge, just after 5am, Mark's phone rang. Mark was a Tactical Advisor and planner for the policing of public order events. He had been expecting a call since Saturday, when he had first seen the trouble erupting down in London.

Mark reached across his bed and looked at his phone; it was his boss.

'Sir?'

'Mark, we need you in,' he was told.

'I thought you might,' he replied.

'There's some urgent work that needs doing in response to what's happening in London. We're looking at the potential mobilisation of PSUs within our force, just in case. We need to know what staff we have available for earlies, lates and nights for the next seven days.'

Mark rolled out of bed and went into work. He was surprised that they weren't being deployed to London but he could understand why they were at least making preparations for their area. The rioting had already started to spread and there was potential for it to mushroom even further. Cambridgeshire wasn't exactly a hotbed of terror but it was better to be ready, than not.

Still, he couldn't help feeling disappointed not to be sent down to the capital.

By 7.15am the report was sitting on the boss's desk. But it had all been a ruse; it had never been about Cambridgeshire at all. It was in preparation for deployment to London – they just didn't want Mark knowing about it. Not yet, anyway.

0800 hrs
Edmonton

After a slow, tedious night, morning arrived with a welcome, fresh breeze. Darren was tired and hungry. He hadn't eaten or had anything to drink all night, and he and other officers were now complaining about the lack of refreshments. They figured they had been forgotten about, but it was the same for most officers across London. Anything they needed to keep going during long shifts spent fighting, such as food and water, had not been arranged. Feeding the officers and keeping them hydrated was something that hadn't been catered for.

As Darren leant back, resting against the building line of shops, his round shield held down by his feet, he lifted the visor on his helmet and allowed the cool air to wash over his face. Then, out of the corner of his eye, he saw a handful of local residents approaching. *Maybe they're coming over to complain about the lack of police response again*, he thought, and braced himself to remain polite at all costs. But they weren't the same people he had spoken to earlier that night. Instead of questioning why the officers were guarding shops, these people came over to thank them, and to say, 'Well done.' Darren felt undeserving of their gratitude and praise. As far as he was concerned, all they had done was stand around protecting shops, and chase off a few youths. But as far as these residents were concerned, they were heroes.

Then he saw a sight that immediately woke him from his weariness. A lady was walking towards them with a tray of tea and toast. She gave it out and then disappeared, returning with more and more – more than enough for everyone on his unit. Twenty-one mugs of steaming, sweet tea, with round after round of hot toast, all brought out for the officers. A huge tub of butter was also provided and they pounced ravenously – but gratefully – at their unexpected and very welcome breakfast.

1000 hrs
Cambridge
At around 10am Mark received another call, this time in his office. London was requesting assistance. Mark went to speak to his boss. 'Sir, the mutual aid call has just come in from The Met.'

'Yeah, I know.'

Mark was confused. 'You know? But it's only just come in.'

'I was told last night that they would call. I've just been waiting for it to come in. Why do you think I called you in so early this morning? It's got fuck all to do with Cambridgeshire, but if I had told you the reason at 5am you'd have been like a dog with two dicks. You would have got nothing done.'

Mark was a touch irritated, but there were no hard feelings because he understood the reasons why he had been kept in the dark. His boss had got the work completed that he needed done, and so Mark hadn't wasted his time. The reports containing the figures and numbers of officers available were used to put together the Cambridgeshire PSUs and just forty minutes later they were ready – 1 inspector, 3 sergeants and 18 constables, plus three to drive the carriers. In addition, they brought two medics. Many other forces across the country were doing the same.

A short time later they set off for London.

71

South Norwood

As had been predicted by Tom, 7am came and went. He and his fellow officers were cold and exhausted. Eyes were raw and muscles ached. It wasn't until after 10am that the early turn shift eventually arrived to relieve them. The Croydon officers finally boarded their carrier and made their way back to South Norwood, where they could de-kit, book off duty and finally get home for some much needed rest and sleep. At least that was what they had thought – and hoped for. But at South Norwood, those ideas were immediately crushed.

'Right, you need to stay on,' they were told by a sergeant. 'You need to re-parade at 2pm for your normal late turn shift.'

Their shift pattern meant that they worked two early shifts, followed by two late shifts following by two night shifts. They had been on their first late shift when they had been taken away for Tottenham. Today should have been – and now was again – their second late shift. It never occurred to them that they would still be required to work it after what they had been through in Tottenham. It didn't matter that they had just spent the entire previous day and night fighting on those streets. It was almost as though the previous night hadn't happened. The officers were drained and weary to the point of collapse. They had been on duty for hours – all afternoon, all night and into the morning. They hadn't eaten or had any water. Nothing had been arranged to have their late shift covered and now they were expected – ordered – to stay at work and continue into their regular shift pattern, working from 2pm to 10pm.

Some officers tried to complain on the grounds they had kids to take to school or other commitments that morning. Other officers were carrying injuries from the previous night's rioting and needed to recover. But they were all told the same thing: they were staying on.

The officers decided to try to make the most of the handful of hours that they had to themselves, hoping to grab a couple of hours' kip before their shift was due to start but they were told that they couldn't use any of the offices or rooms at the station to rest in, as they were needed for briefings, and besides, there was only one blow-up mattress in the entire station anyway.

'Why don't we go down to Homebase or somewhere, and get more beds?' one of the officers suggested. 'We can find somewhere to put them. Just give us some money and we'll go and buy them.'

This request was quickly refused.

Tom gave up and slipped away to his car, which was parked in the police station yard. He made himself as comfortable as was possible on the back seats and did his best to get any snatches of sleep that he could.

During all this, officers were made aware of messages had been circulating since the previous night which said that Croydon was to be attacked. 'Everyone out to Croydon for looting', was one BlackBerry message that had been intercepted. Cans of petrol had been found hidden in bushes, placed there by two youths, no doubt in preparation for the trouble that was being planned for that evening. This was not sporadic or opportunist – it was clearly organised. More messages were circulating to gather in Croydon and to 'Fuck the Feds [the police]'. It was early but trouble was already starting to build.

1100 hrs
Lewisham
Darren and his unit arrived back at Lewisham police station. They had finally been relieved at Edmonton at 10am by other Level 2 officers. Darren didn't even know what borough the officers were from; he was just pleased that someone had finally come to take

over. As he trudged through the station he passed by the gym. He looked in. The floor was covered with sleeping officers, all of whom had spent the night fighting in the riots somewhere or other, and were getting some kip before going back out.

Darren closed the door quietly. *Well, at least they've had a great night,* he thought to himself.

Darren and the rest of his unit were dismissed. Their shift had come to an end and they were allowed to go home. Darren didn't waste any time; he left Lewisham and returned to Catford police station so that he could drop off his riot kit before jumping into his car and heading home. His wife was at work and he had a one-year-old baby boy but Darren's mum had taken his son home with her so that Darren could get some rest. In the end Darren only managed to get a couple of hours' sleep, so he called his mum and asked her to bring his baby boy back.

No sooner had his mum dropped off his son and returned to her own house than Darren's phone rang. It was Lewisham police. Lewisham had already sent a full PSU – the officers he had seen sleeping in the gym – to another borough, where disorder had broken out, but now trouble was starting to spread into Lewisham itself. With their own PSU elsewhere, the borough had been left dangerously exposed. Darren was told to get his arse back into work ASAP.

Darren looked down at his boy, giggling on his knee, and he made his own phone call. 'Mum, it's Darren again…'

Darren arrived back at Catford to pick up his riot kit bag. The station was practically deserted and he walked through the building searching for someone who may be able to run him over to Lewisham. Eventually he found a lone PC. He was young and still in his probation but he was able to drive a panda car, and that was good enough for Darren.

'Mate, I need a lift to Lewisham. I really don't want to have to take a bus to get there.'

'Yeah, of course,' the PC said. 'I'll take you over.'

Darren threw his kit bag onto the back seats of the car and they left Catford police station. Almost immediately they saw gangs of youths crazily charging around the streets. Then, in a surreal moment, the gangs charged at them – running towards their little car.

'What the hell are they doing?' Darren asked out loud.

As some of the youths continued to run towards the police car, others stopped. Darren watched as they dropped an arm behind their backs and then swinging it up again, quickly, releasing whatever it was they had been holding. Suddenly bricks and bottles began to crash down on and around the car. Within seconds, the officers had gone from the relative safety of the police building into a hail of missiles. Road signs, traffic cones, rocks and bottles were all being thrown towards them. They slammed into the body of the vehicle and against the windows.

The probationer looked stunned.

'PUT YOUR FOOT DOWN!' Darren screamed at him. 'FLOOR IT! MOVE!'

The driver was young in service but even he could see the seriousness of their situation, and he didn't need telling twice. He brought the car down a gear and stamped his foot to the floor, diving into what they hoped would be quieter side streets, in a desperate attempt to escape the attack.

At first, no matter where they went, the streets seemed to be completely under the control of the mobs, and there were no other police in sight. The lack of other police units made their own presence all the more dangerous; they were an easy target – the only target around – and the rioters seemed terrifyingly resolute in trying to catch them. And what would they do if they did catch them? It didn't bear thinking about. Every road they turned down, there were more and more people milling around, gathering in numbers and looking for trouble. Darren and his young driver probed deeper and deeper into the side-roads, further and further away from where they were trying to go, to avoid the gangs of rioters.

Swerving around another corner, the road suddenly cleared – no bricks, no bottles and no people whatsoever. It was a deserted residential street and that was just fine as far as the two officers were concerned.

With their hearts still pounding, they finally made it to Lewisham. Somehow they had made it in one piece. Even the car seemed relatively undamaged despite the hammering it had taken. Darren thanked the probationer, feeling for him, as he knew that he now had to make the return journey back to Catford alone.

Inside Lewisham police station, Darren found his way to the IBO – the Integrated Borough Operations office – where he figured that there would be someone to direct him to where he needed to be, and where he was expected. A lone female PC was sat in there, staring at a computer screen and scribbling notes onto a piece of scrap paper. She looked stressed, and paid little attention to Darren.

'I was told to come here to parade,' Darren said, breaking the silence.

'Okay,' she replied, sounding busy and impatient. 'Well, who are you?'

Darren told her his name but he doubted that she even heard him.

'Where am I meant to go?' he asked. 'Is there a briefing?'

The officer snorted. 'No,' she told him. 'Just go out and deal with whatever you see.' And she handed him a small bottle of water from a stack in the corner of the room.

Darren stared at the water and then looked up at the female officer, taking in what she had just told him. She was now back at work, and clearly had more on her plate than one officer was meant to handle. Darren looked around the room. There was no one else here.

Then he realised the seriousness of the situation: there were no more police officers. Even worse, it seemed to Darren that there was no one in charge, no one organising the police response to what was happening in Lewisham. Had it really become so desperate, so hopeless that they were at the point where they had no choice but to send out officers on their own? That was what he had just been told to do – go out onto the streets alone. The danger of doing that during these riots was obvious – the drive over from Catford had made that perfectly clear – but then, what choice was there? These were exceptional circumstances. Even so, he knew that if he were spotted by a mob his life would be in serious danger.

Darren thought for a few more seconds. Then he went back to his kit bag, picked up his shield and his riot helmet, stuffed the small bottle of water into a pocket, and stepped out of Lewisham police station, alone – a one-man riot squad.

Outside, he pulled on his helmet, lowered the visor, and looked around him. He picked a direction, and began to jog.

1300 hrs
Guildford, Surrey
Richard was now at home, trying to relax. He'd started work at 10am on Sunday morning, and hadn't got off duty until 11am the following morning – a 25-hour shift that consisted mostly of

having bricks and bottles thrown at his head. Getting any rest, though, was proving to be impossible. As his phone rang for the umpteenth time, Richard knew what it would be: another officer from his TSG unit wanting to know when exactly they would be getting deployed again. It was the worst rioting for a generation and they were supposedly the elite riot trained officers. Yet they were all sitting at home, watching it on TV. All were willing to come in to work – all *wanted* to come in and work. Like racehorses at the starting gate, they were desperate to get going and do the job they were trained for.

Richard felt the same way as his colleagues, and he had been calling their station over and over, offering up himself and his officers for duty. He was told the same thing repeatedly: 'No, you aren't to come in.'

'But I have officers calling me up,' he explained. 'My phone is hot! I have people texting me, asking what they should do. Telling me that they are by their phone, just waiting for the call, asking if they should come in.'

'Under no circumstances are you to come in,' he was told.

'But I am just sitting at home, watching it happening on TV!'

'Don't come in. There're no plans for you to come in. Everything is all right. You're not needed. We don't need any extra TSG officers.'

Richard looked at his TV, and saw images of buildings in various London boroughs burning to the ground, police cars and other vehicles burning out of control, and police officers desperately trying to take back control of the streets against overwhelming numbers of rioters. Worst of all, he saw police colleagues being petrol bombed and led away covered in blood.

'Everything is all right. You're not needed.'

Richard couldn't understand it.

Minutes later his phone rang again. It was another officer calling up. Another officer – like him – wondering why the fuck they were all sitting on their arses at home doing absolutely nothing to help.

1400 hrs
Croydon

At 2pm Tom and his team paraded for late turn as ordered. But it felt ridiculous to them; this was never going to be a normal shift. Croydon had already been hit and they'd had more intelligence suggesting it was going to get worse as the evening went on. Under the mutual aid system, officers from other boroughs were being drafted in to help, including from Greenwich, which Tom thought was ridiculous as he had heard that Croydon officers had been sent on mutual aid to Greenwich. *Where's the planning? Where's the common sense?* he thought to himself, while imagining the Croydon PSUs and the Greenwich PSUs each waving as they crossed paths on their way to the other's borough.

After their normal late turn parade, the officers set out on patrol. They were dressed in their regular uniforms, patrolling like it was a regular day. Some officers were even posted to cars on their own, single-crewed. Again, Tom was left scratching his head. Single crewing was normal practice but surely not at a time like this. *Why are they trying to pretend it's business as usual?* he wondered.

Tom set off from the station, wondering why on earth he was going around taking calls from people who wanted their friends arrested for saying bad things about them on Facebook. This sort of thing wasn't important on normal days, let alone right now when there were no officers left in the box and everyone knew it was going to kick off at any moment. But any complaints landed to deaf ears. 'Just do your core work,' they were told.

The officers were scattered across the borough, from Norbury to Addington, reporting 'domestics' and acting like everything was fine. But an hour later the panic button was pushed. Croydon was now kicking off in a big way. It was still daylight but gangs of masked youths were attacking shops and businesses – smashing and looting. Surrounding stations were contacted in a bid to get more resources, and nearly a hundred public order officers were being sent down from Central London. Serious, large-scale disorder had broken out.

Tom continued to patrol the streets as he would on any other given day. While still recovering from the previous night's rioting in Tottenham, and suffering from a serious lack of sleep, he turned a corner into a deserted residential street. As he did so, his radio suddenly came to life.

'Anyone who is Level 2 trained, go to Croydon now! Get your kit and get out there!'

Tom and his fellow officers stopped patrolling and made their way back to the station as quickly as they could.

1500 hrs
Ealing
Keith arrived at Ealing police station. He had been waiting since Saturday to come to work and he couldn't understand how, as London burnt and rioters ran wild, he hadn't been called in sooner. Despite the fact that he was a Level 2 riot-trained officer, he had sat at home watching on TV as streets, buses, police cars, shops and homes were all destroyed. He had even telephoned his station in desperation, offering to come in to work, but to his astonishment he was repeatedly told to stay at home. Finally, after

two nights of the worst rioting the country had seen in a generation, he was told to come in.

And now here he was, standing in the near-empty station yard at Ealing police station. If tumbleweed had blown by, it wouldn't have looked out of place. But at least he had finally been called in, as had other officers from his station. All were pleased and relieved to be finally heading to the riots. The only issue they had now was the lack of a riot carrier, and they were certainly going to need one, ideally with a protective metal grill that could be pulled down over the windscreen. But the only vehicle left in the yard was a 'Level 3' carrier, which was nothing more than a basic minibus; the type of thing cub scouts were transported in. It had zero protection and was utterly unsuitable for a riot – no blue lights, no sirens and no grills – but it was all they had, so it would have to do.

Keith looked at the other officers. Many were young in service and some had never been involved in any public order situations before. A few weeks previously, working towards a promotion, Keith had taken his sergeant's exam. Even though he was still a PC, the exam, along with his experience as a Level 2 public order officer and 15 years of police service, would mean that many of the younger officers would be looking to him for direction and leadership. He also knew that due to his height – he towered over many of the other officers – he would also make a good target for the rioters.

The officers threw their kit bags, containing their flameproof overalls, arm and leg guards, gloves and riot helmet, into the minibus but none of this equipment was much use without shields. Riot carriers were equipped with enough shields for each officer but this minibus had nothing, and there were none to be found in the station – they had all been taken already. With no better option, Keith and the rest of the officers set off regardless, hoping that they would manage to find some shields somewhere before they reached the frontline.

With or without shields, they'd been ordered to get to Hackney, where the disorder had increased to such a level that there was real concern the streets and neighbourhoods would be completely lost to the rioters. Keith and the rest of his crew didn't know it but they were heading into the most dangerous rioting of the troubles so far, and without much of the protective equipment they would need. They were heading into serious, serious danger.

Central London

The Cambridge PSU arrived in Central London, and the unit inspector went in for a pre-deployment briefing, leaving the rest of the Cambridge officers to wait in their carriers. The officers were buzzing. All around them were police units and PSUs from across the country. Officers were coming and going, vehicles were turning up and leaving, bosses were speaking urgently into mobile phones while carrying bundles of papers and maps – it was all happening and they were now, finally, a part of it. There was the rush of adrenaline knowing that they would soon be heading into the riots. But their excitement was about to be crushed.

The inspector came back out a short while later, looking despondent. The buzz that had been circulating thorough the carriers suddenly ceased.

'Guv?' an officer said, as the inspector climbed back onto the carrier.

'We're being deployed to Oxford Street for high-visibility patrols and public reassurance,' he told his officers, glumly.

Everyone was disappointed. They had all mentally geared themselves up for the frontline, and now here they were being told to walk around London's tourist spots. It was not what they were expecting or what they had hoped for. Some wondered if they were being fobbed off because they were from Cambridgeshire, leaving the London officers to deal with the real trouble.

As the carriers set off, it quickly became apparent that no one actually had any idea where they were going. In their rush to get down to London they hadn't had any time to prepare, so no one had a map and Cambridgeshire didn't fit the carriers with satnavs. The Met hadn't given them anything either.

'Pull in here,' the drivers were told, as they approached a petrol station.

Officers jumped out, ran inside and bought some London A-Zs to share among the carriers.

Then another problem presented itself. The Metropolitan Police were not using the national standard mutual aid radio channels – they were using their own Met channels, which the Cambridgeshire carriers and other county forces' carriers didn't have. It wouldn't have been so bad if the Met had at least provided them with a handheld Met radio, but they hadn't even given them those. The only way they could communicate with each other was by mobile phone. Not having radios in a regular police incident was bad enough, but in a riot?

As they left the petrol station, the inspector received a call on his mobile; they were to redeploy immediately to Upton Park, where there were reports of a bank on fire, with people and police officers trapped inside and under siege.

Everyone looked at each other. This was it. The moment they had all wanted so much. Finally, they were on their way to the frontline. The driver switched on the blue lights and sirens, and waited while his operator flicked through the newly acquired A-Z, working out how to get to Upton Park.

Lee

Having managed to snatch a couple of hours sleep after getting home from Brixton, Alan was once again driving towards his TSG base in Catford to parade for work. As he turned off Bromley Road into Aitken Road, where his TSG unit was based, he saw around thirty men hanging around at the top of the street. The men looked out of place, like they were waiting for something, and they eyed Alan darkly as he drove slowly past them.

Are they planning to attack the base? Alan wondered.

Other officers from Alan's unit arriving for work had had the same fears. Although Alan had to move a bit slower – his right shoulder was still causing him pain – everyone got kitted up as quickly as they could in case they had to defend their own building. But no attack came and the men remained gathered at the top of the road. Instead, Alan and his unit were ordered onto their carriers. They were to head straight out to Lee, just to the south of Greenwich Park and Blackheath, where, they were told, mayhem had broken out.

Driving out of the base and back up Aitken Road, Alan took another look at the men on the corner. Something wasn't right about them. Then the carrier drove past the Bromley Road Retail Park, with stores including PC World and Currys. *Was that their intended target?* Alan wondered. Maybe, but whatever the men were up to, whatever criminality they may or may not have been planning, someone else would have to deal with them. The carrier drivers switched on the sirens, and speeded up.

In Lee, local shops had been attacked and rioters were running amok along Lee High Road. The large, glass windows of the Dirty South pub, which faced directly onto the street, were all completely smashed in. Reports had come through that the rioters were attempting to burn it down. Next door, the Xin Long

Chinese take away had also had its windows put in. Across the road, Mino's Hairdressing had all of its windows smashed. Its owner stood inside among piles of broken glass, guarding what was left of his small business. Nearby, the constituency office of local Labour MP Heidi Alexander (who was, at that moment, in New York enjoying the first day of her honeymoon, which she cut short because of the riots) also had its windows smashed, and the door had been kicked in. Looters had entered the building and stolen laptops. The laptops, however, were encrypted which made them useless to the thieves.

Further along the road, the BP petrol station too, had been attacked. As with all the other businesses, its windows were smashed, with glass covering the ground inside and out. Bins had been overturned and litter and debris lay everywhere. Shop after shop, business after business had been smashed up and looted. But the local Nando's chicken restaurant – a favourite with many, criminal and police alike – had escaped untouched. Reports were also filtering through that customers drinking in the nearby Wetherspoons pub had even been robbed in what was described as a 'mass mugging'. Lee had been hit hard.

Alan's unit pulled into the area. The streets were filled with youths. Many had their hoods up. Others had scarves over the bottom parts of their faces. Some had both. The arrival of the police was immediately met with a barrage of bottles and bricks. The officers quickly left their carriers, helmets strapped on, shields held up, batons drawn. The rioters had had the run of Lee for some time with little interference from the police, despite being just yards from Lewisham police station – the largest police station in Europe – but that was all about to change.

The officers lined up, stretching out across the street. The sergeants and inspector stood behind them, ready to organise and direct the officers. Bricks, bottles, traffic cones, pieces of wood – the usual variety of improvised missiles – came tumbling down on them.

'VISORS DOWN!' a sergeant shouted from behind the officers' line. 'TO THE NEXT JUNCTION! FORWARD!'

The officers jogged towards the next road junction, about 50 yards ahead of them. The youths continued throwing whatever they had in their hands. Bricks and bottles smashed at their feet. Some of the missiles reached a target and officers felt the solid impact on their shields. A few others felt the heavy weight of the missiles striking the toes of their boots or slamming into exposed parts of their bodies – legs, shoulders and arms.

'HALT!' the sergeant ordered.

They had reached the junction. With a danger that officers wouldn't notice the junction they were aiming for due to the red mist of adrenaline or because their visors had fogged up with condensation, the sergeant had screamed the order to stop as loudly as he could. The officers themselves then repeated the order to each other to be doubly sure everyone heard it. Alan could hear shouting coming from all directions: orders being called out by sergeants and inspectors, fellow officers warning each other of incoming missiles, and from the crowd came the usual screams of abuse – 'Fuck the pigs!' and 'We're gonna fucking kill you!' All around him was noise.

The rioters, who had begun to fall back at the approach of the police line, started to shuffle forward again, picking up any discarded missiles, and inching closer. The police held their position. More of the mob moved back up. Then they began to lob the bricks and bottles again. The officers calmly parried away any missiles that had managed to reach them, with their shields and waited for the next order.

'TO THE NEXT JUNCTION... GO!'

'GO!' the officers shouted back in unison.

They were now sprinting along the road, leaping over bottles and bricks that fell in front of them before scuttling along the ground. The rioters turned and ran once more.

'HALT!'

And then again, with more urgency, 'HALT!'

A couple of officers, not hearing the order, had kept moving but were quickly pulled back in line by colleagues, who reached out with their gloved hands, grabbing them by the collar and firmly yanking them backwards.

The officers had passed shop after shop that had been attacked. A blanket of shattered glass lay across the ground, dotted with tiny islands of smashed bricks and concrete. It was as though an enormous builder's skip had been emptied along the road. The area looked ruined, but the police advances were working. The gradual pushes were forcing the rioters back, and Lee High Road was being retaken and cleared. Other police units then started to move in, although Alan couldn't see if they were TSG, local officers, Level 2s or 'county'. It didn't matter anyway; they were winning.

No sooner had Alan's unit completed the series of short shield advances, clearing the High Road, than they were suddenly ordered back to their carriers. It would be the start of a period where they would dash from one location to the next, frantically clearing away rioters and looters all across south London. Their next deployment was to Peckham, which was quickly descending into violence.

That afternoon, Robin arrived at Ealing police station to start his usual late shift. The place looked deserted – he knew many Ealing officers had been deployed to Hackney, where serious trouble was breaking out. But despite the disturbances that were happening elsewhere around London, normal policing still needed to done, and Robin was no longer a riot officer. With well over 30 years of police service under his belt, his days of running around with a plastic shield and having petrol bombs thrown at his feet were well and truly behind him. He had spent several years in the TSG, and had kept up the training after coming to Ealing, becoming a borough Level 2 officer, but the constant cancellation of his rest days to work at football matches had convinced him to give it up.

But he had plenty of experience. Robin worked through the Brixton and Tottenham riots of the 1980s, at one point fighting for his life in the heart of Brixton after being ambushed by a large group. He remembered clearly the crowds of angry men throwing petrol bombs and bricks at police officers – at him. Once, as he stood in a line with other officers in Brixton, men armed with machetes tied to the tops of long poles had tried to stab him. A week later he was sent to Broadwater Farm in Tottenham, arriving there the day after Keith Blakelock had been murdered. The Simple Minds song 'Alive and Kicking' had been in the charts, and since then he couldn't hear it without thinking back to that terrible time. Now he was living and working through a whole new period of unrest and disturbances, and those terrible days from the 1980s would come back to haunt him.

Despite all he had seen and been through, Robin still loved being a copper. He could have retired on a full police pension years ago, but he refused to, and instead he turned up for work as eager as a probationer just starting out.

Robin now drove the 'Q Car' – one of the unmarked robbery cars that operated on the borough – and he loved his job. He also loved Ealing. He was an Ealing boy born and bred, and still lived there. Many of the local youths knew him and he had even picked up a nickname from the kids along the way: 'The Terminator', or just 'The Term'.

Ealing wasn't Hackney. It was a generally calm, pleasant, neighbourhood in the west London suburbs, with million-pound homes, trendy restaurants and pubs. It was also home to the legendary centre of filmmaking, Ealing Studios. But that was mostly around Ealing Broadway and Ealing Common. Further west, along Uxbridge Road, the borough morphed into Southall, Hayes and Harlington. Million-pound homes became scarcer and the streets slightly rougher around the edges. But Southall was a good area, a well known Asian neighbourhood with large collections of Asian jewellers and restaurants. It was colourful and vibrant, busy and energising, and a world away from the less exotic Ealing Broadway.

These differences in neighbourhoods was one of the features that made Ealing Borough an exciting place to work but even with those difference, it still wasn't Hackney, and Robin felt quite sure that whatever was happening elsewhere around London, life would continue to plod along as normal where he was.

But Robin couldn't have been more wrong.

At the briefing before they left the station to start their patrol, Robin and the two officers he was posted with – Michelle and Sergeant Ashton – were given an update about the rioting happening in other boroughs. Much of what they were told, they were already aware of; like everyone else, they had been glued to the TV news for the past couple of days. They had heard a few rumours that Ealing could be hit but Robin didn't think it would happen here. This was the west London suburbs, not the inner city. He figured that any trouble makers that they did have on the borough would be heading to other parts of London to take part in the looting and rioting that was already going on rather than hanging out in Ealing.

The three officers left the station in their unmarked Ford Mondeo, and headed towards Ealing Broadway. It was a nice, pleasant afternoon but very quickly Robin noticed small pockets of youths – youths he didn't recognise – hanging around the streets, or sitting on railings outside high street shops. It was a little strange but still, he didn't think anything would happen here. Perhaps they were just gathering before heading elsewhere.

Outside Ealing Broadway rail station Robin noticed a small group of local youths – eight of them – hanging around, looking like they were planning an evening of trouble; they had their hoods pulled up, despite the warm afternoon weather. Robin pulled up outside the station. The car was unmarked, but all the local kids knew it on sight. If they were lucky, the unmarked car gave the officers inside a few extra valuable seconds before being noticed. Sometimes criminals were too excitable to even distinguish them from the regular cars on the streets, but in calm circumstances like this, the kids spotted them a mile off.

Robin stepped out. The kids all smiled – it was 'The Term'. Around them, regular commuters were hurrying past, walking away from the small station entrance and towards Haven Green, the tidy garden square that this neighbourhood surrounded.

'We've been hearing rumours that Ealing is going to get done tonight,' Robin mentioned to the small gang.

'Nah. It ain't gonna happen here,' one of the youths said. 'We're off to Hackney. That's where it's happening.'

And with that, the kids walked away towards the station platform to catch a train to the riots.

Robin turned to Michelle and Sergeant Ashton. 'That's what I figured,' he said.

The three officers jumped back into the car. Robin turned the key, started the engine and drove slowly away from Ealing Broadway station and back towards the town centre, just a short distance away. As they drove, they began to receive text messages on their own phones, warning them of the latest rumours for trouble. BlackBerry Messenger (BBM) was apparently going into meltdown. All the kids and gangs were using BBM to communicate and messages where flying around that 'Ealing's going to kick off tonight'. Still, Robin felt sure that nothing was going to happen on his borough. After all, hadn't he just seen a bunch of youths saying that Hackney was where it was at tonight?

All this talk of Ealing kicking off is just bollocks, Robin thought.

But he couldn't ignore the fact that things were feeling different now. Along the High Street Robin once again noticed gaggles of youths hanging around, waiting. But waiting for what? There was a weird vibe in the air – eerie, almost. None of the youths were wearing masks over their faces, as he had seen on the news, but still, the groups looked out of place.

As he drove slowly along the road, with the rest of the evening traffic, he wondered if the rumours were true after all.

Robin brought the car to a stop, at a set of red traffic lights. 'Something's not right,' he said out loud. 'Something does not feel right.'

At that moment a group of youths sprinted towards them. Robin didn't know why they were running, but they charged towards the line of traffic he was sitting in. As the youths reach them, they jumped onto the bonnet of the Mondeo, and the car bounced under their weight. It had happened so suddenly that all Robin, Michelle and Sergeant Ashton could do was watch in silent disbelief as their car was trampled on. A second later, the youths had disappeared into the traffic, and across the street.

The officers looked at each other.

'Something is definitely going to go on here tonight,' Michelle said.

At that moment another youth jumped over the bonnet of their car and as he did so, he peered in, grinning crazily at the three officers. 'Waaaahaaaayyyyy!' he shrieked, excitedly.

'Yeah, I've got a feeling you could be right,' Robin said to Michelle.

The traffic started to flow again and as they continued on, a regular call came out. There had been a robbery earlier in the shift and two uniform beat officers had spoken with the victim, taking some notes about the incident and getting a description of the suspect. Ealing Borough prioritised robbery reports and one of the most important jobs was to take a description from any victim or witness whilst it was still fresh in their mind, and get it written down into an Evidence and Actions Book (EAB). The beat officers had taken the description and now wanted to hand the EABs over to the Q Car for filing with the robbery team, who would then take on the investigation.

Robin arranged to meet the officers on a nearby corner and as he drove down the street, ahead of him he could see the two officers in uniform standing around, and talking. One of the officers was holding the distinctive blue EAB in his hands. Robin pulled up alongside the pair. The officer with the book took off his beat helmet and bent down to lean on the open, front passenger window.

'It's all in there,' the officer said, handing the book over. 'A full description of the suspect. Usual thing though – all dark clothing, face covered, etc, etc.'

'No problem,' Robin replied. 'How has it been otherwise? Anything else going on?'

'Usual stuff,' the officer said. 'A few unfamiliar faces hanging around, though.'

'Yeah, we've noticed that too. Just had a bunch charge over our car. Hopefully nothing will happen, but be careful, it could still all go to shit.'

The officers told him they would and placed their helmets back on their heads, before turning around and strolling casually off, down the street.

'How about we drop this book off and grab a bite to eat?' Robin suggested to Michelle and Sergeant Ashton.

'Sounds like a plan,' Sergeant Ashton said.

Everything was starting to seem normal again, just like any other day. As they drove back, through the early evening traffic, Robin paid a little more attention to the groups of youths that were gathering. Perhaps like the ones he had spoken to earlier, they were meeting up before heading off to Hackney, he thought. Then his phone buzzed. Messages from friends and colleagues were still coming through to him stating that Ealing was to be targeted that evening; that Ealing would be 'going up', and that it was going to 'kick off'. Increasingly concerned, his friends warned him to watch his back. But Robin still wasn't sure – lots of rumours about lots of places had been flying around for some time.

Ahead of him was Acton police station. Robin slowed down, checked his rear-view mirror and turned on the left indicator. Then he checked the nearside wing-mirror to be sure it was safe to turn and that no cyclists were slipping down the side of the car. It was clear and he began to slowly turn the steering wheel, looking forward to grabbing something to eat.

And then the call came.

'URGENT ASSISTANCE! URGENT ASSISTANCE! WE'RE BEING ATTACKED!'

Robin recognised the voice; it was the officer who had just handed him the EAB.

'WE'RE UNDER ATTACK! URGENT ASSISTANCE!' he screamed.

Robin spun the car around. He switched on the sirens and covert blue lights and rushed back towards the officers. They were in danger. Serious danger. Other than the sound of the engine and the sirens, the car was silent. No one spoke. All three people inside were focused on reaching the uniformed officers.

Over the radio, the two officers told Robin they were running for their lives, away from a mob. He listened as, at the corner of Bond Street, the officers ran into a 7-Eleven store, and quickly pulled down the metal shutters, locking themselves inside. For now, they were safe and the mob quickly moved on. The two police officers stayed where they were, waiting until other officers could later come and get them out.

Things were now moving quickly. With the two officers safely locked inside the 7-Eleven, Robin turned towards the WHSmith on The Broadway and pulled up outside. Word was now coming through that there were 'smash-and-grabs' in progress inside The Broadway Shopping Centre. Jewellers in particular were being targeted.

'I know exactly where the looters will come out,' Robin said.

He pulled back out, into the traffic and roared around into the High Street. As he did so, around twenty masked and hooded men charged out of the building and ran across the front of the car. Each had their hands full, with boxes of jewellery and watches. Operating on instinct, Robin went to open the car door.

'Don't get out! Don't get out!' Sergeant Ashton said. 'There aren't enough of us to take them all on.'

Robin knew that she was right – two officers had already been attacked and chased – but they also couldn't just stand by and allow the mob to run off with arms full of stolen loot.

'Right, we're going with them,' Robin said. He put the car in gear and began to drive alongside the sprinting looters.

Some of the hooded men looked over at them and realising who they were, called out to the others that the 'feds' were chasing them. The looters picked up their pace. At the end of the High Street, some split from the main group, jumping over a fence and running into Walpole Park but Robin stayed with the group that continued into Mattock Lane. Ahead of him, scattered randomly across the street, Robin noticed 4 or 5 cars with engines revving and doors open. The cars were waiting for the looters, who quickly dived into the passenger seats, slamming the car doors behind them. The drivers roared away, down the narrow, residential street. Robin, with the car's sirens and blue lights still going, put the call out over the police radio that he was now in pursuit. Ahead of him was a chain of getaway vehicles.

The car he was directly behind careered along Mattock Lane. The junction with Culmington Road was coming up, and Robin heard another officer on the radio. The officer was driving a police van and coming to back Robin up. He was just turning into Culmington Road from Uxbridge Road. At the junction, the getaway car swung sharply to the right, into Culmington Road. By now the police van was racing down the road towards Mattock, and on seeing the flashing blue lights ahead of them, the driver of the car panicked, swerving across the junction and slamming the car into a metal bollard on the corner of the road. The car came to an immediate halt as it hit the post.

Robin quickly pulled up behind the stacked car. The station van raced towards them and came to a halt in front of it. As the officers were leaping from their vehicles, the car occupants were doing the same, their eyes wide in panic. Robin dived onto the driver, and the pair fell to the floor. The driver was a man in his twenties, and he began to struggle desperately to get out of Robin's grip. As they fought, stolen jewellery and watches began to tumble out of the man's pockets, scattering across the road. As the man continued to squirm, Robin managed to get a firmer grip on his arm, bending it round behind his back, and the driver of the police van, who had now joined him, snapped one end of his handcuffs onto the guy's wrist. It was game over. As Robin stood the man on his feet, he peered into the open doors of the car that the man had decamped from. The foot wells were covered in even more stolen jewellery and watches. The men hadn't just pinched one or two items – they had absolutely gone for it, stealing armfuls of expensive gear.

A uniformed officer approached Robin. The officer was a probationer and keen to make an arrest.

'Do you want to arrest him for burglary?' Robin asked.

'Yes!' the officer replied.

Robin gave the probationer the facts and told him that he would write up his statement a little later, once all the craziness had died down.

Robin watched as a couple of other handcuffed men were brought out of the park, where they had been chased and caught by other officers. Leaving the uniform officers to it, Robin, Sergeant Ashton and Michelle went back to patrolling the streets.

More people had begun to gather in and around Ealing Broadway, and Robin gave updates to the control room about the size and locations of the various groups.

Most of the groups were gathered on corners and junctions along the Uxbridge Road so Robin took to driving up and down a short section, keeping a close eye on them, and continuing to update the police control room. As the groups grew in size, Robin became increasingly concerned. And then, suddenly, without any warning, the gangs of youths started kicking the hell out of shop fronts. All along the street he could see large plate-glass windows bending under the force of the repeated kicks until eventually one after another, the windows gave in, and shattering.

Robin watched in horror. 'It's started,' he said.

Lewisham

Darren trotted up the road, looking all around him, checking junctions and side streets. He was totally alone. The streets were deserted, and he was seriously exposed. His pulse was racing with adrenaline, his heart thumping in his chest. He thought that he must have looked like a character from some apocalyptic zombie flick – a lone survivor wandering the streets, looking for signs of life, while all the time hoping not to find any.

A breeze blew along the road, picking up random pieces of litter and tossing them about at low-level, in the gutters. He stopped for a moment and lifted his helmet visor, looking up and down the empty street, and at the closed and shuttered buildings. He wondered what he was meant to do if he came across groups of rioters. After all, he knew what they would do to him if they got the chance. *You'll find out soon enough*, Darren told himself. And then he pulled his visor back down and picked his pace back up, still completely alone. The only sounds he could hear were the rhythmic stomping of his black boots on the ground, his heavy breathing and the beating of his heart.

Darren was relieved that the streets were quiet, but the stillness soon took on an eerie, ominous feel. He knew that if something happened, if he did come across some rioters, there would be no one to help him, no one to witness what happened to him. The streets suddenly felt a lot smaller, more confined, as if the surrounding buildings were tightening a grip on him. Then he saw someone up ahead. He lifted his shield, defensively. His visor was already misted up with condensation and as he lifted it, for a clearer view, he realised that the person was another police officer, also in riot gear and also alone. Darren jogged towards the officer, who had also now seen him. It was a sergeant that he knew, and she seemed as pleased to see him as he was to see her.

'Fancy meeting you here,' she said, smiling.

'I was told to go out on my own,' he told her.

'Me too,' she said.

The pair teamed up and jogged up the road together. As they did, a police minibus drove towards them. Most of the side windows had been smashed in, and the four officers inside looked tired and on edge. Whatever they had been through, they had clearly taken a battering.

'Need a lift somewhere?' the driver asked.

Darren and the sergeant hopped inside. They were glad to have found more officers to team up with and happy to have a set of wheels, even if it was a smashed up, unprotected minibus. But it was better than nothing.

Darren thought about the situation they had all found themselves in. No one had been briefed, no one had been spoken to by anyone of rank, and no one had been told what the hell was going on or what they were even meant to do. But at least they had managed to find each other before any rioters had got to them; that was something.

The driver parked the carrier on a street corner. As the officers wondered what they should do or where they should go, the voices of local officers – officers Darren knew personally – came screaming over the radio.

'URGENT ASSISTANCE! URGENT ASSISTANCE!'

The desperate officers were at the Bromley Road Retail Park, to the south. It was where Alan had earlier seen a group hanging around. Alan's concerns about the men wanting to attack the retail park had been proved right, and now there were a total of just six PCs and PCSOs from a local Safer Neighbourhood Team there to protect it. Wearing basic beat uniform, with no protective riot equipment other than a couple of short shields between them, that handful of officers was seriously outnumbered. Darren thought they didn't stand a chance.

The retail park was a collection of modern warehouse-style buildings facing a car park. It contained half a dozen stores including a couple that would prove to be of particular interest to the mobs – PC World and Currys. The fact that the retail park was located pretty much next door to a TSG police base didn't seem to bother the would-be looters in the slightest. Perhaps they already knew that most officers were dealing with trouble elsewhere, and that there was little chance of any officers being there to come out to stop them. Or perhaps, in this anarchic new reality where the streets appeared to be ruled by criminals, they didn't care. To the half a dozen officers at the retail park, who were hoping desperately for reinforcements to show up, it felt as though there was some kind of rage overtaking everyone's minds. People seemed to be oblivious to the consequences that would surely come their way; if not now, than at some point in the near future.

All the mob seemed to be able to think about was the here and now.

The officers stood in a line outside PC World. A gang of around fifty youths were standing about thirty metres from this truly thin blue line, and were shouting aggressively at them. The officers were seriously and dangerously outnumbered but they held their formation. Their only other option was to make a run for it, and it was something they had all considered; after all, was it really worth risking all of their lives for the sake of a few shops? No, not by any logical analysis. But the six of them wouldn't leave, even when faced with this dire situation. They were the police, and these businesses were on their patch. As outnumbered as they were, they weren't going to just give up. The officers were going to hold their ground.

'We're gonna hit PC World and there ain't nothing you gonna do about it,' a yob yelled at the officers.

The officers looked around, watching as the mob moved in closer. Some in the crowd were holding house bricks, while others had bottles, and even fence posts. The officers had their batons drawn and held up, doing their best to show some sign of strength with genuine intent behind it. But they were wearing just their regular beat uniforms, and had only two shields between the six of them, and the rioters didn't seem worried at all.

Then the first brick was thrown. It landed a few feet in front of the officers, the rioters still too far back to be within range. The rioters moved closer, and more bricks were thrown. They were now close enough for some of the missiles to reach the officers, slamming into their bodies and legs. The officers held their line as the two of their number holding the small round shields did their best to protect the other four from the bottles and bricks. Then the mob – screaming and shouting obscenities and threats

– charged at the tiny group of police. It was fifty violent yobs against just six unprotected officers. If they had finally decided to run at this critical moment, could anyone blame them? Was it really worth risking all of their lives for a bunch of shops? Again, not by any logical analysis.

But the shops were Lewisham shops, and they were Lewisham officers. These were their streets, their businesses to protect, and if they didn't do it, then who would? The officers would not leave, and so they knew what they had to do. They could stand there and be overrun, attacked, beaten or even worse, or they could fight back. As the rioters rushed towards them – some picking up the rocks and bricks that they had previously thrown – the officers made the decision to charge. They waited until the rioters got a few yards closer towards them, and then the officers raised their batons in the air.

'GO!'

The six officers charged towards the mob – a far larger force – and the mob charged towards them. As they came together, the police officers started to swing their batons down upon the crowd.

'GET BACK! GET BACK!' the officers shouted.

The mob immediately began to retreat, dropping their bricks as the officers moved towards them. The six officers stopped and took a couple of steps backwards, careful not to move too far away from their original defensive position.

On seeing the officers retreating, the rioters' confidence came back. After arming themselves once more with bricks and bottles, they started to move forward again. And again, the officers desperately tried to protect themselves from falling glass and masonry – still with just two shields between the six of them. They were taking a battering; by now all the officers were bruised, and some had cuts on their arms. And although their offensive tactic had worked once, they knew they would be lucky to pull it off again. As the attack continued, it didn't seem likely that the rioters would be so easily spooked a second time. Rocks, bottles and bricks slammed into the officers' legs, arms and ankles. The situation was desperate, and as far as they knew, no one was coming to help them. Their courage and commitment was unquestionable, but the size of the crowd facing them was beginning to make those qualities irrelevant. How long could six injured officers hold off a mob of many times their number?

Hackney

At Bow Road, Sergeant Darin Birmingham stared in disbelief at the vehicle that he had been allocated. It was one he had been in many times before, just not in these circumstances. The vehicle was a basic police carrier – a minibus, effectively. It had no protective metal grills on the front windscreen to stop any bricks from coming through, and from what he had been seeing and hearing, a protective, metal grill on the windscreen to stop bricks coming through was exactly what they needed. In no way whatsoever did he believe that this vehicle was suitable for what they were likely to face. But this was the least of his problems. Not only was the carrier unprotected, so were the officers he was leading. They were a ragtag group with various levels of training, experience and skills. They had no riots shields, no helmets, and no other kind of protective equipment.

Darin, whose looks were often compared to the actor Ross Kemp, worked for the Safer Transport Command (STC), under the control of Transport for London (TfL). Their job was to tackle crime on the city's transport network and in and around interchanges, which meant bus and train stations. They were generally an effective outfit, but right now they had a serious problem: TfL didn't permit Level 2 public order trained officers. This meant they were all Level 3 officers – the lowest of the three levels of public order trained officers. They'd had no specialist training, and had no riot kit.

Darin was an experienced officer and he had spent his career in frontline roles, leading operations against gangs and firearms, working in forward intelligence and investigating football related violence. He considered himself a 'copper's copper' and he didn't suffer fools. He was well known for speaking his mind. But looking at their situation now, Darin was getting extremely worried about his officers' safety. He already knew that large parts of north London had gone to shit, so he figured that if they were being called in, there was no one else left. The situation must have been desperate. And Darin was keen to help; he loved London. As far as he was concerned it was the greatest city in the world, and he had always believed that its citizens deserved the best policing they could get. So despite his concerns, he knew that there was no choice but to get on with it.

The officers had already been told that if any of them had any old riot gear in their lockers or at home, they should go and get it. Many officers in London had done the same; gone home and dug out old riot helmets and overalls and equipment, ready to squeeze back into it should they need to. Some of this stuff was seriously outdated, but the officers figured that was a better option than heading out into a riot with nothing at all.

Some of Darin's TfL officers had previously worked on the TSG or had been Level 2 trained, so about a third of them had their own sets of riot uniform. The others had nothing.

Darin boarded his carrier. There were seven other officers with him. Two other sergeants had the same number of officers on their own equally unprotected carriers. The team inspector climbed aboard the first carrier and the three vehicles set off in convoy, heading towards Hackney. As they made their way through the streets, Darin looked at the seven officers he had with him. A couple had come from the Cab Enforcement Unit, the group within TfL which deals with incidents of touting or illegal drivers involving taxis and minicabs, and he didn't even know when the last time those guys had even worn a uniform, let alone fought in a riot. Even so, those officers had grabbed what little equipment they could, and come out with the rest of them, willing to put themselves in danger, and that said something.

Darin then looked over at the equipment his carrier was loaded with. They had just four, short shields and three riot helmets between the seven of them.

They reached Hackney at around 3pm, and the carriers pulled into Mare Street – the A107 – the main road that ran north and south through the borough. Everywhere they looked, it was total chaos, mobs fighting and looting, windows smashed, rubble on the ground. It was utter lawlessness, and their vehicles came under attack immediately, targeted with bricks and bottles. It felt to Darin as though the whole of the criminal world had got together to attack the police.

Rocks, glass bottles and masonry came flying out from all directions, slamming into the sides of the vehicles and windows. Officers instinctively ducked down or lifted up a hand in defence. All around them young men were charging about, picking up previously thrown objects to throw again. Huge, twisting balls of smoke filled the street, pumping out from burning cars, burning bins and burning barricades. Above them, Darin could hear the angry chopping sound of a helicopter's rotor blade.

From side streets, ahead and behind them, he could hear police sirens screaming urgently. The crowd was shouting and cheering.

Glass was smashing all around. Over the police radio channels, officers were screaming for help. There were too many 'Urgent Assistance' calls coming in to count. It was total mayhem. Everyone seemed to have just gone berserk.

The inspector in charge of the three carriers called over their radios that he wanted to brief the officers right there, on the street.

Darin looked out of his window. It looked like a medieval battle. Did the inspector really wanting to brief them in the middle of all this? On the street? Yes, that was exactly what he wanted to do, so the officers left the relative protection of their carriers, and gathered on the side of the road. Predictably, bricks quickly began to fall on them.

Just thirty and forty metres away, rioters were setting fire to cars, attacking and looting buildings and shops, and attacking police officers. Darin could barely believe what he was seeing, and he knew that he and his officers needed to get into the fight quickly, alongside the other units who were already taking on the rioters.

After a few brief words from the inspector, the TfL unit formed up and got ready to enter the riot. Ahead of them they could see other officers from other units trying to hold their line, and blocking falling missiles with their shields. Others were being ordered to charge groups of rioters in an effort to push them back. Riot carriers, with the blue rooftop lights flashing, were held behind the foot officers, ready to back them up as they moved forward.

Rioters would occasionally run off as the officers charged at them but some – either feeling brave, showing off, or wanting the opportunity to hurt a police officer – would hold their ground and join up with others who felt the same. These groups charged back at the officers. Batons and, for those who had them, shields, were brought down and punched forwards against the rioters. They were literally fighting hand to hand.

Darin and his unit now became part of that chaos, sticking closely together but joining the blue lines of police ready to take on the mob. Groups of rioters immediately moved in on them, wanting to fight, not afraid to stand their ground, not afraid to take on the police.

'GET BACK! GET BACK!' the officers screamed at the rioters, holding an open palmed glove at their attackers, trying desperately to keep some distance between them.

Other officers swung their batons into the gap between themselves and the rioters. 'GET BACK!' they shouted, over and over.

Darin had his own tactics: anyone getting too close to him felt the full force of his baton. He whacked it down, hitting his attackers on the arms and legs and body. He knew that if the rioters had the opportunity, they would kill a police officer. The danger of being dragged into the crowd and set upon by the mob was very, very real. He continued to strike out at the rioters whenever he could.

Around him, some officers were still shouting, 'Get back!' and warning off the rioters rather than actually hitting them. Darin knew why they were holding back: they were afraid of getting a complaint made against them. It was an extraordinary moment, even on a day like this. Bricks and bottles were being lobbed at the officers. Rioters were setting fire to cars and buildings, destroying everything they could. Mobs were trying to kill police officers, and yet all around Darin, coppers were being cautious because they were petrified of doing something wrong, or hitting somebody when they weren't sure if they should or not. It was shocking.

Darin knew that if ever there was a time to pull your baton out and start hitting people, it was now. They were coming under a sustained attack, they could get seriously hurt – or worse – but still these young coppers were holding back because they were afraid of getting into trouble ('It's not worth it, is it Sarge?' they would later say to him). It was a dangerous fear to have at a time like this – one that could get them and their colleagues killed. They needed to fight. But as bricks and rocks and bottles came pouring down from the sky, it became obvious that the TfL officers weren't equipped to deal with the level of violence that was being directed at them. Without that extra training, and without proper riot equipment and shields, they were casualties-in-waiting.

'Back on the buses!' the inspector called out. 'There's too much coming over. There's too much flak.'

Darin and his officers retreated and boarded their carriers; he knew that there was no other choice. Missiles continued to crash down, but at least they were now in the relative safety of their vehicles.

They sat there and watched as better equipped officers moved against the rioters, taking missiles themselves but batting the bricks and bottles away with their shields. As the lines of riot officers moved forward, taking ground from the rioters, there were brief but intense volleys of missiles from the crowd before the waves of falling bricks and rocks lessened, stopping altogether as the officers grabbed the upper hand, rushing forward. Then the missiles would start again as the officers stopped to hold the ground they had just taken. Then rioters moved forward, picking up discarded and previously thrown objects, to throw at the police once more.

Once the Level 1s and Level 2s had pushed far enough ahead,

Darin and his unit were ordered back on the street again. The commanders intended to keep hold of the ground that had been fought over, and the TfL officers were now used to hold junctions and discourage anyone who may try and get around the back of the police line. As the riot officers continued to push further on, Darin and his unit stood around, with folded arms, guarding the burning roads as further shield units moved up.

Upton Park

Carriers from various county forces – including Mark's Cambridgeshire PSU – arrived at the bank in Upton Park. It had taken them some time to find their way there, and all they really knew about their location was that it was somewhere near the West Ham United football ground. For a moment they wondered if they had gone to the wrong place, because all was quiet – there was no fire, no smoke, none of the expected chaos – and it quickly became obvious that the call had been a hoax. Still without a radio, the inspector used his mobile phone to try to find out what was going on. He was told to stay where he was, and to remain on stand-by. The carriers from the other forces began to enter the car park at the rear of the bank, but Mark told the drivers of his own vehicles not to follow.

'What's the problem?' a driver asked.

Mark pointed out that the car park had only a single way in and out. As Tactical Advisor it was his job to recognise these issues, and to bring them to his inspector's attention. They had already been brought to the bank on false pretences, so who knew if anything else was going to happen? It could be one big set-up.

'Once you go in there, you become a sitting duck,' Mark explained. 'If the entrance gets blocked, if rioters shove a burning car across it, we won't be going anywhere.'

The inspector agreed and instead they parked along the road, outside the bank, as carriers from the other forces continued to enter the car park. Shortly after, bricks and bottles were thrown over the walls around the car park, landing on the carriers that had parked there. Maybe it was a trap, after all – although it seemed like a rather trivial one. The carriers quickly drove back out of the car park, this time stopping alongside the road as Mark's carrier had done.

As the officers sat in the vehicles, bored and waiting for another deployment, they heard a loud bang. Then there was another, and another.

'What the hell was that?' asked a PC at the back of Mark's carrier.

'GUN! GUN!' an officer shouted from the street.

'Fuck me, I think someone's shooting at us!' Mark said.

Suddenly there really was chaos. Each carrier began to move quickly, turning in the road, or driving immediately away. Everyone looked around, to try and see what was going on, or where the gunfire was coming from. With the heat of the day, as well as all the other uniform and padding that they had to wear, no one had bothered to wear their body armour, having removed it to try and stay cool. Instead, there was a pile of bulletproof vest slung together at the back of their carriers.

Remaining where they were wasn't an option, and the Cambridge carriers bolted, moving away in convoy, as the inspector once again used his mobile phone to call in about the incident, and to find out what was going on and what they should do.

They drove away, heading back into the unknown streets, trying not to get lost but knowing they would, and that it was better than getting shot at. Mark watched the wing mirrors for any trouble but no one was following them and there were no more gunshots. Then they heard the sound of police sirens getting closer towards them. There was nothing unusual about that, especially today, but Mark guessed that it was in response to the gunfire. Moments later a couple of 'Trojan' units whizzed by – armed officers from the Met's Specialist Firearms Command – heading towards the bank. Later Mark was told that a man with a gun had been standing in the middle of the road shooting at the carriers.

They continued to drive away from the scene, finding a fire station about half a mile away, where they pulled onto the forecourt and came to a stop.

'Right, everyone get your body armour on!' the inspector ordered.

1700 hrs
Sutton

Sutton, a few of miles to the west of Croydon, was calm. There were few people or cars on the streets, and that was fine as far as anyone was concerned. The rest of London was going up in smoke, so if Sutton was quiet, all the better.

On the whole, Sutton is a peaceful, middle-class neighbourhood that seems a world away from other parts of south London. Even so, Sutton could have its moments. It was very much an evening and night time economy, with bars and nightclubs, which could, on occasion, present the usual drink-related problems and crimes. But normally Sutton was a nice place to be. The local population was supportive of the police, crime was low, and there was an almost village-like feel to the area. Despite being just five miles west of Croydon, there was no reason that Sutton would suffer from any of the issues that had been breaking out elsewhere.

The borough Commander, Detective Chief Superintendent Guy Ferguson, had been at the station most of the day. He was the on-call Acting Commander for a number of areas as well as his own at Sutton. With so much happening across London, he kept a close watch on those other areas – Kingston, Richmond, Merton, Wandsworth and Croydon. With serious trouble breaking out in Croydon, command of the public order response had pretty much been transferred over to other senior officers, but he still kept a close watch.

Guy had already released the early turn shift from Sutton, so that they could be re-deployed to Croydon but other areas had been calling up for support and with Sutton struggling to justify hanging on to officers, he began to release more units to help elsewhere.

Fourteen Sutton officers had already fought at Tottenham on the Saturday, and Guy wasn't sure if they had even been requested. He suspected the officers had taken it upon themselves to go there anyway to do what they could to help. The violence they had faced had been extreme and two had required hospital treatment – one was knocked unconscious by a brick to the head. Having fought in Tottenham, the officers had been attacked again as they stopped to fill up with petrol on their way back to Sutton. All 14 officers had been injured. Despite this, those officers had all come back to work. Even those with serious injuries had volunteered to come in and work 'inside duties', so others could be released onto the streets to help other boroughs. Guy was proud of his station, and of his officers. They were a good bunch and morale was high among them. They looked out for each other, and were there when he needed them. But still, with so many now dotted around other boroughs, he was running low, and all he could spare were 'penny packets' – perhaps just one sergeant and half-a-dozen PCs – nowhere near a full unit.

Although Guy hoped that his quite little area of London would avoid the violence and destruction seen elsewhere, he was still very aware of the potential. If trouble did break out here, he could have serious issues. With that in mind, he had already ordered in as many of their special constables as he could get to help bolster his officers' numbers.

Guy knew that if anywhere in Sutton was going to see trouble it would be the High Street, with its concentration of shops. He also knew that Sutton would be alone. There was no one to give support, so no one would be coming to help them if things kicked off. With so few officers available to him, he wanted to be prepared, and, if possible, ahead of the game, so he decided to get out and try to judge the current mood on the streets. He put on his hat and his stab-vest and stepped outside, heading for the High Street.

Like many others, Rob, a Sutton team sergeant, had been sitting at home watching the riots on his TV. He was meant to be on annual leave, but after seeing what was happening around London and elsewhere, he picked up his phone and called his station, offering to cancel his leave and come back into work. He had been told repeatedly to 'stand by', and finally, in the early afternoon, his phone rang. Could he come in?

Rob was a former TSG officer, and although he had transferred to Sutton on promotion as a sergeant, he still had his knowledge and skills from his public order days, and was keen to put those experiences to use.

At Sutton, Rob reported immediately to the duty officer – an inspector.

'I'm here and I'm available,' he told him.

'Great, come with me on parade.'

Rob joined the duty officer in the station parade room, where four PCs sat with their pocket books open and pens ready to write down their duties for the day. On a normal shift Rob would easily count twenty to twenty-five officers.

'Is this it?' Rob asked the duty officer.

'This is it. Although we are calling in some special constables.'

Great, Rob thought to himself cynically. *Specials. Just what we need. Unpaid, part-time, volunteers.*

He wasn't at all convinced they would be able to deal with any trouble should it start in Sutton. But he understood that desperate times required desperate measures.

After the parade, Rob stepped out of the police station and headed into the nearby town centre alone, to see what – if anything – was happening. The streets were mostly quiet, which wasn't particularly unusual for Sutton, and he strolled along the pedestrianised High Street. Then he spotted the borough commander, Guy Ferguson, and went over. Guy was pleased to see him.

Small groups of youths were hanging about the streets, and they spotted some that they knew. Rob and Guy walked over to talk with them. The kids were staring at mobile-phone screens and passing them around so that others could see. They were all quite animated.

'What's going on lads?' Guy asked.

'It's all gonna kick off, officer,' one of them said, excitedly. 'Apparently it's gonna happen at 9pm.'

'Asda is already burning!' said another.

Guy looked over in the direction of Asda, just a hundred yards away, at the top end of the pedestrianised part of the High Street, where they were all standing. There were no flames, no smoke.

'I don't think that's quite right, do you?'

The kids looked over and shrugged their shoulders.

Guy and Rob stayed a while to talk with the kids. It was all good-natured banter but as the kids were clearly getting further information over their phones and BlackBerrys, they continued to try and gain as much from them as they could.

'It's all going to go wrong tonight!' the kids said.

'Here, in Sutton?' Rob asked.

'Yep, that's what we're hearing. People are saying that they are going to come to Sutton because it's an easy place to hit.'

Rob looked around the street. Sure, it would be an easy place to hit – there were virtually no police for a start – but still, it was Sutton. Why bother? Perhaps it was just kids talking stuff up and getting over-excited, Rob thought.

Gradually though, information began to filter through from police sources that gangs really were planning to come to Sutton, to loot. The gangs were aware that Sutton was virtually un-policed and they intended to take full advantage of it, and as the evening went on, more youths began to fill the streets.

As they walked around, Guy noticed a car parked along the kerb. It was full of young men. Guy didn't recognise any of them. The way they were looking at him convinced Guy that they weren't from the local area. He knew many of the youths in Sutton, and something about the attitude of these men was wrong. He now began to seriously fear that Sutton would, after all, be targeted.

'What do you think, Guv?' Rob asked Guy. 'If it all kicks off, what do you want to do?'

Guy had been a copper for a long time. He had worked the miners' strikes in the 1980s, the Poll Tax riots in the 1990s, plus Wapping, and many other moments of serious trouble over the years. He knew what was needed, and he knew not to be afraid.

'The way I see it,' Guy said. 'We can either stand here allowing them to start throwing things at us or we can take the initiative. My approach has always been to take the initiative away from them.'

Rob smiled. It was exactly what he was hoping to hear. 'I couldn't agree more Guv.'

'If it kicks off and they get the advantage, we could end up taking casualties. If I'm going to get injured, I would rather get injured doing something positive as opposed to standing there and being a target. If I'm wrong, I'm wrong. But I would much prefer to get bollocked for actually doing something – and doing something that I think is right – rather than just standing there taking a pasting. And I'm not prepared to take a pasting.'

Rob understood, and they returned to Sutton police station. Together with the duty officer they gathered the handful of officers left at the station. The four PCs who had paraded at the start of the shift were now joined by two CID officers, who had been working in their office. By now nine special constables had also arrived. Rob wondered if the specials would end up being a hindrance, but at least they had come in, that was something, he guessed, and with so many Sutton officers fighting rioters elsewhere, those nine specials practically doubled their number.

No sooner had Rob gathered his band of officers, than staff in the CCTV control room started calling up on the radio. Gangs of youths had been spotted gathering at the top of the High Street.

The officers left the station, unsure of what they would find or what was going to happen. At the back of their minds was still the belief that this was Sutton, and that meant nothing serious would happen, not here. This wasn't Tottenham.

Rachel's day was coming to an end. Having worked the middle shift, from 10am until 6pm, she was feeling good. She hadn't had to get up too early and there was still some of the evening free. The day had gone like most other days on a regular response team – they had dealt with some calls, helped out the early shift, completed some paperwork, and now she and her team were in the process of handing over the cars to the late shift. The officer Rachel had been working with for that day said goodbye, and set off for home but she had a few emails to send, and some admin to sort out first. Besides, she was young; she only had two years of police service and was just out of her probation, so she was keen to show willing and hang around a little longer. She was also a team player. In her downtime Rachel played hockey and she enjoyed being part of a team – both on the field and at work. She liked nothing more that to get stuck in with her colleagues and was never one to hang back. What was about to befall Peckham, however, was like nothing she had ever experienced before.

Everyone was aware of what had been happening in Tottenham, and there had been some expectation that the trouble would filter down to Peckham because, well, it was Peckham, and things like that tended to happen here. But so far everything was fairly normal. But as Rachel pressed the 'send' button on an email, out on the streets a police officer was pressing the emergency button on his radio.

The sound of an alarm on the radio jolted everybody. Two late shift officers, who had also been sending emails, suddenly jumped up and rushed out – any officer hitting the emergency button on their radio was guaranteed a good response from their colleagues.

Rachel didn't know what was going on, other than someone

needed urgent help, and so she dived out of the office with the two late turn officers, and jumped into the back seat of their car. They roared out of the station yard, and the officers headed towards nearby Rye Lane, where the officer needing assistance was located.

'What the hell is this?' the driver suddenly asked out loud.

Rachel peered between the two front seats. Everywhere she looked were gangs of young men with covered faces and hoods pulled up over their heads. They were roaming around, looking for trouble. Some were armed with bottles and bricks.

The riots had reached Peckham.

These crowds were the reason the police officer on the street had hit his emergency button. Another unit had now safely picked him up, so Rachel's driver continued down Rye Lane to see what else was happening. As he drove, there was a loud thump against the side of the car. No one had seen what had caused the noise, but it was obvious an object had just been thrown at their vehicle. They continued on. Buses lined the road, and the officers decided to pull alongside each one to tell them to get the hell out of there, for their own safety as well as that of their passengers.

'You need to cancel your services,' the officer in the front passenger seat told the bus drivers. 'Tell your controller there are already buses on fire in Tottenham, and you all need to get out of here fast.'

The drivers didn't need much convincing, but they were still stuck in the early evening traffic.

Trouble in Peckham was now starting to bubble ever more quickly. Other officers were now reporting gangs of youths milling around and objects being thrown.

The duty inspector that day wasn't an inspector at all – he was a sergeant who was 'acting up' in the absence of the actual inspector who wasn't at work. With trouble starting to flare, the sergeant made a quick decision and got on the radio. 'I'm not happy with this, guys. Everyone back to the nick,' he ordered.

Leaving officers out on the streets on their own – or even in pairs – and without riot equipment, seemed unwise to say the least, and on hearing the order Rachel's driver turned the car around and headed back.

At the station the officers were told not to go back outside without authority. They were to wait until support from Level 1 and Level 2 riot officers arrived. The handful of regular shift officers weren't equipped to deal with what was happening, and they certainly weren't equipped for what was to come.

But not everyone had heard – or perhaps listened to – the sergeant's order. Just a few streets away from Peckham police station, a handful of officers from the Safer Neighbourhood Team had come out of their small, satellite police office, which was little more than a shop front on Bellenden Road. One of the officers came on the radio to warn that youths were smashing the windows of the nearby Burger King. But then, seconds later, the crowd caught sight of the officers and they immediately turned on them. Masked, hooded youths started throwing sticks and rocks at the officers, and then charged at them. Hugely outnumbered, the officers turned and bolted. Suddenly emergency button after emergency button was going off. The officers were screaming and shouting down the radio for help as a crowd of fifty youths armed with lumps of wood, bricks and other weapons chased them through a car park.

Rachel looked at the driver of the car she had jumped into earlier. He looked back at her. 'You know what?' he said. 'We're going back out there. Sod the order.'

Other officers had made the same decision, and as Rachel ran into the station yard, two other police cars, along with the station van, went screaming out onto the streets, their blue lights flashing and sirens blaring.

Rachel jumped into the back seats again but the car's operator from earlier hadn't got out quick enough so the driver went without him, sitting in the front alone.

The police vehicles drove in a rapid convoy down Peckham High Street and quickly turned into Bellenden Road. Ahead of them was the surreal sight of a large mob chasing a tiny number of police officers. The sound of the sirens immediately drew the crowd's attention away from the officers they were running after, which was a relief for them, but not for everyone. There were people everywhere, and now they all charged directly towards the police cars. Bricks, lumps of wood, even a chair, were all flung at the cars. Rachel stared at the mob, horrified.

Then there was a huge crash. A brick slammed into the front passenger window, and shattered it. Hundreds of tiny shards of glass exploded into the car.

The other police vehicles were also being attacked, with bricks and other missiles being hurled at them. It was total mayhem – a blur of masks, hoods, bricks and bottles, all happening to a mixed soundtrack of sirens, screaming and shattering.

As the vehicles were being attacked, the officers who were originally being chased stole the opportunity to make a sprint back to their satellite base. There was no chance that the vehicles would be able to pick them up with the ferocity of the attack they were under, but at least they had been a big enough distraction for the officers to key in the security code on the door, get inside and literally bring down the shutters – barricading themselves inside.

By now there were up to eighty rioters attacking the cars.

Remaining on Bellenden Road would have been suicidal and stopping the vehicles would have resulted in them being overrun by the mob, dragged out of their cars and beaten, or worse. With little other choice, the cars and the station van made a dash for it as well.

One of the vehicle operators came over the radio as the small convoy negotiated their way through the mob and away from the street. 'Is everyone okay? Anyone hurt?' he asked.

'Yeah, we're okay!' Rachel called back excitedly. She could hear the adrenaline in her shaky voice. 'We've been hit but we're all right. Driver and passenger both fine.'

No one had been expecting a mob of that size, and no one had been expecting bricks to be thrown through the windows of their vehicles.

Realising that they had to avoid the main roads, which were now starting to see the effects of the rioting, with gangs roaming the streets and debris littering the ground, the Peckham police cars darted down some side streets.

As soon as they reached the station Rachel jumped out of the car. As she did, tiny pieces of glass fell from the bottom of her trousers and tumbled to the ground.

'I have no idea how that glass could have got *inside* my trousers!' she said to the driver, who was inspecting a couple of cuts to his arms.

Then they took a closer look at the vehicles. Each of the cars had smashed windows, as did the van. They were all in a terrible state. The car Rachel had been in had been hit a number of times, and it was just as well that the operator hadn't joined them, because the brick that had come through the side passenger window would have hit him directly on the head.

The Safer Neighbourhood Team were now securely barricaded

inside their small building, and the rest of the officers had come away relatively unharmed, all things considered. But as Rachel and the other officers remained at the station, waiting for the riot officers to arrive, some of the mob had also decided to make their way towards them. Gangs of hooded youths, armed with petrol bombs, were now descending upon Peckham police station.

Lewisham

Darren's impromptu unit of six officers were still a good couple of miles from the Bromley Road Retail Park at Catford. The officers there were in serious danger, so the driver of the minibus that Darren was now in drove quickly, passing shuttered shops and ruined streets. There was no one else around – no rioters, no other police officers – just six coppers in a wrecked minibus, driving along the middle of the road, towards overwhelming odds.

As they continued along, desperate to reach the retail park and help their colleagues, a group of about fifteen youths suddenly appeared from a side street. They spotted the officers, and the officers spotted them. The youths blocked the road and there was a noise that almost sounded like a cheer, coming from them. Moments later, bricks and bottles and even coins, were being thrown through the air, towards the minibus.

The driver stopped and the officers stepped down from the vehicle and drew their batons. The stood for a brief moment, in a line – six riot officers standing behind six round, riot shields.

'Let's get them,' Darren heard one of the officers say.

Without another word, the six officers all charged forward, directly into a wall of falling debris and missiles. They blocked anything that was flung at them and continued towards the youths. They in turn dropped what they had and ran, heading off down the side streets, and quickly disappearing. The officers at the retail park were still screaming for assistance, so Darren's small unit continued along their way. As they did so, more youths appeared and more missiles were thrown at them. Each time it happened, the officers had no choice but to get out and repeat their tactic of charging at the youths until they ran off. There was no time to form a cordon or to take junctions slowly and methodically. There weren't enough of them anyway, even if they wanted to. They employed as much of their public order training as they could but stopping wasn't an option. It would effectively put them on offer, giving the rioters time to build their numbers and possibly surround the officers. They just had to keep moving: forward, forward, forward.

They passed through Rushey Green, with its lines of high street shops. Some of the stores had already been attacked and glass lay like a glittering blanket across the ground. Then another group appeared ahead of them, and the officers once again stepped down from the bus, moved towards the rioters, speeding up from a controlled jog to a sprint. Rocks and bottles tumbled from the sky and settled on the road around their feet. And as before, the missile throwers disappeared as the officers got closer. Darren and his small team pushed on.

During these small skirmishes, Darren was still listening to the urgent screams of his colleagues at the retail park. He knew that even if they managed to reach the retail park in one piece, there would still only be a dozen officers against fifty or more rioters. The situation seemed bleak.

Where the hell is everyone? Darren thought, listening to the radio. *Where the hell are the TSG? Where the hell are all the police?*

Finally, they reached the retail park. Ahead of them they saw a desperate sight. To the left, across the street, dozens of rioters were throwing bricks, bottles and even fencing panels at just half dozen officers, who were on the right, bravely defending the retail park. The officers weren't wearing any riot equipment – they were dressed in their regular beat uniforms. All they had to protect themselves from the volley of missiles were two round shields, between six of them. Darren stared in disbelief for a moment at the scene. How on earth had these officers managed to hold the retail park for as long as they had, when there were so few of them? And why had they stayed to defend it? Then the rioters charged. Darren watched in horror and realised that they had arrived at what was the endgame as far as the rioters were concerned. It looked to Darren as though those six officers were making a brave, final stand.

Then those six officers then did something that astonished Darren: they charged towards the rioters.

Without a word, Darren and the five officers he was with, sprinted towards the rioters. It was ludicrous – three separate groups all running towards each other to fight. Darren's small unit came under missile attack. Darren kept running, ready for the seemingly inevitable hand-to-hand fighting, but then, just like that, the group of rioters splintered and started running off in different directions, down side streets, and away from the retail park. Darren's unit chased after a few, catching some in the surrounding streets. Some of the rioters turned to take them on, perhaps hoping that their brazenness and numbers would scare off the officers, but they couldn't have been more wrong. The officers charged directly into the rioters, striking them with their shields, knocking them backwards. Darren heard muffled shouts mixed in with his own heavy breathing. All around him was a blur of helmeted riot officers, and masked and hooded youths. He saw blurry visions of men with angry eyes and gritted teeth coming at him with clenched fists. People were pushing against his shield and grabbing at his helmet visor. Some rioters moved back but more moved forward, armed with bricks and bottles. There was another shove against the shields, and then batons began to rain down. Though few in numbers, these officers were not going to stand and take it. They were fighting back.

Further ahead, Darren could see other rioters kicking down brick walls – more missiles, more weapons. Then an estate agent's sign was flung though the air towards the officers. The idea caught on, and more estate agents signs whizzed towards them like large, square Frisbees. It was almost comical. But then came something altogether more lethal: the wooden posts that were used to hold up the signs, were now being lobbed at them like javelins, their sharp, pointed ends tearing through the air.

The officers jumped out of the way, dodging the sharp posts. Darren did the same, and one landed next to him. As he looked back up he saw a man running towards him. The man was carrying something large and white in his hands. Darren wiped the condensation away from the inside of his visor. The man was young and muscular. He hadn't bothered to cover his face with any masks or hood. It was then that Darren realised what the man was carrying: a fridge, albeit a small one. At first Darren didn't trust his eyes, but he looked again, and yes, this man was carrying a fridge. And he was about to throw it at Darren, who lifted his shield in preparation but knew it would do little to protect him against something so heavy.

'LOOK OUT!' someone called.

The man threw it and the fridge travelled through the air. The impact would cause serious injury; that was for sure. Darren braced himself. But nothing happened. He peered over the top rim of his shield, to see what had gone on. The answer was, not much, because after being thrown, the fridge had fallen to the floor, landing about three feet in front of the man. Other rioters standing behind the man started to laugh at him, and he peered down at the broken fridge, looking somewhat disappointed. Darren grinned at this little moment.

With the comedy non-threat of the flying fridge now passed, an officer standing next to Darren raised his baton, and shouted, 'GO!'

Darren ran forward. Once more the rioters scattered, and the officers stood in a small side street, ankle deep in smashed bottles, broken bricks and estate agent signs. And one small fridge.

The skirmishes and baton charges went on for some time but eventually they managed to push the rioters back onto the main road and away from the warren of side streets. But then an order came through for them to leave. Darren didn't know who had given the order but they were told to leave the rioters – to let them go. Instead they were to guard a nearby Halfords store, back up towards Rushey Green.

Darren couldn't believe it. They had just spent the best part of an hour battling with rioters and now they were ordered to leave them and guard a shop? Matters were made worse by the increasingly urgent calls for assistance coming over the radio from other police units. Rioters had been brandishing knives. Some were even said to be showing off guns. Darren became increasingly disheartened as he heard the near-constant sound of police emergency buttons being sounded. Officers, clearly fearing for their lives, were pressing on their radios in desperation, hoping that someone would come to their aid. The officers needed more units, they needed help, but Darren and his team were told to remain at Halfords – guarding a shop rather than going to the aid of fellow police officers.

How stupid is this? Darren thought. *Officers are calling for help all over the place and here we are, guarding a fucking shop!*

1900 hrs
Sutton

Guy Ferguson stood with Rob, a handful of special constables and a few regular officers. Ahead of them, at one end of the High Street, were dozens of hooded youths with scarves pulled across their faces. No sooner had the officers arrived, than the youths began to throw glass bottles, which smashed on the pavement in front of them.

Other than the occasional car, which drove quickly through the area, there was no one else on the streets – just the bottle throwing mob and the thin blue line of officers. Rob knew that things were about to go very wrong for Sutton. He had spent long enough on the TSG to know that this crowd wasn't going to back off without some encouragement.

As the youths began to advance on the police line, Rob looked around at his small band of inexperienced officers. Being Sutton, those officers weren't used to the level of violence that was about to confront them, he knew that. But these few officers were all that Sutton had; all that stood between anarchy and order. Rob didn't fancy the odds at all but there was nothing either he or anybody else could do about it; they had to either back off or go for it. He and Guy Ferguson had already had the discussion and he knew what was needed: they would have to fight.

Guy Ferguson had been keeping a close eye on what had been happening in Croydon. Things were getting seriously out of control there, and as he watched the youths ahead of him, jumping around in nervous excitement, getting read to cause trouble in Sutton, he thought to himself, *Bollocks to this. I'm not having it. Not in my borough.*

Rob wondered how many other borough commanders were standing on the streets with their officers that night. Not many, he ventured. But that was Guy Ferguson for you; a well liked, very well respected senior officer, who was out there, just like any other officer. This was his borough, and his responsibility but still, he could just have easily hidden himself away in the CCTV control room, watching events safely on a screen, and directing officers via a radio. Instead, realising how grave the situation was, he had stepped up to take his place on the frontline.

Guy looked over at Rob, pleased to have someone with him who had real public order experience. He gave him a nod and Rob knew instinctively what that meant: it was time to go.

'SHOW OF STRENGH!' Rob ordered the officers.

Everyone raised their baton in the air, in the hope that the crowd would run off rather than face being struck by the police. But the gesture had no effect at all, and the bricks and bottles continued to rain down on them.

Rob told the officers to prepare to baton charge the crowd. Bottles continued to smash down on the pavement in front of them, sending shards of glass across the ground and skittering towards the officers' feet, while other bottles that didn't smash bounced wildly towards the police line. Rob looked down at the fallen bottles. Sutton had quite a large bar and nightclub culture, so the skips and bins were full of handy missiles for the crowd to throw. Amongst the usual beer bottles, there were also wine and even champagne bottles being lobbed at the police. Being Sutton, the rioters missiles had to be of a higher class. Rob smiled, but he also knew that those champagne bottles were larger, heavier and potentially more deadly than the others.

'ON ME!' Rob called out to the line of officers. He raised his baton in the air, above his head. The officers did the same. 'GO!'

There was a fresh frenzy of bottles. Bricks, too, were now being thrown. Rob couldn't understand where the rioters were getting the bricks from, and as the missiles fell, he continued to rush towards the rioting crowd.

Having thrown the one or two objects they had each been holding, the crowd quickly began to fall back until the short backwards skips became a forward sprint, as they turned and scattered into the darkness.

'HALT!' Rob called out.

The officers repeated the order. 'HALT!' and they all came to a stop.

Their push forward had been a success but Rob knew that if the crowd had been made up of more hardened yobs from Croydon or elsewhere it may have been a different result altogether. If this had been Croydon, it was likely that those rioters would have stood their ground and fought back, and with so few officers the police would quickly have found themselves outnumbered. So Rob was pleased and relieved that the simple and direct, if risky, advance had worked. He didn't want the officers to get too confident, though. It wouldn't take much for the crowds to return, and worryingly, they now knew the fragile strength of the police numbers.

Rob had good reason to be concerned.

Croydon

Tom arrived back at the station, expecting the same set up as the previous day: half-a-dozen or so officers, with a sergeant and possibly an inspector leading them, and a carrier that would make up part of a larger PSU serial. But at the station there were no sergeants or inspectors to meet or organise them – not even the sergeants from their own shift. The PCs were standing in the station yard alone.

'Where are the skippers and governor?' one of the officers asked.

No one knew, and they found themselves milling about in the yard, not really knowing what was going on, what they were meant to be doing or where they were meant to go.

'We can't just stand here doing nothing,' Tom eventually said. 'We're going to have to sort this out ourselves.'

So the officers scratched around for equipment, got themselves ready and then piled into the only riot carrier left at the station. They knew that trouble had erupted down in Croydon town centre so they decided to make their own way towards the rioting to see how they could help. In their minds, not having a supervisor wasn't a reason for not going out, and they could only hope that once they arrived in the town centre, someone would know what to do with them. At the very least they hoped someone would be expecting them. But they knew that not having a serial number for their makeshift unit meant that they weren't going to be on any list anywhere, and that they probably wouldn't be accounted for. Anything could happen to them and no one would have a clue.

By now hundreds of hooded and masked youths had swarmed into the town centre. The word had gone out and it seemed that Croydon was to be that night's main target. Rioters and looters were descending on the area from all over the capital.

Tom's carrier parked close to North End. It was a pedestrianised shopping area with a large Primark shop at one end, and was also close to the entrances to the Whitgift mall. The inspector who appeared to be in charge in the area hadn't been expecting them, but any supervisor would have had to be insane to turn them away when so many other places were in desperate need for more officers, and they were quickly snapped up and put to work. The plan was simple enough: to keep everyone out of the shopping centre, which was a looter's paradise, with both large and small stores selling everything from birthday cards to jewellery to high end electronic goods.

Tom and his small unit formed up, and became part of a larger protective cordon of officers. Either side of him were police officers standing in their riot uniform, round shields held on one arm and a long, black, acrylic baton held in the opposite hand. All of the officers had pulled the thin, black strap from the top of the baton tightly around their gloved hand to secure it in place. All were looking dead ahead, in stoic silence. As the officers held the line, Tom watched, horrified, as gangs of hooded youths attacked nearby shops, stealing whatever they could carry. Some were even attempting to torch the buildings, sparking cigarette lighters next to pieces of paper and fabric.

Why are the police just standing there? Tom wondered.

Eventually, he couldn't keep quiet any longer and he spoke up. 'Look! There are people looting those shops over there. Why don't we get them?'

'Hold the cordon,' he was ordered.

'But they're just a hundred yards away and we have a full serial here. We could chase them off.'

'No. Keep the cordon.'

Tom was shocked. Lines of riot officers stood watching as shops were attacked, robbed and destroyed. The shops, although close by, were just outside the footprint of what looked to Tom like slightly more upmarket shops and he wondered if that was why they were being held back. Were the orders to protect the larger, more prestigious stores, and to allow lesser ones to be attacked? He sensed that other officers were also frustrated, watching as these smaller shops were being ransacked while they stood there protecting Primark.

What about the rest of the area? What about the rest of the shops and streets? Who would be protecting them?

Why is one shop more valuable than another? Tom thought to himself. *What is the point of us being here if we are going to allow them to do this?*

Then a group of looters approached the static police line. They waltzed up with their hands held out to their sides, provocatively, urging – daring – the officers to do something. Some pulled scarves and shirts over the bottom part of their faces as they got closer to the lines of riot officers. Then countless bottles, rocks, pieces of wood, and other missiles began to fly through the air towards them.

In a way Tom was pleased, because he was convinced that now they would be allowed to take on the rioters, that they would move forward, shields and batons in hand, and clear the rioters away. That was what they were trained to do, that's why they were here, and he was ready to move. He waited for the order to be called as more bottles smashed around him. He kept his shield raised above his head and batted away flying bricks and traffic cones. Other officers were doing the same. Every now and then he ducked to the side to miss other missiles that he hadn't had time to deflect with his shield. Ahead of him, the mob was jumping around deliriously, screaming in delight every time one of their missiles struck an officer. Tom continued to wait for the order to attack but it never came. They were made to stand fast. No one was to move forward. All were to stand where they were, and take the flak while holding the line.

'This is crazy,' Tom said to the officer next to him. 'I'm not saying we have to nick everyone but at the very least we could chase them away.'

But it went on; the rioters and looters returning every now and then, spending ten minutes or so throwing various heavy objects at the police line before continuing to smash windows and loot shops. Somerfield supermarket, just to the north, on London Road, had now been attacked and set alight, and as the night went on, the road would see far worse with numerous other buildings falling victim to arsonists. Homes and businesses were set ablaze and gutted. They were scenes straight from the Blitz – roofs collapsing and entire building fronts crumbling into the streets. Further south, in Drummond Road, a double decker bus was completely ablaze – a great box of intense fire, with a fat pillar of black smoke pumping into the sky.

More riot officers were urgently making their way from Central London. There was widespread disorder throughout the city, but it was clear that tonight would be all about Croydon, the battle for which was now well underway.

Officers at the other side of North End, by West Croydon rail station, had also been set upon, with over two hundred rioters attacking their lines. It was a huge number, and every one of them seemed to be throwing rocks and bottles at the officers guarding that end of the street. Then came a volley of petrol bombs to contend with, which exploded into balls of fire and heat. There was screaming, shouting and panic all around. It was chaos. The officers were coming under a sustained attack and were seriously – and dangerously – outnumbered. PCSOs, untrained and unequipped for public order situations, were bravely standing side by side with their police officer colleagues, desperately trying to fight off the mob. Officers and PCSOs fell to the ground, casualties of the countless missiles. Then, as if the constant barrage wasn't bad enough, rioters started to drive stolen cars at the police lines – something that had been happening in other parts of London. It was reckless and crazy. They weren't just having a go at the police, they were trying to kill them. As one car careered towards the line, an officer leapt to his side, striking out with his baton, smashing the driver's window. But it was a desperate defence against such a dangerous attack.

Things were rapidly going from bad to worse. A group was spotted on CCTV heading towards Croydon police station carrying petrol bombs, and officers were immediately sent to intercept them. Police cars were burning on the streets and the police helicopter – 'India 99' – was deployed to keep a vigil above the town. Croydon didn't have enough officers to deal with everything that was going on. They had already received hundreds of officers from Central London but some of these had been lost through arrests or injuries, and the pot was now empty. No more help was coming. Out of the 32 London Boroughs, 22 were reporting disorder with looting, fires and fighting breaking out across the capital. It was unprecedented. The situation facing the police and the city was overwhelming.

Then a call came through that more officers were desperately required at the nearby Reeves Corner – an area that had been named after a family run furniture store that had stood there for over 140 years. The store operated out of a handful of buildings, which also contained a number of occupied flats and homes. As officers had been battling hordes of rioters, one man – Gordon Thompson – had broken into Reeves furniture store and stolen a laptop. Once back outside, Thompson shouted to other rioters, 'Who's got a lighter? Let's torch the place!' He then set alight a sofa in the shop window. With the level of violence going on all around, the fire brigade couldn't reach the building and the fire spread rapidly.

Reeves Corner was just a two minute run from where Tom and the rest of his crew were stood, and it was now burning to the ground.

There was an explosion of glass, liquid and fumes. A petrol bomb slammed against the outside wall of Peckham police station. But as the gasoline filled bottle hit the building there was no fire – it had failed to ignite.

The protective shutters had been pulled down on the station's windows, and the heavy wooden doors on the Victorian, three-storey brick building had been shut and locked. Anyone inside the building was now barricaded behind its defences, but also trapped within its walls as the rioters laid siege.

Rachel was in the front office, wondering what to do but knowing that there was nothing she could do. The borough commander was sitting at a desk in the front office calmly completing some paperwork, refusing to leave his officers alone.

Rachel could hear the furious shouting and violent noises outside the building, as further petrol bombs were lobbed at the police station.

'Guv,' Rachel said, trying to get here boss's attention. 'Guv, they're petrol bombing the police station.'

The chief superintendent looked up at Rachel.

'You might want to move,' Rachel suggested, fearing that the front office may end up catching on fire.

The chief superintendent collected his things and left the office for somewhere a bit more out of the way. Rachel remained in the office, holding a fire extinguisher in case anything went up, in case the rioters smashed through the shutters or the doors, and a petrol bomb managed to get through. She cautiously approached the windows and peered through the gaps in the shutters. Outside were gangs of youths holding petrol-filled bottles. The bottles all had rags stuffed into the tops and Rachel watched as they were lit one after another, and the bottles thrown at the police station.

Other officers joined her, looking through the shutters at the petrol bombers, and it became almost a game. No matter how hard they tried, it seemed that the rioters just couldn't get one of the petrol bombs to hit the station and explode into fire.

The next one was flung towards the building but it just bounced off and scuttled along the ground, rolling back towards the rioters' feet.

'Okay, second time lucky!' one of the officers said, mocking the would-be arsonists.

Another bottle, another failed, bouncing petrol bomb.

'They're really shit at this, aren't they?' the officer said.

Another attempt, another bouncing bottle.

The officers all shock their head in disbelief. 'This is embarrassing. Should we just go tell them how it's done?'

After several dozen failures, the rioters finally gave up, skulking away to cause trouble elsewhere.

Despite the bravado from the officers, they all knew that if the petrol bombs had got through the station defences, they would likely have had to deal with the fire themselves. They were well aware that all emergency services – not just the police – were working flat out and were coming under attack from the rioters. The likelihood of the fire brigade reaching them – or even coming out to them – was very slim.

In the station yard, behind tall, solid, fortress-like brick walls, local Level 2 riot trained officers were rapidly getting kitted up into their protective gear. Bags were being rifled through, overalls pulled on, straps tightened, helmets pulled over heads, gloves yanked onto hands. There was a feeling of excitement – officers were pumped up with adrenaline – but also some unease at knowing that they would soon be out on the streets facing hundreds of rioters who would have liked nothing more than to see a police officer killed and their station burnt to the ground. There was some good news, though: Level 1 TSG officers and armoured Jankels were already on their way to help create a protective ring of blue around the police station.

By the time Alan's own PSU pulled into Peckham, much of the work had already been done. As they had been clearing Lee, other TSG units, together with local Level 2s, had been battling on these streets. But shops were still burning, and long flames blew from shattered windows into the road as officers charged past, heading for the small pockets of rioters that were left. As Alan looked out of the carrier's window, all around were gangs of people – some just watching or filming the chaos, a few still threatening police lines, throwing missiles and taunting the officers with threats of violence – but judging by the fires, looted shops, junctions controlled by Level 2 and 3 officers, not to mention the debris covered roads, it appeared that the main trouble was over. What was happening now was the endgame.

On a normal day this would have all looked horrific but with what had been going on, and with what Alan had already seen in places like Tottenham, this was clearly manageable.

Alan's unit were deployed on foot and immediately sent towards groups of troublemakers. The officers followed the same pattern as Lee – short shield advances. They moved gradually up Peckham High Street, passing local shops, banks and fast food places, taking missiles to their small, round shields and occasionally to their bodies. Their forward advances had the usual effect of pushing the rioters backwards, away from the main seat of trouble. Level 2s and 3s moved in, taking the junctions and holding the ground that had been won.

'TO THE NEXT JUNCTION, FORWARD!'

136

They moved again, still taking missiles but easily gaining the ground from the rioters. Other units moved in as well and cleared away the remnants of the rioters. A few brave souls continued to taunt officers, still up for a fight, trying to encourage others but the police here were clearly winning.

No sooner had they completed a bunch of shield advances than they were ordered back to their carriers once more.

'Where to now?' the driver asked the sergeant.

'Walworth,' he was told. 'On the hurry-up.'

Alan's unit had become one of a number of PSUs that were being rushed about from one trouble spot to another, helping out and mopping up. And now it was Walworth's turn, where widespread looting had broken out.

The driver switched on the emergency lights and sirens and they rushed past lines of riot officers, burning buildings and the occasional lobbed brick. Along Peckham Road, grey smoke drifted from an abandoned double decker bus, its windows – the ones that were still there – blackened by a fire that had burnt inside before being extinguished by fire fighters. Peckham was damaged and scarred but it was back in control of the police.

Newham

The Cambridge PSU had spent the past few hours rushing from one part of the city to another, not really sure where they were or where they were going. Most of the time they felt as though they were chasing their tails. Whenever they did find their way to where they were meant to be, they would arrive only to find that whatever had been going on was no longer happening, or else had been dealt with by other officers. They always felt as though they were arriving five minutes too late.

Now they were back at the fire station again watching as

carriers from various forces, including a number of Met vehicles, rushed about in all directions. The Cambridge officers were desperate to help out and get involved. Here they were, an entire PSU, sitting around the East End, doing next to nothing, while absolute chaos was going on. They couldn't understand it, and not having a police radio didn't help their situation. Their inspector was continually on his phone, trying to find out what was going on and what they should do. But time after time they were told to remain on standby.

'At least we have access to a toilet,' someone said, pointing towards the fire station.

Moments after hanging up his phone in frustration, the inspector's mobile rang again. Finally the Cambridgeshire officers were being directed somewhere. They were needed in East Ham, south London. Close to City Airport, gangs of looters were targeting a Sainsbury's supermarket. As the Cambridge drivers negotiated their way through the streets, directed by an officer flicking through an A to Z, more information came though over the mobile phone. Around twenty masked teenagers had smashed their way into the store, attacked security guards and were now stealing laptops and mobile phones.

By the time the officers arrived, the youths had already made off, running onto a nearby estate, so Mark and the rest of the Cambridge crew got off their bus, and spoke to the staff about what had happened. In the distance Mark could hear a noise – like workmen on a building site. It was the sound of an electric drill or something similar, although he couldn't tell what exactly. But whatever it was, it wasn't at Sainsbury's.

He looked over at sheets of shattered glass that carpeted the outside of the store. Standing amongst it all were a handful of battered and bleeding security guards. After the youths had smashed the plate-glass windows, one of the guards had rather valiantly attempted to fight them off with a fire extinguisher but he had little chance and was overwhelmed by the vicious mob.

As they spoke with the staff, a Suffolk unit suddenly blue-lighted past them. They were heading a little further south, towards an Asda supermarket where there had been another call.

While Cambridgeshire had been dealing with the attack at Sainsbury's, some bright spark had literally driven a JCB into the wall of Asda. As the Suffolk unit arrived, they found a circular cut-saw – the noise the Cambridge officers had heard – still imbedded in the brick around the ATM.

Mark's unit along with the Suffolk PSU were told to remain where they were. Local officers were making their way towards them and would take the reports and deal with the paperwork, allowing Cambridgeshire and Suffolk to be released.

Having been sent here, there and every-bloody-where, they were now ordered to Hackney, where the Cambridgeshire officers' night was to become far more interesting – but also far more dangerous.

'How do we get to Hackney?' the driver asked. 'Where the fuck *is* Hackney?'

Great! Mark thought to himself. *We don't have a fucking clue what we are doing or where we are going.*

Not knowing where they were going would put the Cambridge crew in serious jeopardy. The driver would find his way to Hackney but instead of driving towards the police lines, he drove towards the ranks of rioters.

Walworth
Along Walworth Road, huge gangs of looters were trying to smash their way into the small Foot Locker store. More looters were

smashing the windows of other shops on the street. Bins were set on fire, and buses had come to a standstill, blocked by huge mobs of people who wandered freely across the road, moving from one scene of carnage and looting to the next.

At a betting shop, a man swung a fire extinguisher repeatedly at the windows, cracking and smashing the glass. Others had managed to force their way through the shutters of the local Argos, and as soon as people saw a few running in to loot the place, swarms rushed over, desperate not to miss out on the free-for-all. Others were trying to force their way into a nearby Santander bank.

Among it all, regular people stopped to look, shocked at what was happening around them on what was normally a regular shopping street. Old women stepped carefully off buses that were no longer able to make it through the throngs. Men dressed in business suits strolled past, hands in pockets, glancing over but continuing to walk away from the violence. People were walking dogs, riding bikes. Cars, blocked by stationary buses and mobs of looters, rapidly reversed away from the trouble or spun around, heading off quickly in the opposite direction. Shop alarms rang out from different directions. Some people whooped, while others stared in disbelief.

Alan's PSU pulled into Walworth Road. People were running everywhere, holding stolen items in their arms, laughing and smiling, like it was some kind of carnival.

Local officers in regular beat uniform, some with shields, were working their way down the street, together with some fully kitted Level 2s, doing their best to clear the road and prevent the looting. Among them, officers wearing regular clothes – jeans and t-shirts – marched down the street alongside their uniformed colleagues. All had their batons in their hands, outnumbered but up for doing whatever they could to take back their streets. Officers tried to hold people away, yelling 'GET BACK!' at anyone who attempted to push past them. 'You can't tell me where to go!' people said to them, walking up to their riot shields, putting their faces up to the officers' visors, openly challenging their authority.

Alan's carrier came to a stop outside some shops, which looters were ransacking. Most of the looters hadn't even noticed them, and the officers charged out of their carrier as excited looters ran in every direction. The officers reached out, grabbing at anyone they could get their hands on, like it was some sort of game. People struggled violently, desperate to get away. Anyone they caught was immediately handed over to local CID officers, who had been sent out to pick up prisoners, leaving the uniformed officers and TSG to continue to try and clear away the looters and rioters.

Local people were stepping out onto the streets, pushing up to riot shields, trying to get past the police lines. Arguing with officers for not letting them move as they pleased. It was clear that the Level 2s and 3s were in danger of losing the street. Alan's unit were brought back together, along with other PSUs. They stood behind the local officers, with the carriers stopped behind them; the engines running and blue lights flashing. Then the order came. They were going to push forward and clear the Walworth Road. Enough was enough; the police were taking back the street.

The huge line of riot officers jogged forward, like a long, dark blue snake, moving down the centre of Walworth Road with the riot carriers following from the rear. Most people began to move out of the way, whilst other hung around on the pavements, watching to see what the police were going to do. An order was shouted and the officers charged forward. Different police units suddenly broke away, independent from the main group, rapidly moving into the road junctions to the left and the right, using their shields to force people back and away from Walworth Road. People jostled, some pushed back but the strength and speed of the officers gained the advantage, and lines of shield officers now held the junctions, preventing people from getting back onto Walworth Road. Fires raged in bins all along the street, and glass lay shattered in piles outside shops, but the police were now back in control.

Alan's unit held a junction at one of the residential side street. A few men stepped forward shouting abuse at them, angry that they had been forced off the main road and held back. A few bottles were flung at the line.

'TO THE CAR!' a sergeant called out.

Ahead of Alan, parked along the kerb was a silver car – their target – and the crowd was level with it.

'GO!'

They charged forward, batons held up and the small, round shields out.

Women in the crowd screamed but the mob quickly fell back, fearing that the police were going to attack them.

'HALT!'

They reached the car and came to a stop. One man walked back towards the line, shouting at the officers, swearing, calling them names, but then the crowd suddenly dispersed.

At one end of Walworth Road, a large crowd had gathered again, having found a way around through the maze of back streets. Officers were redeployed back onto the Walworth Road and stood in a line across it, facing the crowd. There was a standoff, with the crowd unsure as to what to do next. Then, from behind the line of riot officers there was a shrieking of police sirens. The line of officers split and a trio of enormous, dark blue, armoured Jankels moved through, driving directly at the crowd. Carriers followed the Jankels through. Like many people – police included – most, if not all in the crowd, had never seen Jankels before. The crowd darted left and right into the side streets once again, and once more the officers moved in, holding them back.

Level 2s and 3s moved forward again and, Alan's unit were ordered back to their carriers. They were to return to Peckham police station, back to protecting the building.

Hackney

That night, in Hackney, the police became direct targets. 'Kill the police!' became a mantra heard shouted repeatedly through the streets, and the rioters seemed to mean it, as the small police unit from Ealing were to find out.

Hackney was in chaos when Keith and the Ealing officers arrived. The dark streets were full of roaming gangs of youths. Debris from the rioting lay everywhere, and the Ealing vehicle bumped along the roads, driving over smashed glass and lumps of concrete and bricks, occasionally having to weave around makeshift barricades of shopping trolleys and large commercial bins that had been set alight. Acrid smoke had settled into the narrow streets, and the entire area felt almost post-apocalyptic, anarchic and full of dread.

There was no slow build up to the start of their fighting. No getting ready for it, no preparation. The officers drove straight into Hackney, and straight into a hail of bricks, bottles and rocks. Anything that could be picked up and thrown was aimed at their undefended, vulnerable minibus. Crowds of rioters focused their violent attention upon the Ealing vehicle, which had driven innocently and unexpectedly into a mob. The officers had already put on their riot gear, which was just as well as the loud bangs against their vehicle suddenly became a terrifying smash as one of the side windows gave in. The officers ducked down, and the minibus continued moving.

Looking for somewhere to park in safety, they found a quiet side street where they stopped and got out. The officers stood on the corner, unsure of what to do next. Without shields they felt that there was no way they could enter the murderous arena that the streets of Hackney had become.

'We need to get some kit, right now,' their sergeant said. 'Start looking for some shields.'

But where? Someone mentioned that they had seen a bunch of unmanned riot carriers which they had driven past just a moment before, and as a group they jogged up the road towards them, praying they wouldn't be ambushed by rioters along the way. Incredibly, the carriers had been left unlocked. The officers they belonged to were already battling with rioters elsewhere.

The Ealing officers wasted no time. They opened the doors of the carriers. Inside it was clear that the officers had left in a hurry; sweet wrappers and half-drunk plastic bottles of water lay scattered over the floor, and kit bags lay opened and abandoned all around. The insides of the vehicles smelt musty and smoky, but that wasn't unusual for riot carriers, which were used for carting around officers in uniforms that were often soaked with the odour of petrol bombs that had been thrown at them during training.

The Ealing officers quickly pulled out any shields that had been left inside and each carrier was scavenged until every officer was holding a shield of his or her own. Keith slipped his arm through the large metal ring on the rear of his shield and held it tightly against his body. Now he felt a whole lot better about things. Lining up with the rest of his unit, he stepped out into the riot.

The murky street was carpeted with smashed bricks, lumps of broken paving slabs, shattered glass and burning embers. Ahead of them was a line of police horses. Their determined riders gripped the reins and held the horses firmly as they faced a crowd of rioters a dozen metres further ahead of them. The scene was nightmarish, and the horses looked almost supernatural set against the glow of the fires and flames. The animals jostled restlessly, stomping down with their front hoofs and twisting their heads from side to side. They were frothing at their bits, straining their necks, with bulging, panicked-looking eyes peering towards the violence. The introduction of riot horses usually had an immediate effect at any scene of disorder but something here was different. Keith watched as the rioters stood where they were or even approached them, lobbing things at the horses as well as throwing bottles and bricks over the mounted officers in an attempt to hit the lines of foot officers behind them. The mounted officers stood firm, keeping their line and preventing the rioters from pushing back onto ground officers had already fought to take.

Then someone, somewhere, took charge of Keith's unit and they were ordered to form up and follow two police dogs and their handlers. The plan was to try and get behind a crowd of rioters and box them in. The entire scene was confusing, and Keith didn't really know what was going on. They had been attacked in their minibus, had to steal shields from other vehicles, and now they were suddenly ordered to run around the back streets following two German Shepherds. But he ran. Along with all the other officers, he ran after those dogs, along roads he had never seen before in an area he had no knowledge of. Then the dark backstreets opened up, and the officers found themselves on a main road. Keith paused, taking in the scene ahead of him. The streets were filled with police, rioters and traffic. *Traffic!* Buses and cars were still driving down the road as shop front after shop front was being smashed in.

Then the rioters, perhaps having run out of shop windows to smash, started to throw scaffold poles and lumps of wood through bus windows. Terrified passengers ducked down, trying to avoid the missiles and the shattering glass. It was surreal; a regular high street with shops, cars and buses, but those shops, car and buses were being set upon by swarms of maniacs. Anything and everything that was on the street was being attacked – especially the lines of police.

Keith saw groups of people crouching down and dipping through the smashed window of JD Sports, before coming back out moments later, their arms full of anything they could carry. Watching the mayhem, Keith knew that there weren't enough police on the streets. It was totally out of control. He felt that whoever was responsible for organising the response to the riots hadn't done enough. They should have gone in hard much earlier, but he felt that they had left it too late. Now it was down to the few officers left on the streets to try their best to pull it all back.

Keith re-joined the rest of his unit, creating a line of riot shields across the street – something they had practiced over and over during their riot training – and then they began to move. Marching towards the rioters, they used their shields to bat away anything they saw flying through the air towards them. The rioters began to move backwards as the officers continued to push forward, retaking the street one step at a time. Eventually they reached a large junction and the Ealing officers moved to the left, slotting in behind another PSU. After a moment, the officers began to push forward again, against the rioters, forcing them backwards as the rioters continued to throw anything they could get their hands on. Either side of him, Keith was aware of officers knocking bricks and bottles out of their way just as he himself was doing. Then they came to a stop. They had pushed the crowd back far enough to create a sterile area behind themselves, where further police units could gather in preparation for a larger assault on the rioters.

Ahead of him, Keith saw a row of a dozen officers holding onto long shields. These officers were now taking most of the impact from the missiles. That was what the transparent, body-length shields were for, and the bricks and rocks mostly bounced off after striking them. The shields had become targets and the officers crouched down to ensure the top of their heads weren't exposed, scuttling backward and forward a few feet at a time, taking the flak as the missiles rained in on them.

Keith stood behind them, with his short, round shield held protectively in front of his body, occasionally lifting it above his head as yet another rock or bottle dropped down on him. Then it was time for him to move forward again and take over from the long shields, and become the frontline.

Until that moment, and as serious as it was, the riot had seemed like nothing more than a large bit of public disorder that had gotten out of hand, but as he stepped forward to the front, Keith realised that it was far worse than that. This was more than just some unrest that had gone wrong. For the first time, Keith could see for himself exactly how serious it was. Standing there, on the frontline, he had a clear view of the rioters. There was everything from eleven-year-olds to thirty year-olds. That was shocking in itself. But far worse were their eyes and their faces – there was actual hatred in them.

These riots were different to anything else Keith had seen in his years of service. These rioters weren't just trying to goad the police. Keith felt certain that if these people got the chance, they would kill an officer, and then as many more as they could. He had never seen this level of crazed loathing before, and he knew that he never wanted to see it again. For the first time in his career as a police officer, Keith thought to himself, *Do I really want to be standing here?* He pushed the questions out of his mind. They were for later. Right now, he was busy fighting for his life.

The officers at the front were being struck by increasing amounts of missiles, including objects that Keith had never seen thrown at police before, objects which should never be thrown at the police or anyone else. Lumps of concrete so large it took two people to lift them were now being hurled through the air, mixed in with the usual things: bricks, bottles, scaffold poles, and lumps of wood. Some rioters had even taped knives to broom handles and poles, using them as deadly spears.

The officers needed to push forward again, against the rioters who were becoming more brazen and restless as the officers stood holding the junction. But they couldn't move without becoming isolated in the centre of the junction, so they had no choice but to hold their ground and continue blocking the missiles with their shields, their arms growing increasingly weary every time they took a heavy impact.

Then Keith heard the sound of glass smashing near him and an instant later, smelled petrol, followed by a heavy whooshing noise, bright orange light, and a sudden, violent heat. He turned around. Some of the rioters had managed to get behind the police lines, and now petrol bombs were hurtling through the air towards them. And these weren't the half-filled milk bottles that got thrown at their feet during their training; these were litre-sized bottles, aimed directly at their bodies. As the bottles smashed upon the ground, officers were showered in glass and burning petrol. Keith watched horrified as all around him officers were going up in flames.

Cars were also catching fire but they were ignored as the officers used the fire extinguishers they carried for only one thing – to put out the fires on themselves and each other. Anything else that had been hit had to be left to burn. Officers dashed to each other's aid, aiming the extinguishers at the flames until they ran out, and then doing their best to pat out the fires with their gloved hands. The situation was becoming increasingly hopeless.

Keith knew that there was only one way to deal with petrol bombs, and that was to target those rioters who were armed with them in order to keep them far enough away to make it difficult to reach the officers with their throws. And so pairs of officers charged at individual petrol bombers, rushing them, and forcing them back, before returning to the relative safety of the police line. The petrol bombers then retook their positions and the order for the officers to charge, came again. The pairs sprinted forward, doing their best to stick together. They held their small, round shields in front of them, and leapt over the debris on the ground, knowing that tripping could be a fatal mistake because it would make them such an easy target. The petrol bombers skipped backwards, lobbing the petrol bombs at the officers' feet as they ran towards them. The bottles exploded into walls of fire. Fuel splattered the officers' overalls and boots, igniting them, but the officers still ran through the flames, ignoring their burning uniforms, and chased off the petrol bombers.

Then the officers, still facing the crowd and taking hits from missiles, skipped backwards themselves, looking over their shoulders, moving back through the flames towards their own lines. The officers continued with this tactic until they had managed to push the rioters far enough back to be out of range of the petrol bombs. For a second the rioters seemed to have disappeared into the shadows, and the officers through the fight might be over now. But even if it was, the police couldn't turn and run – to do so would invite a mob to chase after them, and the consequences of doing that could be horrific.

The officers looked around themselves, trying to get their bearings. Throughout the fighting in the surrounding streets and the pushing back of the petrol bombers, they had been advancing on the crowds, and without realising it they had ended up on the Pembury Estate. Across the door to one of the large, four-storey brick blocks, Keith read the words 'FUCK DA POLICE', which had been painted in large red letters.

Built in the 1960s, the Pembury Estate was a warren of passageways and alleys – a haven for anyone whose business was violence and terror – and the domain of armed gangs. To make matters worse for the officers on the ground, each floor had an open corridor leading to the doors of the flats, and they had ended up in a kind of courtyard, surrounded by corridors and balconies. They looked up, and realised how perfect the buildings were as high ground for the rioters to throw things at them. The rioters were one step ahead, and the bombardment started, the usual missiles falling on the officers. The mob they'd been charging, the one that had melted away into the shadows, reappeared, and this time they had extra numbers on the floors above. The officers desperately scanned around themselves. It was like standing in the middle of a gladiatorial arena, surrounded by a baying crowd eager for blood, or being trapped on enemy territory.

Tall flames raged from bins and out of indistinguishable piles of debris. The burning light threw huge, menacing shadows across the labyrinth of brick buildings as pillars of angry fire reached into the night sky, and murky phantoms of black smoke swirled around, trapped within the high walls of the estate.

Without warning, an officer standing next to Keith dropped to the floor. The officer had collapsed as they moved forward, and now lay in a heap on the broken ground among large splinters of glass and smashed masonry. Keith didn't know if the officer had been hit with a missile or had just tripped over some of the wreckage that littered the ground. Either way, remaining down there would be fatal.

'Are you okay? Are you hurt?' Keith called down at the officer.

The officer was still moving and looked to be trying to get back to his feet. Keith quickly reached down, grabbing hold of the top of the officer's body armour and pulled him back up. The officer retook his position, adjusting his helmet visor and the shield on his arm. He nodded, and Keith knew that he was okay.

The intensity of the missiles had grown to such a rate that it was impossible to avoid being hit. As Keith lifted his shield above his head and whacked another bottle away to the side, he caught glimpse of a lump of concrete about a foot wide flying through the air. It was too far to his left to hit him but he watched as it dropped down towards his sergeant. The sergeant, who stood with his shield held in front of his body, hadn't seen the concrete block. Keith opened his mouth to shout a warning but there was no time. The slab slammed into the sergeant's head, and he crumpled to the ground under the weight. The sergeant lay on the floor, not moving, with more objects raining down on and around him. Keith looked at him, and saw that the sergeant's helmet had a huge crack running from the front to the back.

The sergeant was still on the ground, prostrate among the debris and broken glass. He didn't move, and no one knew if he had even survived the impact. Officers close to the sergeant remained frozen where they were. Keith looked over, wondering why no one was moving forward to help their sergeant. But he quickly realised the young officers were terrified, and who could blame them? No amount of training had prepared them for this. They were fighting for their lives, and now one of their own sergeants – their leader – was lying motionless on the ground, out cold, or, for all they knew, dead. This was the stuff of police nightmares.

At the same time, the rioters on the floors above the officers became delirious at the sight of the injured sergeant. The mob roared triumphantly, and the intensity of the missiles raining down increased as they looked for ways to injure more officers. Their bloodlust made them barely seem human. They were more like characters from some horror film. But this was real, and Keith knew someone needed to do something, and quick.

Keith grabbed hold of two officers with long shields, pulling them backwards towards the downed sergeant in an effort to protect him. As he did so, something large and heavy slammed into Keith's own shield, knocking him back. It was another huge slab of concrete. It shattered the top of Keith's riot shield, and as he fell backwards, the concrete chunk ricocheted under the visor on his helmet and hit him in the face. With rocks and bottles crashing down all around him, Keith stumbled backwards some more, momentarily stunned. He could feel the blood on his face and he could taste the blood on his lips but he was conscious, thinking clearly, and there was still the sergeant to worry about, prone on the ground and in a far worse way than he was. He shook his head to re-focus and reached down, grabbing hold of the top of the sergeant's overalls, dragging him backwards along the ground and through the debris in an effort to get him out of range of the rioters' missiles. Two other officers saw what he was doing and ran forward, helping him to drag the sergeant away.

Chunks of paving slabs, bricks and glass bottles were coming down and the officers felt their backs being struck repeatedly by hard, heavy objects as they pulled the sergeant along. The rest of the officers, unable to hold their ground against the barrage, began to fall back with them but they were too slow and the rioters, seeing the officers in retreat, surged forward. This was exactly why the officers hadn't taken a step backwards so far – the mob would react by chasing them, and that would bring even greater danger.

Keith looked up in dismay. No one was hitting the rioters. They were getting far too close, and if they reached the downed sergeant, they would tear him to pieces. Missiles continued to fall on them, and he could see the rioters breaking things up – anything they could get their hands on – and throwing it at the cluster of officers.

'KILL THE PIGS!' the attackers screamed. The chorus of murderous cries was followed by an increase in bricks and bottles that filled the grey sky.

Still no one was using force against the rioters. Keith, still dazed but managing to keep hold of the sergeant, looked at the officers ahead of him. *Why the hell weren't they fighting back?*

'KILL THE POLICE!'

'HIT THEM!' Keith suddenly heard himself screaming at the officers, in desperation. 'FUCKING HIT THEM!'

The order jolted the officers into action, and they finally lunged forward with their batons, striking anyone who had come too close. But it wasn't enough to keep the mob back, and the officers had no choice but to continue to retreat.

'ATTACK FROM THE REAR!' an officer suddenly called out in alarm.

Keith turned around. Some of the rioters had doubled back

and got behind the police lines again. It was their estate and they knew the rat-runs. More bricks, more petrol bombs followed, now coming from all angles: front, back and above. The officers had no choice and quickly moved against the rioters. Then, as before, the rioters seemed to melt away into the darkness.

The reason for their disappearance quickly became clear. There was another smashed bottle, the toxic smell of petrol, the rapid rush of flames and burning heat, and then the onslaught of objects began again. Wave after violent wave of bricks, bottles and petrol bombs filled the sky, cascading down upon the officers without pity. And once more the shout came, 'ATTACK FROM THE REAR!'

Through it all, the officers were still guarding their injured sergeant. No one knew how badly he was hurt, and no one knew what to do with him. The ambulance crews couldn't get to them, and although police medics were doing all they could, they had no idea if it would be enough.

Unknown to the cornered officers, there was a hospital just a few hundred metres away.

As Keith and the Ealing officers fought for their lives, Mark and the crew from Cambridge had finally found their own way to Hackney. Ahead of them they saw a group of more than 200 rioters attacking a group of Met officers and police dog handlers. There was debris everywhere. Shops were smashed to pieces, and vehicles were burning out of control in the streets. It was total bedlam. And then they realised they were in the wrong place.

'Shit,' Mark muttered.

Somehow the Cambridge officers had managed to come in behind the crowd, not from the front as they had hoped, and Mark again cursed the Met for leaving them without any maps, guides or directions.

Being behind the rioters left them isolated and exposed, and if word spread through the mob that they were there, the trio of carriers with a total of 21 officers on board wouldn't stand a chance.

'What the hell do we do now?' the driver asked, turning to Mark.

'Drop the grills,' Mark told him.

'The grills?'

'Yeah, the fucking grills! Drop 'em!'

A scaffold pole suddenly smashed down on the carrier's windscreen and the driver quickly reached up to release the leaver, dropping the heavy, metal grills over the glass. The other carriers immediately did the same.

'That's fine for you at the front but what about us in the back?' an officer said, slapping the side windows with the palm of his gloved hand. 'This bandit glass isn't as good as it's supposed to be.'

Mark looked behind him at the officers sitting at the back of the carrier, in the dark. More missiles were starting to smash into the vehicles. The mob had spotted them and the three Cambridgeshire carriers were now the focus of their attack.

Shit, Mark thought to himself. *We're sitting ducks.*

He stared out at the crowd and as more bottles and bricks rained down on them he knew there was only one option.

'Fucking go!' Mark told the carrier driver.

The driver looked at him, unsure by what he meant.

'DRIVE! We have to go through them!'

The driver put his foot down and the three carriers drove straight into the dense, frenzied sea of rioters, having no idea if they would manage to make it through, but clear as to what would happen to them if they didn't.

155

Sutton

Word reached the Sutton officers that the youths were beginning to gather. The CCTV operators had kept a close watch on the area, and had spotted groups of youths forming up again close to the Benhilton housing estate before they had started to head back down the High Street. Shops were being targeted again, and officers returned to deal with the trouble.

The High Street wasn't the only area being hit. Away from the town centre, where there were few, if any, police, other shops were also being attacked. Rose Hill, to the north, was starting to suffer damage and in Hackbridge, to the east, shops and warehouses were being looted. But it was the High Street that was seeing the worst of it. Asda, JD Sports, Argos and HMV were all now being attacked by the mob.

Following the previous charge up the High Street, Guy Ferguson had returned to the police station to check on how the other areas were doing and to get the latest briefing on what was happening across London in general. But he was now back on the streets and continuing his walk through the town centre. As he walked, he noticed a local council leader, also out to see what was happening, and they joined up, patrolling the streets together. As Guy filled him in on what had happened earlier, they headed toward the HMV store and saw that things had started to get ugly again. Plain clothed officers from the Sutton Crime Squad were dealing robustly with gangs of youths who had been attacking the shops.

As they went forward to help, Guy suddenly heard one of his officers shouting.

'If you run away again, Freddy, I'm going to baton you! Do you understand?'

Guy looked over and noticed one of his female officers standing down a narrow side street. She had her ASP baton in her hand and standing in front of her was a 6' 6" lad, who towered over her tiny, 5' 4" frame. Despite her warning, the young man bolted down an alley. The female officer sprinted after him, still waving her baton.

A pang of pride came over Guy, but he also realised what a risk the officer was taking chasing him on her own, so he joined her in the pursuit. A hundred yards further on, they managed to catch the guy, grabbing hold of him and placing him in handcuffs.

'What did he do?' Guy asked his officer.

'The windows at HMV have been done. He was standing by them at the time, so I thought he was involved. But when I tried to speak to him, he just ran off.'

Guy considered calling up for some transport to take them and their prisoner to the station but then changed his mind. The station wasn't too far away and with so few officers on the streets and with trouble breaking out once again, he didn't want to divert anyone away from their patrols. So instead he and the female officer walked their man to the station.

Despite the Crime Squad rounding up as many youths as they could, more had appeared, ready to take on the police again. Having seen some of the news footage on TV, Rob was now well aware that Croydon was burning to the ground, and elsewhere around London things were becoming increasingly desperate. He didn't want Sutton to go the same way.

The officers redeployed back to the bottom end of the High Street, ready to do their best to clear it once again, while knowing that the rioters had become more violent, and seemingly less concerned about the presence of the police. The officers began to move slowly forward until they reached the youths, who, feeling braver than before, held their ground. Rob started to push people back. 'Move away. Move away,' he ordered. The youths stumbled backwards with each shove. No one was fighting back, yet.

Other members of the mob had managed to regroup at the end of the High Street, and now they turned on the police. Bricks and bottles dropped onto the officers' line.

'SHOW OF STRENGTH,' Rob called to his officers. 'TO THE NEXT LAMPPOST... GO!'

The officers surged ahead in a single line, towards the lamppost marker that Rob had pointed out. As they ran, a few final champagne bottles and bricks clattered to the ground, smashing at the officers' feet, as the crowd flung whatever they had before running off once again.

The officers stopped running, holding their ground, batons resting up on their shoulders. They stood and watched as the mob moved away from them. But this wasn't the end. Further north, along another stretch of the High Street, looters were now attacking the huge Matalan store.

Guildford, Surrey
Richard sat on his sofa at home, watching the evening news. Despite being told that he and his officers weren't needed, he still hoped that his phone would ring and that he and his officers would be ordered to come in and work. He didn't just hope for it, he expected it. But instead, he sat there feeling frustrated and antsy, watching the evening news which right now was showing Clapham Junction going up in flames.

'I might as well have a beer now,' he told his wife. 'I can't get into work even if they wanted me to now. I can't get the train and I can't drive through a riot to get to my base, so I may as well have a few beers and watch it on the telly like everyone else.'

Richard went to his fridge and pulled out a couple of cold cans of lager. He sat down, pulled the ring on the first can and took a long swig.

His phone would never ring.

Clapham Junction

What Richard was watching on TV was all hell breaking loose in Clapham Junction. This vibrant, dense, largely Victorian south London neighbourhood with the busiest railway station in the UK in terms of train traffic, had up until then managed to avoid any real trouble. But that had all changed now. Word had got out that looters were going to target the area, and residents and business owners had started to gather on the streets, intending to protect their homes and livelihoods. But they didn't stand a chance.

By late evening, with police resources already stretched and committed elsewhere, hundreds of rioters had descended upon Clapham High Street, breaking into shops and taking handfuls of whatever they could carry. They targeted Currys electronic store and Ladbrokes betting shop. The large Debenhams store on Lavender Hill, which occupied the historic and much loved Arding and Hobbs building, had its large display windows smashed in. The looting spread around the surrounding streets and residents were left standing, watching the chaos and wondering where the police were. It would be close to another hour before the first police units would arrive, so the rioting continued and looters smashed their way into a local fancy dress shop – Party Superstore – on Lavender Hill. The small business occupied the lower floor of a four-storey Victorian gothic, terraced building, with the upper floors containing residential flats. Looters stole masks and brightly coloured wigs, using them as disguises and to taunt the police. Then one looter decided to take things a step further, setting fire to a costume that was hanging up in the shop. With the store being full of clothing and fancy dress paraphernalia, it took no time at all for the fire to take hold. The building would be completed gutted and half a million pounds worth of stock destroyed.

2100 hrs
Croydon

The scene that greeted the Croydon officers seemed unreal. A huge, fiery glow illuminated everything in blinding oranges and yellows. In the background were the buildings at Reeves Corner, fully and spectacularly ablaze. In front of them were silhouettes of hundreds of people jumping around like maniacs. The scene was like an illegal rave in Hell. Everyone was shouting and screaming – some in horror but many in crazed excitement. In the sky, against the dazzling flames of the fire, pieces of wood, bricks, street furniture and bottles were all raining down on lines of police officers, who were desperately trying to reach the fire engines that had themselves come under attack from the mob, and were now taking a battering from the countless missiles as they tried to get to the burning buildings. The flashing blue lights of the emergency vehicles were being swallowed and lost within the colour and ferocity of the fire as flurries of hot grey ash floated gently down from the sky like dirty snowflakes. The glass, the violence, the bloodlust, the fire and the chaos – it was the officers' very worst case scenario.

Then Tom saw something that was both astonishing and appalling: people were jumping for their lives from the windows of the burning buildings. There were people still trapped inside, yet the rioters were continuing to prevent the fire engines from reaching them. This was crazy. People were going to die.

The sight of desperate people leaping from windows added an extra shot of urgency into the Croydon officers as they sprinted towards the crowds. Moments later they found themselves diving into a pitched battle with the rioters as they desperately tried to reach the fire engines.

The officers charged into the mob and fought their way through, using their shields to force people out of the way and baton striking others who attacked them, and, as they pushed on, deflecting missiles and punches that rained down on them in the crush of bodies. They worked desperately to stick together as one group, only too aware of what would happen if any of them were separated from the rest. Then a man grabbed hold of the top of Tom's shield, trying to wrench it from him. Tom pushed forward with the shield, knocking the man off balance, and brought his baton down, striking the man on the top of the arm. The man fell back but other attackers moved forward, grabbing at the officers, trying to pull them into the crowd and down onto the ground. Another officer had been caught in a headlock and rioters were attempting to yank his helmet off his head as he reached up, trying to punch them off. Two other officers charged forward, hitting the attackers with the full force of their shields and knocking them to the floor. They took hold of their fellow officer and pulled him back into their own line before surging forward again, into the main body of the mob.

In the midst of the fighting, the abuse and the attacks, Tom noticed something altogether more sinister. As he fought his way through the violent mass of rioters, he saw a young man reach into his jacket pocket. A moment later the youth pulled out a knife. The flash of metal was unmistakable. The youth twisted the knife in his hand, ensuring that Tom saw the deadly blade. The knife was being openly brandished. It was a display of outrageous and terrifying bravado. Tom turned to his left and right and noticed more youths doing the same, drawing knives. It was a blur of masked, hooded faces and glistening blades, all reflecting the deadly colours of the inferno. Knife welding thugs had surrounded the Croydon officers.

The danger of the situation was clear: if just one of these armed men stabbed an officer, it could lead to an uncontrollable frenzy of killing. Tom pushed ever more desperately through the crowds, along with the rest of his unit, fighting to get past the armed men, while half expecting to feel the force of a blade being pushed into his body. It was pandemonium and Tom felt, for the first time in his career, that things were genuinely and completely out of control, and he seriously wondered if they – the police – were going to be able to stop it all.

They continued to push through and saw up ahead that some officers from another serial had managed to fight their own way through the crowds and had reach the fire engines. The officers were now doing their best to protect them from the rioters, and escort them to the fire. They were literally fighting every step of the way towards Reeves Corner, fighting both for their own lives and for those stuck in the burning building.

Tom's unit had now also managed to push through. People were still trapped inside the building, so Tom and his colleagues rushed forward and went straight in.

Everything was ablaze. Smoke filled the dark corridors and an intense, deadly heat swept through the narrow passages. Fire was climbing up the walls and dripping down from the ceiling. There was a sickening, crackling sound as the timber around them burnt in the tight grip of the furious, spitting flames. Tom faced the first door he came to and kicked it down. The wood shattered as it ripped away from the frame.

Tom lifted his visor and called out urgently, 'IS ANYONE IN HERE? IS ANYONE HERE?'

Other officers began to do the same, going door to door, booting them down and quickly calling out for anyone who may still be left inside. People came sprinting out, shouting and screaming in panic whilst others didn't want to leave at all, too frightened to move, until the urgency of the officers pleading made it clear that there was no other choice: they could either run outside and take their chances with the rioters, or they could stay and burn to death.

Opposite the store, in a small flat above a shop, Polish shop worker, Monika Konczyk answered her ringing phone. It was her sister, telling her to get out and to leave Croydon. But it was too late. Embers from the Reeves fire had landed on her building and it was already alight. She was trapped by the fire and terrified that she would burn to death. Her sister begged her to jump from a window but Monika was on the first floor and outside police were battling with gangs of rioters. But she had little choice. She could either stay and die, or leap for her life.

As Monika leaned out of her window, riot police, seeing her inside, had gathered on the street below. Other people had already jumped for their own lives and now it was her turn. Her sister pleaded for her to jump, and police officers held out their arms, ready to catch her. All around her were ferocious fires. People were screaming, shouting, throwing missiles and fighting. The police officers called out for her to jump. They were waiting for her. They would catch her. And so she jumped, sliding down some damaged awning and straight into the arms of the waiting police. Her home and possessions were gone but she was safe. She was alive.

Inside the burning buildings, officers were climbing up staircases, shouting all the way, kicking in more doors, determined that all the residents would get out. The fire engines, though protected to an extent by a ring of riot officers, were still being guided through the crowds, unable to rush because they were under such a furious attack. At the same time, other officers were battling further groups of rioters all around Reeves Corner, baton charging them or fighting hand-to-hand. Tom could hear them – the faint murmur of shouting and rioting and screaming had managed to penetrate the inferno. By now, walls had started to give way and ceilings began to collapse. Tom knew that Reeves Corner would soon be lost, and he knew that they didn't have much time left. He kicked down another door, frantically searching for anyone still trapped in the burning building.

Lewisham

At Halfords, Darren had eventually been relieved by a serial of Level 3 officers. He, along with the group of officers he was with, had been told to return to Lewisham police station. Sitting down in the station yard, by the empty stables, Darren took a long swig of water. Having a rest and having something to drink felt good, but officers still on the streets were continuing to call for help and 'Urgent Assistance'. Despite this, Darren and the other officers with him had been told to remain at the station while senior officers held 'community meetings'. Darren's group were the only serial left not currently deployed. But they were ordered to wait until the meetings were finished before being sent out.

'This is a joke,' an officer said. Darren looked over at him and nodded his head in agreement. 'We're all sitting here while officers are out there calling for help. Who cares about these community meetings? The community is gone!'

The officers had been sitting around for the best part of an hour while their senior officers spoke to community leaders about how to deal with the trouble. But as far as the officers were concerned, it was too late for that, or at least not the right time for it. For now, the streets needed retaking. The rioting and looting needed to be stopped. They didn't feel that senior officers holding meetings with local community leaders was going to do that, especially while screams for help from distressed officers continued to be heard over the radio.

'Sod it,' the sergeant finally said. 'Let's just do something about this ourselves.'

By now an inspector and a chief inspector had joined their ranks and were in agreement. This was not the time for more meetings; they needed to get out and help people. There was just one problem – they still didn't have any vehicles.

'I've got an idea,' Darren said, grinning.

Lewisham bus station was just a short walk from the police station, and Darren's idea was to commandeer a bus. It was a crazy plan but these were crazy times. The inspectors and sergeants looked at him for a moment, wondering if he was being serious. He was. Then they stared at him a little more, wondering if it was a good idea.

'Can't hurt, I guess,' a sergeant said, finally.

The sergeant and another PC jogged over towards the bus station, where they were met by a couple of bus drivers, wiping their hands on dirty, oily rags.

'We have a problem,' the sergeant said. 'As you know, there are riots breaking out all over the shop. The problem we have is that we don't have any vehicles to get to them.'

The drivers looked at the sergeant in silence.

'So…we were wondering if we could take one of your buses?' More silence.

'I know it's a big ask,' the sergeant said, 'but we are getting a bit desperate.'

'Do you know how to drive a double decker bus?' one of the men asked.

'No.'

The drivers looked at each other, with raised eyebrows. Then another bus driver walked over. He was a short, dark-skinned man. 'Come on, I'll drive you,' he said, in an accent which managed to be both strongly London and strongly Turkish at the same time.

'Really?' the sergeant asked, amazed.

'No problem; I don't get off for another hour anyway.'

Minutes later the bus pulled up outside Lewisham police station.

'What the hell is this?' the inspector asked.

'It's a bus,' the sergeant replied.

'I can bloody see that. But it's a double decker!'

The inspector stared at the big red bus parked outside the police station. Then, after another moment of silence, he said, 'Everyone on the bus.'

One of the PCs rang the bell. 'All aboard the riot express!'

'Where to?' the driver asked.

'Sydenham, please, driver.'

Radio calls had been coming out the entire time. Officers were continually under attack and in desperate need of support. At a Sainsbury's supermarket, in Bell Green, Lower Sydenham, a couple of police dog handlers were calling for help. The store was being attacked, and the two dog handlers were trying to take on the looters with just their dogs for back-up.

The bus set off. A few minutes later, on a deserted road, the bus driver stopped at a set of red traffic lights.

'Why have you stopped?' the sergeant asked.

'The lights are red.'

'Never mind that! Go through them!'

'Go through a red light? I've got a load of police officers on my bus!'

'Exactly! We're telling you to go through them! We can't stop here. We need to get to Sydenham.'

The driver looked ahead at the lights and put his foot down, driving straight through them and towards Sydenham.

Before the bus reached Sainsbury's, the dog handlers came back on the radio to say that the looters and rioters had run off to cause trouble elsewhere. The inspector on the bus decided to hang around the area in case they were still on the streets.

As the officers headed along Sydenham Road, the area's main shopping street, they saw around sixty youths who had been attacking shops and businesses. Darren peered out of the bus window towards the mob. They were gathered outside a Ladbrokes betting shop, just a couple of doors up from a small Costcutter supermarket that had already been targeted and attacked, with packs of cigarettes and bottles of alcohol stolen. There were still cars and buses on the streets but everything was moving at a slow crawl as the rioters blocked the road, running back and forth around the vehicles.

The officers on the bus suddenly realised they were as good as invisible. Their bus blended in with all the other traffic on the road, and so the rioters paid it no attention. The mob was looking out for police vehicles and riot carriers, not red buses, which were everywhere. The officers now had an advantage.

'Creep along,' the driver was told. 'Get as close to them as you can and then park up at the side of the road.'

The driver drove slowly along Sydenham Road, but by now

the traffic had come to a virtual stop, so the driver pulled up where he was and looked back at the officers on his bus. They were lined up along the bottom deck, facing the middle doors, like shoppers waiting to get off.

'Okay, open the doors,' the driver was told.

The doors swung open and twenty-one riot officers steamed out, sprinting towards the rioters. The mob was caught completely by surprise. They hadn't even noticed the bus, which was just another vehicle stuck in the traffic jam they had created. The officers ran past the trapped cars, dipping left and right, as the drivers and passengers looked out. Some rioters were already armed with weapons – lumps of wood, bottles and bricks, and with reports of officers seeing knives and guns, it was important that the rioters were reached quickly and dominated. As he ran towards the men, Darren turned to look behind himself. The rest of his unit were still about fifteen feet behind. Darren had been the first off the bus, and in his enthusiasm to get to the rioters he had sprinted off at quite a pace. He decided to keep going, figuring that the rest of his unit would catch up in just a few moments.

Darren ran towards a hooded man. The man was holding a glass bottle and Darren watched as he spun around to face him. The man's eyes widened at the sudden appearance of the police. Darren had never seen anyone look so shocked before. But then the man raised the bottle in the air, ready to throw it or strike down with it. But it was too late, Darren had already reached him and he slammed his shield into the man's face. The top rim of the shield pushed up, into the man's open mouth, so that for just a moment it looked as though he were trying to take a bite from it. The man went flying backwards, landing on his backside. Another rioter moved towards Darren, reaching out to grab him. Darren swung around and brought his baton down on the man, striking his shoulder. The man stumbled backwards. By now the other man had picked himself off the floor and both men ran off.

The rest of the crowd also began to run off, heading towards the Hazel Grove housing estate. The officers didn't chase after them and instead, held their position. The inspector ran up to the officers.

'Who just did that? Who just went in on the rioters?'

Darren turned to face the inspector and lifted his visor up to show his smiling face, but wondering if he would be in trouble for going in on his own or going in too hard.

'Darren. I should have known it would be you... that was great. Let's do a bit more of it!'

It was just what Darren and the other officers hoped to hear, and just what they felt was needed in order to show the rioters that the police were still in charge.

'GO!' the inspector shouted.

The officers surged forward again, towards the rioters, some of whom had stopped running and had retaken their positions along Sydenham Road. The determined advance of the officers convinced the mob to keep retreating and by pushing forward, the officers managed to clear the rioters off the road and onto the estate.

Darren looked back at the traffic. The cars and busses were flowing normally again, as if nothing had just happened here at all.

'How weird is that?' another officer said to Darren. 'You would never have thought this place was just the scene of a riot.'

Parked up, along the side of the moving traffic, the double decker bus was waiting for them. The driver was gripping his steering wheel and peering out through the windscreen, with a broad grin across his face.

As Darren walked over to the bus, he looked back at the street, reflecting on what had happened. It had been a quick battle but it was a battle they had won. It had probably been the first time that those rioters had seen police taking the initiative; the first time they had had police charging at them. And it had worked. They had spent a long time guarding Halfords and listening to people having 'community meetings' when what they felt had been needed was some firm, assertive policing. And here was the result – the looting had been stopped, the rioters had run off and Sydenham Road could get back to normal. The rioters clearly hadn't enjoyed being taken on like that and Darren – like so many officers – knew instinctively that was the only sort of police response which was effective. The police hadn't been doing enough of it, and the result had been brazen gangs of youths doing whatever the hell they liked with little fear of any kind of comeback. Darren had been angry and frustrated but now he finally felt that they were doing what they were supposed to be doing.

'We should have done this hours ago,' Darren said.

'Hours? We should have done this days ago!' another officer replied.

The bus driver had been an absolute diamond, but he was worried about his boss, who had been calling up wondering where his bus and his driver were. Darren and the unit inspector did their best to reassure him. 'Don't worry,' the inspector said. 'We'll sort this out for you.'

Another officer rang the bell. 'I want to get off!' he called out, jokingly.

'This isn't your stop,' the sergeant growled at him.

The atmosphere on the bus was jovial, and even the driver seemed to be enjoying himself. The band of officers, in their enormous, bright red 'riot carrier' had turned quite a few heads. Now they were headed back to Catford, where they had earlier help chased off the gangs from the retail park. The youths had gathered once again, and as had happened in Sydenham, they paid little attention to the bus.

The doors of the bus opened once more. Twenty-one police officers, wearing full riot kit, charged out, their shields and batons gripped tightly in their hands. Within seconds the officers were on the rioters. Most ran off but some remained, too shocked by the sudden appearance of the police to run. Others, though, were up for a fight. Shields were rammed into bodies, and batons struck down on those holding weapons or moving to attack the officers. Those few rioters who had stayed quickly began to disappear too, skulking off down the side streets and onto the surrounding estates. Over his radio, Darren could hear other police units coming across the scattering rioters. Officers were starting to 'up the ante' and they too were dealing with them more firmly – forcing them off the streets and preventing them from damaging any more buildings.

By now it was time to return the bus to the garage. The driver had been a total star. He had willingly come out with the officers, and bravely driven them into the thick of the rioting. Even as his own boss had been calling him over the radio, ordering him back into the garage, he had stuck with the officers. It was a commitment that the officers would make sure didn't go unrewarded. Without him and his double decker, areas of Lewisham may not have seen any police at all. Rioters would have continued attacking shops in Sydenham and looters would have returned to Catford. In between, they had also managed to provide some relief to other officers in need of a break. All of this had been because this driver came out with his bus. It was a bold and valiant action that none of the officers would forget. Other officers, upon seeing the busload of coppers, would burst out laughing, and when asked how they had managed to commandeer a double decker bus, the inspector said, 'Initiative'.

Woolwich

Monday was turning into the most intense and violent day of the riots so far, and trouble had now spread far outside London, with copycat attacks and disorder breaking out in other cities. In Leicester, police were tackling gangs of missile throwing youths. Rioting had also broken out in Liverpool, and the disturbances would be the worst seen there for a generation. Though contained in a small area to the south of the city, vehicles were set alight, and shops attacked as around 200 youths rampaged through the area. A police helicopter hovered above, looking down on the destruction as officers moved in against a barrage of missiles as skirmishes with the rioters went on for several hours. Half-a-dozen buildings and around twenty vehicles were set alight. The fire brigade came under attack themselves, and seven of their vehicles were subsequently taken off the road because of the damage they suffered.

Nottingham, too, was now seeing outbreaks of violence. Vehicles and buildings were being attacked in the city centre, and petrol bombs were thrown into the yard of a police station. Youths were seen roaming around armed with bricks and clubs and even sticks with nails hammered into the ends.

In West Yorkshire police and vehicles were attacked by masked youths armed with bricks and other missiles. Tensions ran higher as a man was shot in the face, and a youth was bitten by a police dog.

But it was in London where the police were seriously stretched and some corners of the capital were beginning to look and feel as if they had been forgotten about or abandoned. The officers in Sutton had already accepted that when they made a stand against the rioters, they would be on their own. In Woolwich, just south of the river, below City Airport and the Isle of Dogs, other officers were feeling the same strain, but unlike Sutton, it was the rioters who would take control from the police.

Along Thomas Street, eight police officers faced a mob of around 150 rioters. Six of the officers had been paired up with long shields, as two short shield supervising officers stood behind in standard riot control positioning. They stood near the crossroads with Wellington Street and Greens End. On either side of the officers was a mixture of old and modern three storey buildings, made up of shops, offices and flats. Ahead of them, standing within the crossroads itself, was the mob of rioters. Street signs, traffic cones, planks of wood and bottles were all being hurled towards the officers.

Missiles slammed into the long shields, some heavy enough to knock the officers backwards a step. A lump of wood hit a shield on its outer edge, causing the entire shield to twist to the side, momentarily exposing the officer standing behind it. The force of the continual barrage crashing against the shields reverberated through the officers' arms and bodies. The officers behind the shields crouched down, so that their helmets sat just below the tops of their shields. The mob was growing, but it was impossible for the officers to move from their position. To move forward, into the junction, would mean that they would be exposed on three sides, as opposed to the one ahead of them that they were currently facing. Moving forward into the junction would also give the rioters an easy opportunity to get behind the officers, which would mean they were surrounded on all four sides.

As missiles continued to be slung towards them by an increasingly hostile, violent, growing crowd, and with little other option, the order was called.

'WITHDRAW! WITHDRAW!'

The long shield officers began to shuffle backwards, dragging the bottoms of the shields along the ground and keeping them facing the rioters and their missiles. The retreat of the officers was all that was needed to set the rioters into a frenzy. Now they felt empowered, and they charged forward in even greater numbers, throwing everything they could at the withdrawing line of officers. The violence and missiles rapidly increased in speed and intensity. More traffic signs, more lumps of wood, more bottles, rocks, more screams of abuse. Individual rioters, now feeling bolder than ever, ran up to the shields, standing just feet away as they threw their missiles directly at the police. When any normal person, fearing for their lives, would have turned and run, this handful of officers continued with their controlled retreat, moving backwards, taking whatever was thrown at them, watching as the mob swelled in number. Staring at the rioters through the scratched surface of the burned, plastic shields, the officers picked up their pace but kept the long shields facing the crowd, allowing the acrylic to take a majority of the impacts.

Behind the shield officers, further down Thomas Street, a line of police officers, wearing their regular beat uniform and yellow jackets, waited. The shield officers were heading back towards them. As the officers moved further, the mob thinned out, not wanting get too far from the crossroads, where they had control of the major junction.

A jeweller, a bank and other shops had already been attacked and looted, and a police car outside Woolwich Arsenal train station had been set alight, and was now burnt down to a dirty metal shell. Now the rioters set about a pub on the corner of Thomas Street and Wellington Street, smashing the windows and doors. A youth with a scarf tied across his face picked up a four-foot plank of wood and tied a rag around one end. Moving towards a small fire of wooden crates, he lit the rag and ran towards the pub, jumping through the smashed doors. He aimed the burning plank at the highly flammable bottles of spirits, and the alcohol went up in a violent rush of fire and smoke. The fire quickly took hold, catching onto the furnishings.

The youth who had thrown the flaming plank walked calmly away, and joined another group. A short distance from the burning pub, they broke into a shop using a spade, and stole a charity box.

With the gangs of excitable, violent yobs charging round, it was impossible for the handful of police to move back in and escort and protect the fire brigade, who had come to deal with the fire in the pub. So the Great Harry pub was left to burn. As rioters attacked nearby shops, the pub windows blew out and fierce, furnace-like flames flung themselves into the street. The fire had now completely consumed the pub and it was beyond saving.

Images taken on a mobile phone of the retreating officers and the burning pub on Thomas Street were shown on the news, but were mistakenly described as being from Liverpool. It seemed that no one was even aware of what was happening in Woolwich. It was just one more site of violent disorder among dozens of others.

2200 hrs
Hackney
There was a thump on the front of Mark's carrier but this time it wasn't a bottle or a rock – it was a rioter. Then there was another,

and another. The driver wasn't going fast – the mob was so dense that he couldn't have even if he wanted to – but rioters were bouncing off the bonnet as he cautiously made his way through the crowd. The road was packed with people in masks and hoods and they weren't getting out of the way. In fact, some seemed to be intentionally standing in front of them, perhaps thinking – wrongly – that the carriers would stop. But stopping would have been a deadly mistake, so the small caravan of riot carriers persevered through the dense sea of thugs. Faces filled the side windows with vicious shouting, swearing and repeated threats of death, and the protective glass was quickly covered in a slimy coating of spit.

The constant sounds of thumping and banging was now a mix of people bouncing off the bonnet and others punching and kicking the carriers, striking the windows in an attempt to smash them. It was madness. It was surreal. It was like nothing the officers had ever seen before. The carriers rocked back and forth as they were attacked on all sides. No one in Mark's carrier spoke as they held their shields up against the windows in case they finally went in. All stared dead ahead, completely focused on getting through the crowd and reaching the other side.

Finally, Mark's carrier broke through. He snatched his head back, to check that the two carriers following had also made it. They had. They were battered and a little sorry looking, but they had all reached the other side.

The officers quickly jumped out of the vehicles, glad to have made it in mostly one piece and happy to be standing on their own two feet.

As they stood there, checking the damage on their carriers and wondering how they had managed to successfully drive through the crowd, another PSU Inspector walked up to them, shaking his head but smiling. 'Fuck me, that was good!' he said. 'But what the hell were you doing over there?'

'Someone said Hackney High Street,' Mark told him. 'They didn't say which end.'

The Cambridge officers pulled down the visors on their helmets, raised their shields and turned back around, ready to meet the rioters face on.

The fighting in Hackney continued on and off for some time. Groups would appear and throw objects at the police lines before quickly disappearing again but eventually the estates and the surrounding streets became quieter. The rampaging gangs lessened and there were no more surprise attacks. Now, finally, an ambulance was able to make its way to the fallen sergeant. Keith watched as the sergeant was carefully lifted in and taken to hospital. Examinations of his injuries would reveal a concussion, and compression on the neck. The sergeant wouldn't return to work for another four weeks and would suffer with blurred vision and slurred speech.

After fighting continually for about three hours, the Ealing officers were briefly released so that they could go to the hospital themselves and be checked for injuries. Evidential photographs were taken of their wounds. Keith's broken riot shield and the sergeant's cracked helmet were taken away by the 'suits' – CID detectives – who were gathering up as much evidence as they could for later investigations and potential prosecutions. The injuries and damaged equipment were all disturbing proof of the appalling, vicious and sustained attack that the Ealing officers had come under since their arrival in Hackney.

The break at the hospital had been welcome but the officers' respite was to be brief. Having arrived in the middle of a full-blown riot – one of the most intense, dangerous and brutal yet seen – and having fought their way through the streets and housing estates, losing a seriously injured sergeant along the way, Keith and his fellow officers were ordered back out.

Keith had a quick look around the corridors of the hospital, searching for another shield that may have been left or abandoned by an injured officer, but there were none to be found. He was going to have to go back outside without one. During the previous fighting he had noticed a number of officers holding just their batons, and with no shields. He had pitied them but now he was about to find out exactly how that felt. He wasn't looking forward to it but at the same time he knew there was little choice and he wasn't about to abandon the rest of his unit.

A short time later the Ealing officers entered a pretty, residential square of Georgian townhouses facing out onto a small, green, park, and there they immediately found themselves facing more violent mobs. It was unrelenting.

The officers – exhausted, battered and bruised – stood at one end of the square, gazing into it. Crowds of youths jumped around excitedly at the far end. The entire square was a haze. The faint, orange street lighting was made fuzzy by swirls of black, potent smoke; a Portakabin within the square had been set ablaze. With the arrival of the officers, the rioting yobs moved back, disappearing behind the poisonous smokescreen. Then through the smoke appeared volley after volley of bottles and bricks, which rained down on the officers as the Portakabin burned. Keith looked more closely at the small, wooden structure and noticed, to his dismay, what appeared to be gas canisters attached to its side. It didn't take much to imagine the potential of what would happen if the canisters went up, as they surely would if left to burn. The rioters were seemingly unaware of the very real danger that they were in, not to mention the nearby houses and homeowners.

Keith turned to the officer next to him. 'We need the fire brigade to do something about this,' he said.

The officer looked at him blankly before answering, 'They won't come.'

'What?'

'Not while there are people down there, rioting.'

Keith looked back towards the fire as missiles continued to emerge from the smoke, and fall down on the line of blue uniforms. Then some of the rioters started to come through the smoke and into the square, where they began shouting abuse at the officers. It was as though they were gearing up for a battle on the square.

It was clear what needed to be done. Despite the risk of the canisters going up, the officers had to push forward and clear the rioters out of the square. It was the only way to get the fire brigade in and to ensure there wasn't an explosion.

The officers formed up and began to advance on the rioters. As they got closer to the burning Portakabin, the level and intensity of missiles grew, tumbling down on them as they fought to push the rioters back. By now the officers were standing close enough to the burning hut to feel the powerful heat of the flames and the taste of the stinging smoke, knowing that the gas canisters could explode at any time. Homes could be destroyed, people could die and still, bottles and rocks and bricks teemed down on them. The rioters wanted it to burn.

The fire grew more intense and there was a greater rush of flames. 'The canisters!' an officer shouted at Keith, in panic.

'Just keep pushing. If they go, they go. Just keep pushing past them,' Keith shouted back, desperately trying to knock bottles away with his baton, like a warped game of baseball.

As the officers advanced, Keith could again fell the heavy, painful thuds of rocks and bricks slamming into his body. Each one knocked him back slightly and each one sapped away a little more energy, a little more confidence. Without a shield he had little chance of blocking all of the missiles but he pushed forward with the rest of his unit regardless. There was more sharp pain, this time on his leg and he could feel one of his plastic leg guard crack under the barrage of rocks.

The officers, determined to get past the gas canisters, forced their way onto the rioters' ground. Young officers who, just a few hours before, froze as one of their own sergeants was taken out, were now battling like veterans – calm, methodical and effective – as they gradually pushed the mob away from the Portakabin.

Finally the rioters began to fall back, allowing the fire brigade to come into the square. The officers held the line and watched the sky as missiles and debris continued to be flung at them. Then, perhaps realising that the officers were batting everything away and were clearly not going to give up the ground they had fought to take, the rioters turned away from the police line and instead began to attack cars that had been parked in the street by the local residents. Some of the cars had already been moved by the rioters to create roadblocks, but the officers had no choice but to hold the line and ensure the safety of the fire brigade. Dealing with the Portakabin and making the canisters safe was the priority. So the officers stood and watched as cars were attacked and set alight in front of them. The air became hotter and the street filled with even more black smoke. Once again it became hard for the officers to see the missiles tumbling down through this new smokescreen. But worse was the smoke itself. Without breathing gear, getting oxygen into their heaving, burning lungs was becoming increasingly difficult. But they continued to hold the line, only falling back once the fire brigade gave the all clear and the canisters had been made safe. Without the focus of the burning hut, the rioters now lost interest in the square, and Keith watched as they ran off, no doubt looking to start trouble elsewhere.

The crowds facing the Cambridge officers had also appeared to lose interest. The missiles stopped and people began to disperse. Mark stood on the cordon with his shield held up, ready to take any flak that could still come his way. But ten minutes later the mob had mostly gone. Then, before the Cambridge officers had a chance to catch their breath, they were suddenly redeployed to Leicester Square.

The officer standing next to Mark looked over at him. 'It's going off in the centre of town as well!' he said.

But the officer was wrong. Leicester Square was empty and, once they were in place, the officers guessed that the commanders just wanted them there as a presence, to walk around and be seen; as had pretty much been the plan right at the start, when they had first been told to deploy to Oxford Street, even though they never actually made it there.

Walking around a deserted West End, the boredom and time of night played on the officers' minds and bodies. Fatigue set in, followed by hunger. The officers hadn't eaten all day but they soon found a nearby McDonalds, where they got coffees and plenty of food. They would remain in Leicester Square for the rest of the night, feeling that they had never really been given the chance to get stuck into the riots.

Ealing

As Robin drove along The Broadway in Ealing, he saw a marked police car ahead of him. Masked youths were jumping on it, kicking in the windows and attacking it with bats and lumps of wood. The officers the car belonged to were nowhere to be seen.

Everywhere there were gangs of youths attacking shops, buildings and cars. It was mayhem. Then a crowd charged up Springbridge Road, by the side of the pretty, sand-coloured Christ the Saviour Parish Church, heading towards Haven Green – a large public garden square opposite Ealing Broadway rail station. Facing the crowd was a ragtag, makeshift line of police officers. Most were wearing a basic police uniform of flat-caps and bright yellow jackets. Only a few had any real protective riot equipment.

Robin quickly drove around, coming behind the police line to face the rioters. He looked ahead of him into the darkness and then continued past the police line, driving closer towards the advancing crowd of rioters. He wanted to get a better idea of how many there were, and to see if he could figure out their intention. His eyes widened as he drove closer. Ahead of him was a huge mob that he estimated to be around 200 strong. His original plan had been to try and push the rioters back; there may have been just three of them in one unmarked police car, but Robin knew from experience that sometimes just the sound of the police siren and a flashing blue light could be enough to make at least some of them run off. But to Robin's horror, rather than legging it away, the crowd stood firm. Then came a barrage of bricks and bottles and other missiles.

Robin quickly put the car into reverse. He turned to Sergeant Ashton and Michelle. 'Tactical retreat,' he said.

With the police so outnumbered and coming under such a ferocious and sustained attack, the line of officers couldn't push forward against the rioters. The mob had moved forward and the usual volley of bricks, bottles and other random objects was falling from the sky. Rubbish bins had been tipped over in the road and set alight. Some larger, commercial bins had also been tipped over and placed across the road as a burning barrier, or else rolled towards the officers' lines. Other litter and debris crackled and spat as it burnt in the gutters all around. Hundreds of rioters were now holding one end of Springbridge Road. It was a narrow street and the only way onto it was from the north or from the south, and with the rioters in control of the north end, by Haven Green, which they had also overrun, there was no way to outflank them.

As the street burnt, and the officers held their line, Richard Mannington Bowes, a local man who lived in flat on Springbridge Road, had had enough. Wearing a blue and white plaid shirt and a pair of shorts, he bravely stepped out of his front door and onto the street. The 68-year-old retired accountant was no stranger to dealing with nuisance people, having had issues in the area before. But this time it was different. This wasn't one or two drunks urinating against his front door, this was a full-blown riot with hundreds of violent youths attacking police lines and looting shops. But no matter, Bowes was having none of it. As a fire burnt in the street, he began to stamp on it, in an effort to put the small blaze out. As he did so, a 16-year-old youth – Darrell Desuze – ran up to him. Desuze, wearing a white t-shirt and a distinctive black sweatshirt draped over his shoulders with the words 'Robbers and Villains' printed across the front, punched Bowes in the jaw, knocking him unconscious. As Bowes fell to the ground, his head slammed against the solid, concrete pavement.

'No! No!' someone in the crowd shouted. 'He's just an old man!'

But it was too late. As Bowes lay on the floor, surrounded by dozens of rioters and burning bins, he was robbed of his wallet and mobile phone.

As the rioters continued to hurl missiles at the static police line, Desuze returned to Bowes' motionless body as other rioters began dragging him further onto the pavement. Then Desuze left again, returning to the riot and heading off to continue looting shops and restaurants around Haven Green.

As Robin drove back towards the police line, officers had already started to move up, heading towards the same rioters that he had just retreated from. Robin stopped the car and watched as the thin lines of officers passed by his windows. They had been joined by some Level 2 officers, wearing full riot equipment, but many others still weren't properly equipped for the danger that they were heading into. They were wearing shirtsleeves and carried small, extendable ASP batons in their hands. These officers were just the PCs and PCSOs from the local policing team that had happened to be on duty at that time. Robin recognised many of them.

As the officers moved up, creating a line across the road, the mob went berserk. They threw anything they could get their hands on. More burning bins were dragged across the road, and as more litter was tipped out, the fires blazing in the gutters grew. But the officers held their line, refusing to retreat under the bombardment.

Then the officers began to advance further up Springbridge Road. As they did, Peter Firstbrook, a 60-year-old neighbour of Richard Mannington Bowes, rushed out to see what was going on. Some of the youths approached him, and one of them said, 'There's one of your lot over there and he's injured.'

Despite the rioting that was going on all around, the youth had spoken to him politely and had even sounded concerned about

Bowes's welfare. Firstbrook forced his way through a crowd of rioters and saw Bowes lying on the ground with his legs dangerously close to the burning debris. He tried to pull him away from the fires but Bowes was a dead weight. He called to some youths to help him and three came over, also seeming concerned about Bowes's condition. They helped to drag Bowes body towards a nearby alley but then disappeared again, into the crowd. Firstbrook tried to speak to Bowes, and checked his airway and pulse – basic first aid – but there was no response. Then he noticed blood coming from Bowes's ear, which meant he had a serious internal head injury.

At the same time, the police were continuing to push up, slowly forcing the rioters back onto Haven Green. Seeing Bowes on the ground, surrounded by burning rubbish, officers, still coming under fire from the retreating rioters, stopped to help, removing their riot helmets and bending down to check on the injured man. As they did, another officer began to kick away the burning piles of litter that blazed by their feet. The few officers carrying long shields moved forward to try to give Bowes and the officers treating him some form of protection from the rioters' missiles. The officers and Firstbrook were desperate to do whatever they could to help but it was no good. Bowes died in hospital three days later without regaining consciousness.

Desuze, from Hounslow, west London, had originally planned that night to head out to Harrow. Instead, following a text message saying there was going to be trouble in Ealing, he changed his plans. Those changes had resulted in the death of an innocent man.

Robin decided once again to try to gauge the size and strength of the rioters. He reversed from the police line and drove the wrong way around the far side of Haven Green, in an attempt to get behind the crowd. As he drove, he could see the shops on the east side of Haven Green being attacked by crowds of masked looters. The local officers were already engaged in a pitched battle with the other crowd and there was no one left to deal with the blatant criminality that was happening all around. Every business was being attacked, windows kicked in and goods looted.

A huge mob then descended upon the small Tesco store on the north east side of Haven Green, and gangs of masked youths ran past Robin's car, their arms filled with bottles of alcohol. Restaurants, still with their customers inside, were having bricks thrown at the windows. Robin watched as customers and staff cowered inside. It was sickening to witness, but there was nothing he could do about it. As he watched, the crowd saw him in the unmarked police car, and realised who was in it. Suddenly bricks and bottles were being thrown at them as well. There was a blur of hooded men, fire and missiles. Murderous shouting mixed with excited screams and the sounds of thumping as the car was struck again and again. The mob was moving in, getting closer, surrounding the car. Robin put his foot down and roared away, towards the High Street.

A safe distance away, Robin pulled into Bond Street, a small business street that ran south, off The Broadway and down towards Ealing Studios. Turning in from The Broadway had meant that he was once again driving the wrong way down a one-way street, but he had seen some people moving around and the only people on the streets now were either police or rioters, so he was keen to see who they were and what they were up to. As they pulled into the road, Robin stopped the car and the three officers stepped out and started to walk further along Bond Street. Ahead of them was a small group of officers in riot gear, and in front of them were a group of masked men who had been trying to get into a Bang and Olufsen shop. One man, wearing dark clothing, with a black hood pulled over his head and a black scarf pulled across his face, was whacking the huge plate-glass window with a metal bar. The glass had started to crack and others from the group had gathered to watch. As the glass started to bow, the group began kicking at the window, trying to force their way in. The officers watched as one after another the men charged the window, but only succeeding in bouncing off again. Behind the masked group, three cars were burning in the street.

Although they had no shields, Robin, Sergeant Ashton and Michelle had their batons drawn and they stood with the riot officers. An order was shouted by one of the riot officers, and the others raised their batons in the air. Then they charged. The group of rioters stopped attacking the shop and fell back, away from the window and away from the onrushing officers. A few objects were thrown at the police as the gang retreated towards the burning cars. One of the cars had been dragged across the end of Bond Street itself, where it had been rolled over onto its side and set alight. Now it was just a huge, flaming barricade.

Some of the rioters slowed their pace and stopped in the centre of the road, their arms outstretched, encouraging the officers to continue forward. Robin, Michelle and Sergeant Ashton stopped, along with the riot officers. More masked men suddenly began to step out from other streets, bolstering the group that the officers were already facing. They weren't many – maybe just twenty or thirty – but they still outnumbered the officers by three to one. The group moved forward again, towards the police line. Robin raised his baton once more and the three officers sprinted with their colleagues towards the mob. The group fell back. Then they stopped and regrouped. They had realised that they outnumbered the riot officers and began to push forward again, this time ready to fight it out, or worse.

For the officers, it was becoming increasingly dangerous. Bottles tumbled out of the sky again, smashing down on the officers. Without helmets, shields and other protective gear, Robin, Michelle and Sergeant Ashton were in real danger of getting hurt. One thing no one needed right now were three police casualties lying on the street, so the three officers decided to get back to their car and try to get around the back of this group, to see what was happening further towards Ealing Studios and to see if there was another way to deal with them. Robin pulled the car back into The Broadway, and into High Street, moving quickly down towards The Grove pub. There, he saw that the small Ealing Green Local Supermarket was now on fire. The building was burning dangerously out of control, yet it didn't stop looters from streaming in and out, taking anything that they could carry. Above the shop, there were occupied flats, and the residents had had to grab whatever they could and run for their lives, knocking on neighbours' doors to ensure they got out.

Robin stopped the car just a few yards away and the officers watched as the looters ran in and out of the burning building, hoping to identify some of them. But they all wore masks over their faces, and in the darkness, smoke and confusion it was impossible to see who any of them were. Instead, the officers called it over the radio, letting the control room know what was happening on this part of the High Street. Whether anyone was available to come and help was another question, of course.

For Robin, being so close to a looting mob that had already set fire to three cars and a building was dangerous and risky, and after calling in what they were witnessing, there was no alternative but to get away from the rampaging gangs.

Robin drove further down, along Ealing Green and St Mary's Road – a continuation of High Street. They were lined with independent shops and Victorian homes, running down from Ealing Broadway, and past the film studios. It couldn't have looked a less likely place for a riot. As he drove slowly along the road, his eye caught sight of something. Up Grange Road, a residential side street that ran off Ealing Green, he could see a red double-decker bus. It was a night bus, an N11, and it was way off its usual route. Looking closer, he could see that it had been driven onto the pavement and had crashed into a lamppost outside a drama school. The bus's windows were all smashed and someone had tried to set the interior on fire; there were burn marks on the seats but the fire hadn't taken. It turned out that a group of around 100 youths had ambushed the bus, hijacking it and forcing the driver and passengers to flee. They then went for a drive before crashing into the lamppost on Grange Road.

Ahead of Robin, by Webster Gardens, there were two more burning cars, with flames pouring out of their windows and doors. From the burning cars onwards, all the way down the road and all across the small green outside Ealing Studios, there were hundreds of people in hoods and masks. The group on Bond Street had been just a small part of this far larger group.

Some of the group were wearing the 'Scream' mask, a long, horrifying, white face under a black hood, made famous in the movie series. The entire scene was bizarre. Robin had never seen anything like it before – the crowds, the masks, the sheer numbers. And among the hordes was a giant, stocky man, dressed all in black and who towered over everyone else. This man, who Robin judged to be nearly 7 feet tall, appeared to be directing the rioters, like a modern-day Fagin. Robin looked closer at the man, staring through the misty night gloom. The man was also wearing a 'Scream' mask, but it was his hands that really caught Robin's attention, because he was holding a huge machete. This man – this giant dressed in black, wearing a frightening mask – was waving around an enormous blade. It was a terrifying sight.

As the man waved the machete in the air, he gave orders to his hooded minions, who scampered excitedly around him like rats around their rat king. Then machete man pointed towards the famous film studios, and a bunch of his disciples ran towards them, obeying his orders. Some looked back towards their leader, appearing uncertain but he waved the machete repeatedly through the air, as if to say, 'Go! Go! Go!'

What the hell are they going to get from the film studios? Robin wondered. Computers, maybe, but he didn't know for sure. Perhaps the rioters didn't know either. They probably didn't care; the studios were just another place to attack.

More rioters ran up towards the machete man, waiting for instructions. He waved his hands around animatedly, holding court with his followers. *That's one big, horrible bastard,* Robin thought to himself. Then the man appeared to stop talking. He slowly turned his masked face and stared directly towards the three officers in their car.

Robin's eyes widened.

He had already been feathering the clutch on the car, ready to take off in an instant if needs be, and now was quite possibly that moment. But Robin held his nerve; there was still a little distance between his car and the rioters, and he wasn't certain that the man had recognised them as police.

The three officers kept watching as the group the machete man had sent off to the studios, clambered over the metal gates, and disappeared into the darkness of the film lot. Machete man then called over another bunch of masked yobs, and began talking to them. The officers were now focused entirely on him. Then Robin heard the distinctive sound of a diesel engine. He looked in his rear-view mirror and saw a police PSU carrier driving towards them. Robin immediately leapt out of the car, and waved the police unit down. They weren't a local unit but it didn't matter. Here, finally, was some back-up. With a PSU loaded with officers, they now had a chance to take on machete man and his cohorts. They would still be vastly outnumbered, but at least they now had a chance to try and do something.

The PSU carrier slowed down and came to a stop in front of Robin. The driver leaned out the window and Robin showed him his badge, letting him know that he was a local police unit.

He pointed towards the mob. 'We need to tackle this lot,' he said. 'There are more units on their way, so it won't be just us.'

The driver looked over at the masked, hooded crowd. Then he looked back at Robin. 'Sorry mate, can't stop,' he said.

And with that the PSU continued on, driving into the darkness ahead. Robin couldn't believe it.

He looked back at the crowd. Machete man had noticed them again. Only this time, he paid more attention, thanks to the police carrier. Machete man stared at Robin and then started to march towards him, still gripping the machete tightly in his hand.

Robin jumped back into the car and drove far enough away to be out of harm's way but still able to keep an eye on the group, and called in more units. Machete man strolled back to his followers and was quickly swallowed up in the throng.

As Robin waited, police lines soon started to arrive, moving in on the crowd. But Robin, Michelle and Sergeant Ashton were on the wrong side and the police lines were pushing the crowd onto them. They were beginning to get surrounded, so Robin quickly turned into Mattock Lane, in an attempt to get away. In an instant they went from chaos to stillness.

With police units now dealing with the crowds by the studios, Robin drove further away from the area and started heading towards West Ealing for no other reason than to see what, if anything, had been happening down there. He believed – or rather hoped – that things may now quieten down a bit for him and his two colleagues, but the main road leading through the area resembled yet another battlefield. And it was busy. Both sides of the street along West Ealing Broadway were filled with people in hoods and wearing masks or scarves. Shop fronts were being attacked. Blockbuster Video was having its windows kicked, and as Robin drove by, the window finally gave in, and gangs of looters piled into the unprotected store. Other shops along the street were subjected to the same fate. The mobs were kicking the hell out of everything they could see, and the three officers in their battered, unmarked police car were stuck in the middle of it all.

There was still traffic on the roads, but some of the looters had recognised Robin and his car. Perhaps they had seen him earlier, during the chase when the jewellery looters were arrested, or perhaps they just knew him from the area. Whatever the reason, many looters now switched their attention to the unmarked police car. Bricks and bottles began to be hurled towards them, slamming and smashing into the vehicle.

Robin put his foot down once more and headed down Uxbridge Road as a few more missiles were flung towards them. Getting away from the mob, they headed towards a couple of cemeteries further along Uxbridge Road. The area was quiet and empty so Robin pulled up and came to a stop, his heart pounding.

'You both okay?' he asked, turning to Sergeant Ashton and Michelle.

They both nodded their head. It had been one hell of a night. None of them had ever known anything like it. Everywhere they turned, it seemed, there was yet another group of marauding yobs, looking to smash and steal and attack. The mobs were running wild but there were still police on the streets doing whatever they could to regain control, to fight back. So the three officers, in their increasingly battered car, had no intention of calling it a night.

As they drove along the Uxbridge Road towards Acton Police Station, ahead of them they saw a Tesco petrol station. It was being overrun. There were no uniformed police to be seen and no staff at the petrol station either. All of the windows had been put in, and the doors were open. Inside, dozens of people in masks and hoods were diving behind the counter, taking whatever they could get their hands on. People were running past, their hands filled with cigarettes and booze. The ground outside was littered with dropped packets and smashed bottles.

This is bad news, Robin thought, as he watched the mob tearing the place apart.

There was little that the three officers could do against a crowd of this size but once again, they felt that they had to try and do something; they couldn't just sit back and watch. Robin threw on the blue lights and hit the sirens.

Panic followed. Hooded youths burst out of the petrol station, running in all directions. But some remained where they were; the lights and sirens no longer scared them and they began to throw stolen bottles at the car. Once again, as if they were some kind of missile magnet, bricks and glass bottles smashed to the ground around the vehicle. Other bottles, thrown with more force, reached their target, slamming into the body of the unmarked Mondeo. The mob grew braver and stepped closer towards the car, which was now in danger of being overrun. Robin quickly reversed the car away, backing off to a safe distance. There was nothing else that they could do. As much as they wanted to, they couldn't nick anyone; they didn't have the numbers. They put the call up to the control, where no doubt it was added to an increasingly long list of criminality, theft and destruction, that all needed dealing with at some point.

As the officers drove a little further along Uxbridge Road, up ahead they could see a white boy running towards them. The youth looked to be about 16 or 17, and he was sprinting for his life. Behind him, the officers noticed two grown men frantically chasing after him.

'What the hell is this?' Sergeant Ashton asked.

'Perhaps that kid just robbed them,' Robin suggested.

They drove on and as they got closer to the sprinting youth, Robin stopped the car and the three officers leapt out. They had their batons and CS spray out, ready to use in case the situation turned violent but as the youth reached them, the officers jumped on him. He squirmed violently, desperate to get out of their grip.

The two men ran up. 'Oh, thank you! Thank you!' they said.

'What's going on?' Robin asked.

The men told him they were the boy's father and uncle. 'He thinks he's going to join the riots,' the father said. 'But he's not. He's going home!'

Robin picked the youth up off the ground, and his father and uncle took hold of him, and walked him back home.

'That's one less rioter to worry about,' Michelle said.

Robin started the car and they were on the move again. As they headed back towards Ealing Broadway, they saw a PSU of three carriers pulled over at the side of the road. Officers were standing outside in the street, staring at a map. Robin could see that the carriers weren't Met but he couldn't see clearly enough through the smoky gloom to identify what force they were from.

'Need some help?' Robin asked, pulling alongside them and showing his police badge.

'Actually, we're supposed to be helping you, I think,' a sergeant said. 'We're just trying to figure out where we are supposed to be. Ealing Broadway?'

'You're almost there,' Robin told him. 'Follow me. I'll take you to where you need to be. I'm sure the local units will be glad to see you.'

Robin pulled in front of the carriers and they set off along the debris-covered road towards The Broadway. As they reached the North Star pub, on The Broadway, they could see flames to their left, by Ealing Broadway Station. The station faced Haven Green, so they already knew that rioting and looting was going on there, but these flames were close to the station itself, and that bothered Robin. He turned into the road to get a closer look.

A little further up was a crowd of rioters. They were stood behind a barricade of burning bins. The rioters had dragged the huge, commercial bins across the road, and each one had been set ablaze. Burning rubbish sent up huge wafts of black smoke and intense orange flames, high into the air. Some of the bins had been tipped over and litter lay scattered along the tarmac. The rioters, who seemed ready and waiting for any police advance, had already scavenged objects that could be used as a weapon for throwing. With a defended, burning barricade stretched across the street, this entrance to Haven Green was effectively now cut off. Robin wondered if the other access points to the green had also been barricaded.

Were the rioters creating their own area or perhaps planning some sort of final resistance?

Robin reversed away from the burning bins. As he did so, the officers from the PSU he had led in, began to march up the road, their shields held in front of their bodies, their batons gripped tightly in their hands and their helmet visors pulled down. These county officers were ready to enter the fight.

The officers raised their shields as the bricks, rocks, bottles and lumps of wood rained down on them. An order was shouted and the line of officers surged into the burning barricade, knocking fiery debris out of their way and shoving their shields into any rioter that had stayed to fight. Quickly, the rioters were forced back and now other officers were also descending on Haven Green. The rioters' retreat became a rout as they scattered across the northern end of the square. Many turned east, into Madeley Road – a normally quiet, residential street of large brick homes – and Robin would later hear that the rioters attacked every car along that street as they made off towards the North Circular.

But the rioters weren't finished and a short time later Robin's car was called up. Reports had come through that the mobs were now at a petrol station not far away. Some in the group were trying to pour petrol out of the pumps in an attempt to set the place alight.

The officers were bewildered. It was crazy. Actually trying to set a petrol station alight? What on earth were these morons thinking?

Incredibly, it was something that had happened elsewhere in London. Arsonists had attacked a Sainsbury's petrol station in Nine Elms, south London, and one of its petrol pumps had been destroyed. It was only thanks to built-in safety systems that a major catastrophe had been prevented.

Robin didn't know if the mob had any real chance of blowing up the petrol station, but if they did…

He switched on the blue lights and sped towards it. Moments later, he saw the petrol station ahead of him. There was no fire that he could see but gangs of masked youths were jumping in and out of the petrol stations shop and charging around the forecourt. In the chaos Robin forgot to turn off the car's emergency lights and they flashed like a beacon towards the mob. Within seconds, bottles and bricks filled the air around the car all over again.

'Turn the blue lights off!' Sergeant Ashton cried. 'This lot want to kill a copper! They want an eye for an eye!'

Memories of the horrific murder of PC Keith Blakelock came flooding back to Robin. He knew that Sergeant Ashton was right; there were people out there that wanted to kill a police officer at least partly in revenge for the death of Mark Duggan.

Turning the blue lights off achieved nothing; it was too late for that. The rapid thumps and smashes reverberated around inside the car like ball bearings in a tin can. More bricks rained down, one after another, after another, after another. It was madness. With every strike, orange brick dust began to build up and coat the outside of the car and its windows, which were miraculously still holding out against the bombardment, although Robin wondered how much longer they would. And then he didn't have to wonder any more. A brick, perhaps eight inches across, slammed into the front windscreen, which cracked from one end to the other. Then another window, on the side of the car, gave way, and it too cracked. There was only so much more the car was going to take. Robin looked at the petrol station one last time – there were no uniformed police here at all. It was just the brick hurling mob and them. He gave a Situation Report – a 'sitrep' – to the control, and drove away through a new barrage of bricks and bottles; staying there would have been suicidal. All they could hope was that some units, from somewhere, would be available to get to the petrol station and deal with the looters. They gave as much information as they could but no one really knew how many police units there were or if any of them were even free. After all, the entire borough seemed to be under attack. The night had become increasingly dangerous, and increasingly frightening.

Sporadic groups were now popping up all over Ealing, smashing up shops, looting, attacking police. It was impossible to contain it all. But despite the mayhem some people were still – incredibly, or perhaps stupidly – trying to go about their normal business. As Robin, Sergeant Ashton and Michelle inspected their gravely beaten-up car, a call came out to a cash delivery van being attacked in Southall Broadway. They were asked to go check it out.

'Wait. What?' Robin asked. 'A cash delivery van? As in a van delivering actual cash to cash machines?'

The idea that anyone would be crazy enough to be delivering cash on a night like this sounded insane but that was the call, so they made their way to Southall Broadway, wondering if was just a hoax; perhaps even a trap – an ambush.

The call to the cash delivery van would prove to be legitimate, but Robin, Sergeant Ashton and Michelle had no idea that what they were heading to would be the most perilous part of their night. There was a man with a gun on the streets, and Robin was driving straight towards him.

Sutton

Once again, gangs of youths had come into Sutton but, weary of the police on the High Street who had twice managed to chase them away, the youths decided to stray further north, away from the pedestrianised part of the street, and towards the large Matalan store, which was filled with clothing and household goods. A road ran along the front of the store and despite everything that was going on, there was still some traffic negotiating the streets.

The youths headed to the back of the store, to the large car park and rear entrances. The back of the store was dark and deserted. A couple of tall lampposts towered above the car park, gently dropping a weak, grey light down on the tarmac below. As a dozen youths gathered, some hadn't even bothered to cover up, perhaps not realising that they were being filmed on the CCTV cameras, or perhaps not caring.

Across from the car park, a short row of houses and a low level block of flats had a clear view of the scene. The occasional car drove by along the road that ran between the rear of the store and the houses, lighting up the road with headlights that did little to put off the would-be thieves.

Matalan's back doors were large and made of glass, and appeared easy to smash through. Someone had already attempted it with a regular wire shopping trolley, but it hadn't worked and the trolley now lay abandoned on its side across a couple of disabled parking spaces.

One youth walked away, towards some large bins and begins to roll one towards the doors. Other youths joined him, and the group rammed it into the glass doors. Two young women came over and joined in, trying to force the bin through the doors, but they still wouldn't give way. One yob then started to leap at the doors, kicking out at them in an effort to smash the glass. Others picked up rocks and bottles, lobbing them towards the doors before searching the ground for other objects to throw. Cars continue to pass along the nearby road. Then they rammed the bin into the doors some more and one youth climbed on top, trying to force the doors open with his hands. In desperation, another youth used a metal pole he had found and tried to prise the doors apart. But nothing was working.

By now the officers at Sutton are well aware of the attack on Matalan. A decision was to be made about whether or not to take the looters on. There was an argument for allowing the looting to happen – after all, property could be replaced and possibly recovered. There would be a huge policing operation once the rioting had died down and anyone involved in the looting could be scooped up afterwards. Was it worth risking officers being injured for? If more arrests were made, there would be even fewer police on the streets and things could easily get worse, without there being anyone to stop the rioters. But in the end it was decided that they had to be dealt with. One officer pointed out that there was a wood yard nearby, as well as a bunch of houses, and so they couldn't risk the large Matalan building being set alight.

Rob gathered his troops once more, and they moved up the High Street towards Matalan. They walked over broken glass, smashed bricks and rocks, and past shattered shop windows. Rob knew that this next encounter would be the decider – this would be the battle that would either leave Sutton at the mercy of the rioters and looters, or leave Sutton firmly back in control of the police. But the police were outnumbered and the rioters had just found an enormous bottle bank.

As word spread that the police were once again moving in, gangs of youths gathered at the top end of the pedestrianised section of the High Street, and a shower of bottles once more came down towards the officers. Those who had shields blocked the bottles and moved in to protect colleagues who were holding only batons.

Rob looked down the line of officers. Hours earlier most of them had no experience at all of any form of public order work. Now they stood steady, looking ahead at the crowd, determined and ready to move. And many of the officers were Specials – unpaid volunteers. Before tonight, Rob had seriously wondered what use they would be – these part-time 'hobby-bobbies'. But now he knew he had been wrong to doubt them. They had shown him that they were up for the fight. They had completely changed his perception of them. He looked at them now with a sense of pride.

'TO THE JUNCTION…ON ME…GO!'

They ran into a hail of bottles. Huge champagne bottles crashed down. Glass was smashing all around, and while ducking out of the way of the falling missiles, the officers ran forward without hesitation. The crowd fell back, away from the advancing officers. At the junction that Rob had identified, everyone came to a stop. They held their position, regrouping, taking a breath, watching what the rioters' next move would be.

A few of the youths moved forward again, tentatively, picking up discarded bottles and throwing them at the police line. More rioters began to follow the others' lead, moving up and arming themselves.

'TO THE NEXT JUNCTION… GO!'

Another charge. More bottles. Smashing glass. Shouting. Screaming. Running. The rioters fell back further.

'HALT!'

The officers breathed heavily, staring straight ahead. More bottles.

'TO THE NEXT JUNCTION… GO!'

This third charge by the officers was enough for the rioters. They had finally been pushed back to the Benhilton Estate, and it was clear that the police would just keep going, as they had done all night. Sutton wasn't going to be another Croydon – Guy

Ferguson, Rob and all of the other officers had made sure of that. The youths didn't return.

Ealing

Robin, Sergeant Ashton and Michelle stared silently out of their windows as they drove along Southall Broadway, the long, main road that formed part of the Uxbridge Road, running east to west across the borough. It was lined with the usual collection of high street shops, restaurant and banks, but the street also contained a number of jewellers – something that hadn't gone unnoticed by the rioters and looters. Messages calling for people to 'roll thru Southall Broadway' in order to 'hit up the jewellers' had reportedly been circulating amongst the rioters.

Though not as badly damaged as other parts of the borough, Southall certainly hadn't been untouched by the mobs. In an effort to protect their homes, businesses and Gurdwaras (Sikh temples), of which there were four on the Broadway, Sikh men had gathered and armed themselves with hockey sticks, bats and even Khandas – long traditional swords. They were a formidable force, and any potential rioter intent on really having a go at Southall would have had to be insane to mess with them.

Robin drove the car slowly along the street, staring out. Some of the building societies had clearly been attacked; windows were smashed and debris was strewn across the street outside. Then they saw a security van – the heavy, armoured type that was used for storing and delivering cash. It looked utterly smashed up – body dented, windows cracked. There was no one with it. No driver, no security guard. It was just left in the street, abandoned. Whether any money had been stolen from it or not, they couldn't tell. It was anarchy. There was no other word for it. Just anarchy. Robin drove on, heading deeper into Southall.

202

As he drove the car down South Road, he peered into Hamilton Road, a side street, running off to the left. South Road itself was a usually busy, shopping street, full of small Asian stores and fast food places. Hamilton Road was just a tiny residential street, lined with a handful of small Victoria terraced houses and a couple of tiny shops.

He stopped the car in the middle of South Road. His window was wound down and his arm was leaning out as he squinted to see what was happening. He had noticed a group of people – perhaps forty youths – shuffling about further down Hamilton Road. There were also a collection of cars and vans scattered the entire way down the street. As his eyes adjusted, Robin realised what was happening. The youths appeared to be kicking in people's front doors. They were forcing their way into people's homes and taking whatever they could steal from the houses and the flats. It was something that rioters had been doing in other parts of Ealing; taking advantage of the lack of police, who were already stretched across the borough, they had forced their way into houses to burgle them, even as the residents were still inside. To a police officer like Robin, it was sickening. He immediately called the control, to report what he was seeing.

The street was empty of cars. Robin's vehicle was the only one on the road, so he knew that they would have stood out to anyone who was looking.

'This is fucking dodgy,' he said.

Then one guy in the group spotted them, a man dressed all in black. Robin had noticed him directing some of the youths, who were running up and down stairways, leading to some flats. All of them wore masks and hoods. Then Robin heard the man shouting to the youths.

'They're Feds! They're Feds! They're fucking Feds!'

But the shout didn't sound like a warning; it was more of an order.

'Come!' he shouted at the mob. And then they started to run towards the car.

As the guy got closer, Robin noticed that he had a scarf over his face and he was wearing a hood, which was pulled over his head. He was leading the huge gang straight towards them. Some members in the gang were armed with sticks and lumps of wood and other items. Their intent was clear.

'Time to get out of here,' Robin said.

But before Robin had a chance to move, the man, still running towards them, reached into his jacket and pulled out a handgun.

Time slowed. Maybe even stopped, as Robin realised he was directly in the man's line of sight. Then the man stopped running. He crouched, bending at the knees, about twenty metres from the car. Then he raised the gun with both hands and aimed the barrel directly at Robin's head.

The freeze-frame moment was suddenly broken. Someone in the car was shouting at Robin.

'Let's get the fuck out of here!' he heard someone screaming.

Robin floored the accelerator and made a sharp left onto The Broadway, all the time expecting to hear the sounds of gunfire ringing out, but it never came.

About a hundred yards further up the street, Robin stopped the car and called up on his radio. 'There's been a firearm pulled on us. We need some back-up here,' he pleaded. Then, to warn others, 'All officers need to be aware that there are guns out here.'

The control was asking for more information, more detail. They wanted a description of the armed man. Robin gave what he could but all he really had was that it was a man in dark clothing with a scarf over his face and a hood pulled over his head. He knew that he had described half of Ealing.

Suddenly a white transit van tore out of Hamilton Road and careered into South Road and then onto The Broadway. The van pulled out so fast that it skidded, almost hitting the kerb, before roaring away. Then, a moment later, car after car – vehicles that Robin, Sergeant Ashton and Michelle had seen lined up down Hamilton Road – came racing out of the street, following behind the van.

'They're all heading off towards old Southall,' Robin called over the radio, giving any nearby units a chance to cut them off.

Robin put the car back in gear and crept back towards South Road, to see if any of the crowd was still in the area. Five or six more cars came reversing out of Hamilton Road, into South Road and sped off towards Norwood Green. Then the streets were empty again. Bedlam and confusion had turned to stillness, and Southall returned to silent darkness, like an unconscious victim after a violent assault.

Robin slowly turned the car around and headed back towards Ealing.

Just fifty yards further up from South Road, on The Broadway, Robin spotted two people standing on the street, wearing bright yellow jackets.

He looked closer. 'Are they what I think they are?'

Sergeant Ashton and Michelle leaned forward to look themselves.

'They are,' Robin said.

He pulled the car over, alongside two police officers who were guarding a smashed up building society. Both PCs stood with their arms folded, looking bored, in their yellow jackets and regular beat helmets. Robin couldn't believe it.

'Guys, you need to watch yourselves. There's an armed gang down there!'

Both PCs looked in the direction of South Road, where Robin was pointing. 'Fuck. No one told us,' one of them said, unfolding his arms.

After a quick discussion they decided it would be safer just to leave, and the pair trotted up The Broadway, and out of harm's way. Robin, Sergeant Ashton and Michelle also headed away and continued back towards Ealing, where once again they ran into another crowd, this time outside the town hall. The mob was scattered all across the road and pavements but by now Robin had learnt his lesson, and rather than switching on the cars blue lights and sirens, he put his foot down. The crowd, hearing the roar of an engine and not knowing who it was, immediately moved out of the way and Robin drove through without sustaining any more damage to the car – not that it would have made any difference.

Croydon

'IS IT CLEAR? IS EVERYONE OUT?' Tom shouted to another officer.

'IT'S CLEAR! IT'S CLEAR!' he called back, stepping out of the final doorway.

The officers ran back through the corridors and down the stairs. The fire had taken hold even further, and the danger had increased to a level that was far beyond acceptable for the officers to stay inside the building. The heat and the smoke had taken its toll and officers now coming down from the initial adrenaline rush, were starting to realise the gravity of what they had been doing.

And again Tom thought, *No one even knows that we're here.* They weren't on any list of officers deployed to the area. If anything happened to them, no one would know until it was too late.

The fighting continued in the surrounding streets but finally the fire crews made a start on Reeves Corner. It was clear that the buildings were beyond saving but at least the residents were safe. As far as they knew, no one had died, and as the police and fire fighters looked at the inferno, that seemed like a miracle. It was also thanks to the bravery, courage and determination of police officers, including a small bunch who weren't even officially there, but who had thrown themselves into a hugely dangerous riot and then into a lethal fire.

They exited the building and went straight back into the riot, fighting the crowds. The battle of Croydon continued but the tide was starting to turn. The retaking of Croydon had begun.

While officers had been dealing with the chaos around Reeves Corner, other streets and neighbourhoods were effectively lawless, because there weren't enough police around to cover them. Some of the rioters and looters had taken the opportunity to separate from the main group, and had been roaming the outlying areas. Just to the south of Reeves Corner, on the High Street, the local Cash Converters shop was being looted.

As officers had been fighting rioters and battling to reach the burning building at Reeves Corner, Trevor Ellis, a 26-year-old man from Brixton Hill, was sitting in a black Ford Fiesta in Scarbrook Road, a narrow street that was overlooked by blocks of flats, and which was just around the corner from the branch of Cash Converters. Ellis was sitting in the front passenger seat, waiting for his two friends. They soon returned to the car, carrying items that had been stolen from the Cash Converters. Around them were a number of other looters moving through the street, also carrying stolen gear. As the three friends sat in the car, they saw a group of looters approach two Eastern European men, who were themselves carrying a stolen TV. The group attacked the two men, beating them up before robbing them of the TV, now twice stolen.

It was a chaotic free-for-all with thieves openly stealing from other thieves. As Ellis and his two friends watched the men being robbed of the TV, another looter went to the back of their Fiesta, helping himself to a bag from the boot. Having stolen the bag, the man, along with the rest of his group, got into nearby cars and drove away.

The group had driven away in two vehicles – a black Vauxhall Astra and a silver Peugeot 308 – and Ellis's friends decided to go after them to get 'their' items back. The cars ahead sped off and the Fiesta chased after them, following at speed as they turned south, onto Duppas Hill Road. As they reached the junction with Warrington Road, Ellis's friend quickly pulled in front of the Peugeot, forcing it to stop. The occupants of the Astra, which had been ahead of the Peugeot, had seen what had happened, and it too stopped.

Then, on this narrow stretch of the road by Duppas Hill Park, two men stepped out of the Black Astra and approached the Fiesta. One of the men was holding a gun in his hand and Ellis's friend desperately tried to reverse and get away but, with the Peugeot behind him and the Astra in front, they were boxed in. The two men from the Astra reached the Fiesta and the man with the gun lifted the weapon, took aim, and pulled the trigger. A shot rang out and Trevor Ellis was hit. A second shot was fired and Ellis was struck again. The first bullet hit him in the leg; the second hit him in the head.

Just minutes later, a police carrier that had been making its way to the disturbances at Croydon, came across the Fiesta and found Ellis slumped in the front passenger seat. The Peugeot and the Astra had already made off.

Trevor Ellis, a father of four, would die in hospital the following day.

Ealing

Robin almost dared not believe what his eyes and ears were telling him, but it seemed as though Ealing had reached a lull. As he drove through quieter streets, a call came over the radio about a situation at a nearby pub, which had had a window smashed. Nothing unusual about that – not on a night like tonight – but after smashing the window, someone had thrown petrol bombs into the bar. There were people in the pub because when everything kicked off out on the streets, the landlord locked himself and his patrons inside, for their own safety. The smashed window shook everyone up, but at least they were there to put out the fires started by the petrol bombs.

Robin, Sergeant Ashton and Michelle parked up nearby and Robin gave a friendly wave through the glass, at the people inside, and the three identified themselves.

'Police,' Robin said.

The landlord welcomed the three officers into his pub. The patrons, who had been trapped there since the rioting had begun, were gathered around huge TVs that hung from the walls, watching the news channels in intense, shocked silence, while knocking back calming drinks. The landlord offered the three officers a chair each and a table to sit at. They sat down slowly, staring up at the screens. All night they had been travelling across Ealing, getting caught up in one major nightmare after another. Their focus had been on their own borough and their own survival. For the first time that night, they remembered that it wasn't just Ealing that was being fought over. Hackney – where so many Ealing officers had been fighting for their lives – was a war zone. In south London, Croydon looked as though it had burnt to the ground. Then other places appeared on the screens; places Robin didn't recognise. It wasn't just London; it was the rest of the country as well. Police officers across the whole of England, it seemed, were battling against rioters.

As the landlord brought over welcome mugs of hot coffee and fresh sandwiches, the officers continued to look up at the TVs in silence and awe. It was shocking, it was horrifying and it was live. This was London. This was England.

What the hell is going on? Robin thought to himself.

No one spoke. There was nothing they could say. Instead, like everyone else in the pub – like everyone else across the country – the officers sat and watched as burning cities across the nation were fought over by desperate bands of coppers. They watched as lines of officers, despite taking hit after hit, continued to step forward, with little to protect themselves other a riot shield. Some officers had nothing at all. Some of them were even using dustbin lids – as if it were the 1980s all over again.

As he watched, Robin suddenly felt something he hadn't been expecting: hope and faith. Watching those officers on the screens and thinking of the officers he had seen fighting on his own streets, he was touched; touched by the bravery of the officers on the ground, officers that he himself used to look at thinking that they wouldn't be able to handle themselves in a fight. Officers he thought were too fat, officers he used to look at and think, *what the fuck is the Job coming to?* But now everyone was pulling together. Those police officers, special constables and PCSOs, were all out there fighting for their cities, for their country, for each other. Despite all the horror, Robin was impressed.

His radio sparked into life. Trouble was starting to bubble again in Ealing. Robin, Sergeant Ashton and Michelle thanked the landlord. Their break was over. It was time to head back out.

Nigel had seen it all before. So had most of his crew. After all, riots weren't just a London problem. Nigel had been a police officer with Avon and Somerset Constabulary for nearly twenty years, fourteen of which he was part of the force's 'Support Group' – a specialist unit of fully trained riot and 'entry' officers. They were Avon and Somerset's equivalent of the Met's TSG. When a few extra skills were needed, it was the Support Group who were called upon.

Nigel, along with most of the officers on the unit, had already spent much of that spring battling rioters in the city's Stokes Croft neighbourhood. It was an area some claimed to be populated by 'radicals' and arty types. Some people even went as far as to call it 'The People's Republic of Stokes Croft'; it was that kind of place. Bristol had long been a home to a fairly large anarchist population, but they mostly caused trouble outside the city before coming back to Bristol.

But that was before Tesco decided to open a store in Stokes Croft. To do it they had to remove a number of squatters, and that's where the trouble started. Rioting broke out and the disorder proved challenging enough that Avon and Somerset Constabulary had to request mutual aid from Devon and Cornwall, Dorset, South Wales and Gloucestershire. The police eventually regained control of the streets, but when Tesco finally opened, trouble erupted again. Peaceful protests quickly turned into more rioting. Several officers were injured – some had lumps of concrete dropped on their heads. So in Bristol, there had been tension on the streets long before things had turned ugly in London after the shooting of Mark Duggan.

Despite their recent troubles, Avon and Somerset Constabulary still offered – and sent – two PSUs to help the Metropolitan Police with the huge amount of disorder that had spread across the capital. But they didn't forget the potential for Bristol to ignite again, and Nigel found himself back on his carrier with his mates, just in case.

They parked outside the Bristol Fashion pub, by the St James Barton Roundabout, which was known locally as the 'Bearpit'. The roundabout had a large aperture in its centre, with a view into the underpass below. Nigel looked down, searching for any drug dealers that may be lurking in the area. It was a good spot for them to hang out, and therefore a good spot for police to watch. But today it was unusually quiet.

In their boredom, some of the officers on the carrier had resorted to having fun at each other's expense. It was the usual kinds of things: insults, funny stories, banter. Despite Nigel's big build and height – he stood well over 6 feet – the others weren't afraid to target him and he too suffered just as much as everyone else. He had a reputation for not smiling and this was often the direction taken by the jokes against him. And everyone knew that if he did smile, it was usually because he was up to something himself. But during those first few, boring hours, Nigel didn't smile.

Nigel and his colleagues had already been on duty for about twelve hours, most of which they'd spent sitting at the Bearpit. But at about 11pm, when the weary officers were finding it almost impossible to resist sleep, a call came through saying there was a 'little bit' of disorder up in Stokes Croft. The officers pulled themselves up in their seats and an order came through for them to drive up and take a look. They readjusted their belts and tightened up the parts of their uniform they had loosened to make themselves more comfortable. They all knew Stokes Croft well, and they all knew the potential for trouble there. Then, before they had even left the Bearpit, another call came out: 'missiles'. Officers on the ground were now under attack. Very quickly it had gone from sleepy, boring and quiet, to missiles being thrown at officers.

The police may have spent the spring fighting in Stokes Croft, but so too had the rioters. The two sides were now old enemies, and many of the rioters considered themselves riot-hardened veterans. They had fought a number of pitched battles that spring, and now the police and the rioters were about to do it all over again. Same cops, same rioters, same streets. The only difference was the reason, or the excuse, depending on what side you were on.

The PSU made its way to the bottom end of Stokes Croft and the officers decamped from their vehicles before quickly forming up in their lines – one inspector, three sergeants and eighteen PCs. It was only a few hundred metres up Stokes Croft to where the crowd was gathered, and as the PSU moved in bottles and other missiles were aimed directly at them. The officers raised their shields to protect their heads and bodies, and then they drew their batons. This was clearly not a peaceful protest, and most of these people, once again, wanted nothing more than to fight with the police.

The ferocity of missiles increased as the officers grew closer, and the order was given to charge the rioters. The line of officers rushed forward, shields held in front of bodies and batons raised above heads. The officers had to keep lifting their shields in the air to meet the falling bottles and rocks but soon they were on the rioters who had either been too slow or too stupid to run, or else had remained where they were, eager – in some weird and foolish way – to stand and battle with the riot cops.

Batons rather than missiles rained down now, as the officers met the violent mob head-on. In the melee Nigel could see rioter after rioter running at him, throwing punches, kicking out, shouting, spitting. He met each one with a downward strike of his baton or a forward blow with his shield. The rioters started to retreat and the officers charged again, wasting no time in taking the ground that the rioters had surrendered. Soon after, the petrol bombs began, shattering and exploding all around the advancing police lines. Wafts of flames and heat penetrated the officers' protective clothing, rising up under the visors on their helmets, the fumes stinging their eyes and burning their nostrils.

At every opportunity the rioters seemed to be building barricades or setting wheelie bins on fire and pushing them towards the police lines. With so many bins and petrol bombs, it was beginning to look as though the whole of Stokes Croft was ablaze. Everything was either deep black or glowing, blinding orange as the smoke and night mixed together with the angry flames.

Nigel continued to push forward against the rioters, forcing them further and further up Stokes Croft and away from the city centre. But there were many side streets running off to the east and west, and Nigel could see groups of rioters slipping into these roads. He knew there was a danger that the rioters would be able to break out into other parts of the city or even double back and get behind the officers themselves. It wouldn't take much for the officers to suddenly find themselves surrounded. For now though, there was little that they could do about it, and they continued to battle with the rioters on Stokes Croft itself.

The officers' efforts were starting to have some success and the large mob had broken up and scattered into smaller groups. Nigel and the rest of his unit now found themselves jogging short distances, pushing the smaller clusters of youths back and then jogging forward a bit more.

As the officers paused at one of the junctions, a man approached Nigel. He was covered in blood but still, he was walking and he seemed okay.

'Why did you hit me?' he demanded to know.

'What?'

'You hit me!'

Nigel looked at him more closely. Clearly the man believed that he had been struck with a police baton – it would certainly account for the blood that covered his head and face – and it was certainly possible. Of course, it was just as likely that the man had been hit with one of the missiles that had been thrown recklessly and indiscriminately by one of his fellow rioters.

Nigel looked at him again. Nope, he didn't recognise him, and certainly hadn't hit him. He had hit quite a few people as they had battled their way up Stokes Croft, but not this man.

'We've got our rights!' a friend of the man shouted at Nigel, pointing an accusing finger in his face.

Nigel nodded his head and the pair walked away, re-joining another group who laid on some sympathy for the injured man. But it was a riot, what did these people expect was going to happen? People got injured in riots, sometimes badly. If it was a police officer, people seemed fine with that, but they always seemed so surprised – outraged, even – when it was one of their own, as if it was just a game, as if they had some right to attack police officers and destroy property without consequences. But they were wrong.

The officers reached a wide T-junction with City Road and came to another brief standstill, holding their line. Ahead of them was a long strip of fire, rising high into the air. Several wheelie bins had been pushed together and used to create a barrier across the street; all had been set alight, and a burning wall of billowing, black, toxic smoke, pumped out of the plastic bins. The flames created an eerie glow and threw long shadows against the City Road Baptist Church, a tall Victorian building, listed like many along Stokes Croft.

Some of the Level 2 officers moved forward to shove the burning bins out of the way and clear the barriers that had been thrown together by the rioters. Nigel looked around but couldn't see any fire fighters or fire engines. It was just the police.

The officers started to move forward again, passing the smouldering, melting bins before quickly coming to another halt and securing the ground they had taken. They were now just north of City Road and Nigel suddenly remembered something. He spun around. There, on the side of one of the old brick buildings along Stokes Croft, was one of the most famous murals created by the artist Banksy. The large black and white image depicted a huge teddy bear about to throw a petrol bomb at three police officers holding riot shields. At the top of the mural were the words that had become the name of the piece: 'The Mild Mild West'.

Then Nigel heard an urgent shout. He twisted back around, and watched as a real petrol bomb flew through the air, smashing a few feet in front of him, and exploding into a ball of fire, giving off a poisonous waft of fumes. He smiled at the moment, pulled down his visor and marched forward towards the attackers, who quickly withdrew upon seeing the line of officers advancing on them.

The officers eventually reached a railway viaduct – 'the Arches' – just south of Gloucester Road. They had now managed to drive the main group of rioters a mile out of the city centre.

Nigel had been well aware of the smaller groups skulking off down various side streets and the danger they could pose, and there was now another potential complication; the PSU had been pushing the rioters further up Stokes Croft, which meant that fewer officers were left to protect the city centre itself. Nigel guessed that the rioters were also aware of this, perhaps even planning it that way.

The ground the officers had taken hadn't been cordoned off, and as a result it wasn't long before the call came out that it had started all over again at the bottom end of Stokes Croft. Nigel and the rest of his unit turned around and began to make their way back, cutting down some side streets every so often, to chase off random groups of troublemakers.

As they jogged through Ashley Road, about halfway between the Arches and the City Centre, Nigel saw two figures dart out from one of the side streets. As he had feared, some of the rioters had doubled back. He turned to face them, expecting to see more. He raised his shield, ready to defend himself against rocks and petrol bombs but the pair didn't grow in number and they didn't throw anything either. Nigel wiped the condensation from the underside of his visor and squinted to look at the two figures as they walked calmly towards him. They were men in their 20s, wearing dark clothing, and as they got closer, Nigel recognised both of them. They were two of the local drug dealers.

They walked straight up to Nigel, nodding their head in greeting.

'Just to let you know,' one of them said, 'we've seen six people carrying petrol bombs, going down these streets. They're planning to attack you from behind.'

Nigel thanked them for the warning and the dealers walked away with another nod of the head. Nigel guessed that the riots were interfering with their trade – even drug dealers needed to make money.

'You know it's bad when the drug dealers are helping you out,' he said to the officer standing next to him.

They passed the information about the petrol bombers to other units in the area, who would search for them as Nigel and his own unit continued back to the centre of town, checking some of the side streets as they went. The ground was now thickly shrouded in shards of broken glass and blackened debris. Burnt out bins lay scattered and smouldering in gutters. It almost felt as though the regular residents had evacuated the area – curtains were closed, and lights were turned off. The only sound on the street was the crackling of small fires and the sound of the officers' boots crunching over the broken glass. But it wasn't long until the missiles and abuse started again.

As the officers turned into Wilder Street, ahead of them they saw the usual collection of wheelie bins, large, commercial bins, heaps of rubbish, scaffold poles, lumps of wood, masonry, and just about everything else that the rioters could get their hands on, collected into deliberate piles. As the officers had been fighting running battles up Stokes Croft, other rioters had been keeping themselves busy, building more barricades across Wilder Street. And as before, for extra menace, some bins been had been set alight.

The officers' adrenaline was already pumping and they acted swiftly, charging at the barricades and at the rioters. Their PSU carriers followed them up the street, and when faced with a low barricade, the protected vans simple drove straight through them, smashing everything out of the way in a shower of shattering plastic and burning embers.

The officers made controlled, forward surges and as they

stormed the barricades, they caught some of the rioters off guard, perhaps not expecting such a swift counter attack from the police. Many were still holding pieces of the barricade in their hands and immediately used them to attack the officers. Nigel brought his baton down and other officers did the same as they swarmed through the rioters' fortifications, defending themselves against the panicked attacks of the mob, who were throwing everything they could at them – bottles, rocks, pieces of wood, paving slabs, punches, kicks, some choice words. But the officers' surge, along with the vans smashing through the bins, made it clear who was going to take Wilder Street, and the rioters retreated with desperately aimed throws of anything they had left in their hands. As the street cleared, the officers formed a line across it, creating a solid wall of shields as the bins smouldered behind them, and the last remnants of the barricades were shoved out of the road.

Taking advantage of the sudden lull, Nigel hoped to check the news on his phone, to see if he could get any more information about what was going on elsewhere across the country. But he had barely pulled the phone from his pocket when his police radio shattered the moment of peace. Officers were again calling for assistance. There was nothing strange about that – not tonight anyway – but deciding whom to help would come down to who was screaming the loudest, and officers at Nine Tree Hill were doing just that. They were a Level 2 District PSU – local officers – and there was an urgency in their voices that made it sound like more than just inexperienced panicking.

Nigel's inspector didn't wait for any direction from their Bronze Commander – they hadn't seen him all day anyway – and decided to move his PSU up to assist the officers at Nine Tree Hill. It was a good decision but also a ballsy one. Taking it upon yourself to deploy was not the done thing; you waited for orders to move, otherwise you stayed where you were, even if that meant standing still while listening to other officers scream for help down the radio. But these riots had morphed into something bordering anarchy, and the cops needed to take the initiative when they could, or when they had to. As far as Nigel's inspector was concerned, now was that time. They had had no direction from their Bronze Commander for hours. Goodness only knew where he was. Fighting another battle somewhere? Injured? No one knew.

They boarded their carriers, and the drivers turned on the sirens and blue lights, and rushed towards Nine Tree Hill – it was a narrow street leading off Stokes Croft, close to where he had been warned about the petrol bombers by the local drug dealers. It seemed that their warning had been correct and Level 2 officers were taking serious fire in the side streets, and in particular on Nine Tree Hill itself.

The street sloped upwards from Stokes Croft. It was lined with a handful of period houses but it also had a number of old stone walls and Nigel knew those walls would be a great source of missiles for the rioters – just as they had been in the spring. And just off Nine Tree Hill, along Dove Street, was a large housing estate. The area, like much around Stokes Croft, was diverse and young, as well as being densely populated.

At the top of Nine Tree Hill, where Nigel and his unit were heading, was Fremantle Square. It had a pretty little raised garden area in the centre that was surrounded by large, pastel coloured, three-storey Victorian terraced houses. Though close to the areas often considered more hostile, Fremantle Square was a usually peaceful haven. But the raised garden in the centre of the square was held up by another old, stone wall, and as with the walls on Nine Tree Hill, it had also been partially dismantled and plundered for weapons and missiles. No sooner had the PSU arrived than they came under fire from those very rocks. They quickly withdrew, knowing that without a plan it would be pointless and dangerous to just stand there taking the flak.

The inspector gathered the officers together. 'Okay, the way we are going to do this is quite simple,' he told them. 'I'm going to shout, "Go!", and then we're going to run down the hill and just move straight through them.'

The officers looked at each another before one of them turned to the inspector, speaking for them all. 'Yeah. That's fine.' Everyone was nodding. It was a simple plan but that was what usually worked best, and everyone was up for taking the offensive.

Nigel stood next to his mate, Martin. They checked each other's equipment and overalls. They had been fighting now for a few hours and so they took a moment to ensure that straps and buttons were retightened, and that they weren't exposed anywhere – making sure they were protected against the petrol bombs. Other officers were doing the same. It was part of their drills, part of the routine.

'Okay. Ready?' the inspector asked his officers.

They automatically tugged at the tops of their gloves and tightened their grips on their shields and their batons as steam rose from the shoulders of their sweat-soaked overalls. They were ready.

Enfield

With the police so stretched across London, some criminal gangs had felt they were now free to do as they pleased. Just before midnight, as officers continued to fight with looters and rioters across the city, one group – said to be members of the local 'Get Money Gang', or 'GMG' – moved towards the Sony distribution warehouse, on an industrial estate in Enfield, just below the M25. Forcing their way onto the grounds of the warehouse, the gang of around 25 men and boys (some aged a young as 12), smashed their way through a set of glass doors and swarmed into the 260,000 square foot building. As they ran through the storage areas, they grabbed whatever they could carry. Some took so much that they dropped bits of their loot as they charged back out again. As the gang left, petrol bombs were thrown into the warehouse. In a building full of boxes and plastic, the fire spread rapidly. All this happened in just three minutes: the gang broke into the building, looted it, and then set the place on fire.

In what would later be described as 'the largest arson in Europe', the warehouse was totally destroyed by the fire. Enormous towers of black smoke could be seen for miles around. The fire would burn for 10 days, causing £75 million worth of damage and destroying three million CDs.

0045 hrs

Lewisham

After saying their goodbyes to the driver at the bus station, Darren's unit returned to Lewisham police station. By now other officers, along with their vehicles and carriers, had returned from various parts of London. Taking a set of carriers before anyone else managed to nab them, Darren's unit were now, after all these hours, a real, operational PSU.

As they boarded the carriers and set out for patrols around Lewisham, word reached them that Deptford was now seeing rioting. But Lewisham police, having finally got a proper PSU, and having been on the receiving end of the rioters' aggression, were loath to lose the officers again so quickly. As a compromise, the PSU decided to split up. Darren's own carrier – a small party of one sergeant and six PCs – headed out towards Deptford, alone, leaving the other two carriers to patrol Lewisham.

Located south of the river and a mile west of Greenwich, Deptford was an area that was steeped in naval history and historic docks but it was also an area with poverty and social issues. Officers hadn't yet been called there, but they already knew it had potential for trouble. Of all the neighbourhoods in Lewisham, Deptford, with its concentration of gangs, was by far the most notorious, and it could be a challenging place in an already challenging borough. By now it was coming up to 1am and the officers fully expected Deptford to give them their greatest – and most violent – challenge of the night.

Deptford High Street was a long, narrow road, lined with two and three-storey buildings of locally owned shops that catered perfectly well to the resident population but which would hold little interest to any outside visitors. Pawnbrokers, betting shops, halal butchers, and workmen's cafes, as well as a vibrant street market, reflected its diverse population. As they drove into the area, to the officers' surprise, there were only about forty youths gathered. They had been expecting far more. And other than a few minor fires burning in the gutters, there was little else going on. It felt to Darren as if the Deptford gangs had decided to join the party far too late.

The officers lined up at one end of Deptford High Street. The small mob jostled uneasily further down the road. The sergeant ordered the officers forward and they began a steady jog, their batons held up like ceremonial swords and their shields pulled against the front of their bodies. A broken brick landed on the ground inches from Darren's feet as he continued forward. He instinctively looked up, knowing what was coming. More bricks were flying through the air towards them. He heard glass smashing on the ground and noticed some bottles amongst the bricks, glistening momentarily in the light reflected from the lampposts. More and more bottles and bricks began to crash to the ground as the officers drew closer to the rioters' line. Then a flaming bottle swung through the dark sky towards them, smashing down and exploding into a whooshing ball of fire. A second petrol bomb followed the first. But Darren continued to run forward. He pushed his gloved fingers under his visor and wiped away the beads of condensation that had gathered and were fogging up his view.

Officers used their shields to guard against any objects that were targeted at them, and everyone quickened their pace as they gained ground on the mob, running through the barrage of missiles. The bottle and brick throwers moved backwards, lobbing whatever was left in their hands towards the advancing police. The officers continued with their forward momentum; they had the rioters on the run, and they knew it. For the rioters it was clear that these officers weren't going to stop or back down, even with petrol bombs landing at their feet. Despite what Darren and the others had been expecting from Deptford, it seemed as though the gangs just weren't up for it the way they had expecting them to be. As the officers continued to push forward, the rioting group suddenly ran off, towards a nearby estate. Just like that, they were gone. The officers stopped. They stood in the cold, misty glow of the streetlights; smashed glass, rocks and shattered bricks carpeted the ground around them.

'Was that it?' the officer standing next to Darren said, sounding almost disappointed.

0100 hrs
Ealing
Little pleasures, Darin thought as he and his group of TfL officers chomped down on fresh, sticky donuts. Having originally been sent to Enfield to clear the area around the Sony warehouse, his unit had been released in the early hours and Darin, desperate for something to drink, found an open Krispy Kreme shop. He popped in hoping to get some hot drinks for him and his unit.

'Any chance of some teas?' he asked.

'Of course, no problem,' the manager told him and she walked away to make the drinks.

'Stand by,' he called cheerily to his officers, over the radio. 'We're all about to get a nice cup of tea.'

When the manager returned with the drinks, she was also carrying two full trays of donuts and handed them over with thanks for everything that the police had been doing to keep London safe.

Darin was humbled. He was also a little embarrassed, feeling that the public had been let down by the police, but he appreciated the kindness. It said a lot about the true feelings of Londoners when the public were looking out for the police. As long as they were on each other's side, Darin felt sure that there was no way that the rioters would win.

Before being sent to Sony, Darin and his officers had been moved from street junction to street junction around Hackney before they eventually ended up guarding a bus station. They had stood outside it in a protective line, to ensure that no one set the place on fire or stole any more double deckers. They had been standing around various places for hours and all of the officers were starting to feel it; they were drained, so the teas and donuts were a welcome energising treat.

They had been on duty for close to twenty hours and much of that time had been taken up fighting on, and protecting, the streets of north London. Now dozens of areas all around the capital were experiencing trouble and violence. All over London, lines of officers had been desperately fighting against superior numbers of rioters and looters. The police had been stretched and the mobs knew it, taking full advantage of the chaos that had spread.

In Barking, Malaysian accountancy student Asyraf Haziq, who had been in the UK for just a month, was riding his bicycle when he was attacked, punched and his bike stolen from him. The assault left him with broken teeth, and his jaw broken in two places. As he lay on the ground bleeding, surrounded by youths, a man came over to help him to his feet. As he did so, he and another man then rifled through Haziq's backpack, robbing him a second time.

In Camden, a handful of local officers, many in regular beat uniform, including detectives from Camden CID, created a thin line under the famous Camden Lock bridge, carrying out baton charges up Camden High Street against groups of rioters.

After a local Blockbuster Video store had been attacked in Westow Street, in Crystal Palace, a handful of local residents stepped out in an attempt to protect the shops from looters. But as the evening went on, they were forced to disband and allow the looters to do their business. It wasn't worth risking their lives.

In Chingford Mount, in northeast London, three officers, while attempting to arrest looters who had attacked a local clothes shop, were rushed to hospital after being run down by a looter's car.

And it wasn't just Barking, Camden, Crystal Palace and Chingford Mount; all across the city – and now the entire country – police and residents had been desperately fighting back against violent mobs.

The level of violence and destruction across the London boroughs in particular was unprecedented. But finally, in the early hours, all across the city, the police were starting to regain some control of the streets. Groups of officers were standing in cordons, creating blue, human barriers across roads and junctions, ensuring that the streets and neighbourhoods were kept clear.

As some of the areas became quieter, units were made available again – freed from various locations to assist in neighbourhoods that were still struggling. Having been released from Hackney, Darin's unit was now requested to travel over to west London and redeploy to Ealing. Exhausted, they made their way.

While Darin and his unit had been on the streets of Hackney, along with Ealing officers who had been fighting for their lives, Ealing Borough itself had been going up. The town centre was carpeted with glass, rocks, and burning piles of litter. Shops were destroyed and looted. A man lay in hospital fighting for his life.

Darin's trio of carriers pulled into Ealing Broadway. The officers stared out of the windows at the destruction. For the past few hours their lives had been mostly about Hackney. They had had no idea about what had been occurring a few miles away in west London. None whatsoever.

Everything looked as though it had been attacked, with nothing being left untouched by the rioting. Every shop Darin looked at had its windows smashed. Outside the Ealing Broadway shopping centre, which was also showing scars of the rioting, a police IRV, with its headlights still on and the blue emergency lights on the roof still flashing, had been abandoned. All of the windows on the IRV were smashed, and the shattered glass lay on the ground, encircling the wrecked car. Its windscreen had been completely caved in, with a large hole at the centre of a spider's web of cracks. The vehicle's bodywork had taken a pummelling and was covered in large, deep dents. Everywhere they drove, the air was heavy with the smell of burning and smoke.

This is fucking dreadful, Darin thought to himself.

The order came through for the carriers to patrol The Broadway and Uxbridge Road, from Ealing in the east to Southall in the west. They were told to travel up and down the long road, a visible presence that would act as a deterrent to anyone who still intended to cause trouble.

The further west down The Broadway they travelled, the less salubrious Darin felt the area looked. Despite the destruction, Ealing Broadway was clearly the better off part of the borough. As they hit Southall, Darin could see that the area became more Asian – with plenty of the Asian shops and restaurants that the neighbourhood was famous for. There also plenty of jewellers' shops, and many of them had had the shutters either damaged by attempts to remove them, or completely pulled off.

It was easy to see what the main target was here; the rioters had been presented with an easy opportunity to steal and rob.

'What the fuck?' one of the officers in the rear of the carrier said.

'What?' Darin asked.

'Look!'

Darin looked over at a jeweller's that the officer was point at. Some young men were running out through a broken door. They were carrying trays of watches and rings.

'GET THEM!' Darin shouted at his officers, excitedly, his adrenaline pumping once again.

The carriers drove towards the running men, who were ducking and weaving along the murky street. Darin opened his door a crack, in preparation to jump out, and the officers in the rear did the same with their sliding door. Then the carriers came to a stop and the officers charged out, onto the street, giving chase. The officers were physically shattered from their long shift, and they knew they had little chance of catching the thieves.

'STICK 'EM!' Darin shouted.

Officers reached out with their batons at the running men. The length of their batons was just enough to give them the reach they needed to nudge the runners and cause them to drop or throw the trays of jewels on the ground, before picking up their speed and sprinting away from the officers in panic. Most of the officers stopped running and picked up the stolen loot instead, so they could return it to the shopkeepers. But Darin kept up the chase.

Two of the thieves turned and ran down a side street. Darin was determined to keep up and turned into the street after them. His adrenaline was pumping. He was furious at the blatant thievery these men had committed against decent, hard working people.

'I'M GONNA FUCKING HAVE YOU!' Darin snarled at the pair.

The roar was enough for the men to start throwing more of their stolen loot away, chucking trays of rings onto the ground. Darin continued, chasing after the men. As they sprinted down the road, a car pulled up and the men leapt through the open, passenger doors. The men slammed the doors shut and the car then sped towards Darin, aiming straight for him. He watched, as it got closer, before diving out of the way at the last moment. The car roared away.

Darin gave a growl of frustration, and then reality kicked in. *What the fuck am I doing out here on my own?* Darin thought. He walked back, picking up the dropped trays of rings on his way.

Back on The Broadway, he saw an Asian couple – shop owners – standing outside another looted jeweller, crying. It was heart breaking, and Darin felt embarrassed once again. He was ashamed that the police hadn't been able to do more.

As they continued their patrol up and down The Broadway, a call came out to group of a couple of hundred people gathering towards Greenford and Southall. They drove in the direction given and soon spotted them. Other parts of the street were also starting to fill with people – hundreds of them now. They drove closer, not sure of what was going on or what to expect. As they pulled alongside one large group of men, Darin saw that they were armed, with hockey sticks, cricket bats and swords. The men were all Sikh.

'Go and see what's going on, will you, Darin,' the inspector said.

Darin ordered two other officers from the carrier to join him, just in case. They tried to look relaxed as they approached.

'Everything all right, guys?' Darin asked one of the men, casually.

The man stepped forward. Darin held his ground.

'If those rioters come back down here, damaging our businesses and our lives, we'll deal with them ourselves,' he said. 'So we're all right, thank you sergeant.'

'I see.'

'It's not your fault, sergeant,' another man said. 'We know how busy the police have been but no one is protecting us, so we have to protect ourselves.'

Darin told the other two police officers to get back on the carrier.

As he took his own seat again, next to the driver, the inspector asked, 'Is everything okay?'

'Yep,' Darin told him. 'They're all reasonable people. Let's go.'

Bristol

As Nigel and the rest of his PSU stood ready to move onto Nine Tree Hill, word filtered through that a Gloucestershire officer, who was in Bristol on mutual aid, had had a breeze block dropped on his head from the rooftop of a Georgian house on Sydenham Road – the next street to where Nigel was. The injuries were said to be life changing, and Nigel immediately looked up at the buildings. No one was clearing these upper levels; everyone was too busy concentrating on what was happening on the ground.

Nigel stared back down at the street, looking at the rioting crowd and the fires. The sky filled with bottles, bricks and rocks, and then he heard the order: 'GO!'

Then he was running down Nine Tree Hill. The sound of smashing and cracking exploded all around him. The noises of the rioting were mixed in with the muted sound of his own heavy breathing. Out of the corner of his eyes he could see the Level 2s as he ran past them. They were standing, holding the junctions whilst being continuously pelted with a barrage of missiles. Ahead of him, at the bottom of the hill, he could see the carriage works building – a three-storey listed building with arched windows. It had once been described as a 'masterpiece' by an architectural historian but was now boarded up and covered in graffiti. It made for an interesting backdrop.

Nigel's concentration returned to the street he was running down and the people he was running towards. Then he and his unit were upon the rioters. Not all of them had run off on seeing the charging police line; some had stayed to fight or else were too slow getting away. Through his visor, which had become misty with condensation, Nigel could see the braver elements of the mob standing just feet in front of him. He raised his baton and as the police and the rioters came together, Nigel pushed forward with his shield and swung down with his baton.

WHACK! Direct hit. WHACK! And another.

The officers kept the momentum going, moving forward despite the fight back from the mob. Nigel brought down his baton again, feeling the unmistakable thump as it caught another target.

'Will you stop fucking hitting me!' Martin, another officer, said.

'What?'

'You keep hitting me with your fucking baton!'

Nigel lifted his visor and wiped the moisture away. He was left-handed and Martin – his mate – was standing to his left. Every time Nigel had brought his baton down to strike a rioter, he had actually been hitting the top of Martin's helmet. They swapped places and continued down the hill. Then Nigel saw a huge breeze block flying towards him.

This is going to be close, he thought to himself.

Then he felt an impact. The block slammed into his left shin, and pain shot up his leg. He winced in agony, but he kept running, determined that Martin wasn't going to reach the yob who had thrown it before he did.

The intensity of the missiles had increased. The walls that had been dismantled had provided excellent weaponry for the rioters, but so too had the bars and pubs in the area; the backstreets and alleys were lined with huge bins full of empty glass bottles.

Nigel and the rest of his unit meet the rioters head-on once again, striking them and pushing them back as they fought through the bombardment that rained down on them. And they kept pushing them back, all the way to Stokes Croft.

Finally Nine Tree Hill was clear and the officers trudged back up, towards Fremantle Square, returning to their carriers and leaving Nine Tree Hill with the Level 2s once again.

Taking his usual seat in the carrier, Nigel remembered the pain in his shin and lifted up the leg of his overalls. The plastic and foam leg guard that he wore under his flame proof suit had been punctured by the breeze block that had hit him. The block had left a hole where it had managed to smash through, and Nigel noticed some blood seeping out. He undid the straps around the leg guard and removed it but the cut wasn't too bad. Martin handed him the first aid kit and they put a dressing over the wound.

'You okay to carry on?' Martin asked.

'Yeah, it's fine,' Nigel told him.

As they finished patching Nigel up, his phone started to vibrate in his pocket. It was his wife. She had been watching the rioting on the 24-hour news channels and had been texting him messages to check that he was okay. 'Text me when you can', 'Let me know you are all right'.

Nigel sent one back letting her know he was fine and he would call her when he had a chance. She was a former police officer herself, so she knew how these things went. She also knew what Nigel was like, hence the texts. She knew he wouldn't be hanging back from the trouble. His wife, like the partners of other officers, would be following the news closely. She would also see the reports that more trouble had broken out in the St Paul's area of the city. It was a neighbourhood cursed by drugs and gangs, and that was where Nigel was going next.

Many Somali families had settled in St Paul's and some of the kids from these communities had been recruited by local gangs to run their drugs. As they had grown up, some of those young drug runners had gone on to set up their own drug dealing enterprises, recruiting more kids from the neighbourhood. This was on the north side of the M32 – the short motorway that linked Bristol to the M4. On the south side of the M32, in Easton, were other gangs, many of whom were Jamaicans. The groups didn't always get on, and were themselves separated into smaller gangs such as the 'Bloods', the 'High Street Crew' and 'BS5' (named after their postcode). The M32 had separated once united neighbourhoods, and had provided gangs with their own areas to control. It also gave them a reason to fight and sometimes to kill. All in all, this could be a dangerous and occasionally deadly part of town.

Nigel's PSU turned into St Nicholas Road. It was a street of terraced houses and the location of the St Paul's Gardens housing estate. Almost immediately they came under attack and a brick struck the carrier that Nigel was riding in. Then another brick hit them. Then breeze blocks and bins. Anything that could be picked up and thrown was targeted at the PSU. The carriers continued to move through the street, towards Newfoundland

Road, which Nigel could see just ahead of them. There was more banging and thumping as kids from the surrounding streets and estates joined in the attack on the carriers that had driven onto their turf.

There was an enormous crash next to Nigel and he instinctively moved to the side, away from the window he was sitting next to. The window had taken a direct hit from a breeze block and it had completely gone in. Cool air poured into the carrier. With the window now missing, the officers could hear clearer, louder voices coming from the rioters. And seeing the damage they had caused, they were now hooting with delight.

'KILL THE PIGS!' they screamed in their delirium. 'KILL THE PIGS!'

Nigel looked out at the rioters. They weren't just gang members from the estate; they were also students who had come down from Stokes Croft to join in.

He shoved his shield against the open window, holding it in place with his shoulder. The windows were made of Perspex, so at least it hadn't smashed but they were little defence against breeze blocks. Other officers had also placed their shields up against the windows, in case the same happened to them.

The carrier drivers sped up, to get through the street and away from the bombardment. As they reached Newfoundland Road, there was a brief respite. Then the carriers all turned back around, to face the rioters on St Nicholas Road. The mob was gathered across the street, still throwing whatever they could, picking up previously thrown objects to throw again. They were shouting, jumping and running around in excitement. There was a moment of stillness and quiet in the carriers, then the drivers put their feet down and drove directly towards the rioters. The carriers bumped and shook as they drove over rocks and bricks, the sound of glass smashing and crunching under the tyres. Nigel kept his shield pressed firmly up against the open window. The roar of the engines, the speed of the carriers and the resolve of the officers was enough to convince the rioters that the game was up, for now. They ran off, ducking back into the side streets and St Paul's Gardens Estate, disappearing into the darkness.

It was now well into the early hours of Tuesday morning, and as the rioting and skirmishes went on, a small group of looters had set upon the jeweller, Thomas Sabo, in Cabot Circus, smashing its windows with hammers before grabbing armfuls of stock. Police dog handlers were chasing the looters up Bond Street towards Newfoundland but the thieves dashed down a side street, and Nigel and his PSU managed to cut them off, capturing them in nearby Pritchard Street. They were all students from the city's university, and two of them were carrying rucksacks that contained bottles and bricks.

The small group immediately became indignant, questioning why the officers were 'picking on' them. One complained that a police dog had bitten him.

Nigel had had enough. He had been battling all night. He had been running around in Level 1 PSU kit, fighting, dodging missiles, and getting hurt in the worst rioting he had ever seen. He was fucked off with it all. The group started to answer back to the officers, becoming increasingly insolent, to the point where they were starting to behave as though they had the upper hand over the officers. They began to move forward as they argued, as if looking for a way out. They needed controlling quickly; they needed to know who was in charge. And so the officers shoved them up against some nearby railings, immediately taking back control. Nigel wasn't in the mood to stand there and take this anymore. The yobs had had their fun, and now it was time to pay the price. The group were arrested and taken to Trinity Road police station.

After they processed the prisoners, they were placed on standby. The streets were finally started to quieten down. The day crews were coming on duty, which meant that Nigel and the rest of his exhausted PSU would soon be released. But there would be little time for recovery because they would be back on duty at noon.

0400 hrs
Peckham

Alan and his fellow officers had been listening closely to their radios as they sat in their carrier outside Peckham police station. There was trouble all over London but it was clear that Croydon had seen an unprecedented outbreak of violence. Alan's unit were desperate to get stuck in rather than sitting around at Peckham nick. They pressed their supervisors, encouraging them to put their PSU up as available and willing to attend.

Finally they were given the green light, but by then it was more of an afterthought. Fires were burning and building fronts tumbled into the street but the police were finally retaking Croydon. Alan's unit were going to go there anyway.

'Okay, make your way to Croydon,' their inspector told them. 'But we've been told that it's not on an I-grade.'

'Not on an I-grade?' someone said. 'It bloody sounded like it should be an I-grade!'

'Apparently things have started to calm down there now. They just want us there as a precaution.'

They set off for Croydon but as Alan's PSU drove along Whitehorse Road, they saw people running around in all directions. The PSU slowed down to see what was going on. The officers looked over at a large warehouse, a Staples stationery store.

The front doors had been smashed in and swarms of people were running into the building and coming back out with armfuls of goods, including TVs. The looters didn't seem in the least bit bothered by the presence of the police, as though they were expecting the police not to do anything about it, and they continued to make off with various pieces of stolen stuff.

'STOP! STOP!' the sergeant told the driver. 'Stop here.'

The PSU came to a halt and the sliding doors were flung open. The officers charged out and sprinted towards different groups of looters, some of who were still entering the building as others were running back out. Caught up in the delirium of easy theft, many didn't even seem to notice that the police had stopped and we coming for them. The officers grabbed anyone they could. Some of the looters dropped what they had and made a run for it. Others, either too slow, unaware of the police or up for a ruck, fought back. The entire scene turned into a huge brawl.

Alan reached out, grasping a man's arm and taking hold of him. The speed that the man was running at almost dragged Alan to the floor but he managed to keep his grip. The man tried to pull away but by now Alan had hold of him with both hands. Then two other men ran towards Alan and tried to pull him off the man. Other officers rushed forward, pushing the men away and they quickly ran off. Alan and the man fell to the floor, with Alan on the man's back. He took a better grip of the man's right arm, twisting it back and bending it at the elbow. The man was still struggling and looking up hopefully, at other looters, who were either bursting away from the store or fighting with officers. Piles of goods from the store now lay scattered across the tarmac as more looters dropped whatever they had taken in a bid to escape the police. Alan pulled his handcuffs out from the leather holder and snapped one ring onto the man's right wrist.

'Give me your other arm,' Alan ordered the man.

'I wasn't doing anything!' the man said.

'What the hell are you talking about? You were looting the store!'

'I was just seeing what was going on.'

'You were holding a thirty-three inch plasma TV in your hands. Now give me your arm.'

The man did as he was told and Alan placed the man's left wrist into the second ring of the handcuffs. He pulled the man to his feet and saw that other officers had been having similar conversations with other looters, who were all being led to the carriers in cuffs. More officers had entered the shop itself, where some looters were found hiding.

Seeing the throngs of prisoners coming his way, the carrier driver was already calling up on the radio, finding out where they could take their prisoners. Word came back that all custody suites were full.

'What? All of them? The whole of the bloody Met?' Alan asked.

'Every single one,' the driver told him. 'I'm just waiting to find out where we can take them.'

With over 70 custody suites containing over a thousand cells, the Met's holding areas were substantial and the fact that they were all full was another indication of the level of trouble the city and its police had faced.

A few minutes later a call came through on the radio. The prisoners from Staples were to be taken to Guildford, in Surrey.

'Are you telling me that the closest nick with space for prisoners is in Surrey?' the sergeant asked.

'That's the long and short of it, Skip,' the driver answered.

'For fuck's sake,' the sergeant groaned. 'Okay guys, load up your prisoners. We're off to the countryside.'

After dealing with their prisoners in Guildford, Alan and his unit wouldn't get back to their own base until noon the following day, some 24 hours after originally coming on duty. He and his colleagues would be back in that evening.

0500 hrs
Blackheath
Darren and the unit from Lewisham made their way up to Blackheath, an ancient, two hundred acre, flat green that was bordered by handsome Georgian and Victorian houses. It was a protected common, where plague victims had once been buried and armies assembled before heading off to wars. But now it was a little bit of heaven – a village with a pretty Victorian church, sandwiched between Lewisham and Greenwich, two boroughs with many social and criminal problems. All across the large green, police officers and vehicles lay scattered around. Some officers sat in groups, chatting but most lay motionless on their backs, sleeping. As Darren's unit arrived, another went back out, to replace them.

Darren stepped down, off his carrier, and as he lay on the cool, dew-damp grass he felt a vibration in his pocket. He phone was buzzing. They were text messages from friends. They had seen what had been happening in Lewisham, on the news and were checking to see if he was okay.

Darren text back: 'We're slowly winning the fight.'

His phone buzzed again: 'Maybe in Lewisham you are but I think you've lost in Croydon.'

Darren immediately checked the news reports on his phone. What he saw stunned him. Croydon looked like one gigantic fireball. It was utterly devastated.

'I think we may have got off lightly,' Darren said to the officer sitting next to him.

He put the phone back in his pocket, placed his helmet on the shield next to him, and stared up at the stars, listening to the voices coming out over the police radio. Skirmishes were still happening around the area but Lewisham had been retaken and was back in the control of the police.

He closed his eyes and slept.

Croydon

The fires continued but now that the rioters had disappeared, the fire fighters were free to suppress the flames. Everywhere Tom looked there was utter devastation. Reeves Corner was all but gone, and other buildings and shops had also been damaged. Everywhere there was shattered glass and bricks, pieces of smashed masonry and wood. The ground was covered in so much rubble he could hardly see the tarmac. The pungent smell of smoke was everywhere. It clawed through the streets and rose from the officers' overalls, mixed with the smell of their own sweat. There was exhaustion, hunger and cold. People with faces in shock, and blackened with smoke trudged through the streets. Tired, raw eyes peered in disbelief at what had befallen Croydon.

Tom and his small band of colleagues lumbered slowly towards the tram stop by what was left of Reeves Corner – charred, crumbling walls with black, scaly pieces of wood poking out like scorched bones. They fell to the floor, shaking their heads in disbelief at what they had been involved in. They all felt completely spent. They had been going now for two days with barely any sleep and next to nothing to eat. One of the officers lay across a bench while others lay on the concrete, shutting their eyes in the hope of getting at least a little rest. Others lit cigarettes and inhaled deeply, blowing the smoke towards the sky.

By 6am, the group were still at the tram stop. Around them

the fires were still burning. As far as they knew, no one had asked about their welfare or where they were and what they were doing.

With a post-battle calm dropping slowly down over Croydon, the radio traffic had fallen to near silence. The constant, terrifying calls for 'Urgent Assistance' had thankfully ceased – for now.

The door of a nearby pub opened.

'Too early for a pint?' one of the officers joked.

The landlady stepped out and walked towards the officers. They looked over and saw that she was carrying with a large tray of bacon sandwiches and mugs of hot tea. It was better than a pint. Tom could have cried.

Hackney

Back in Hackney, the officers regrouped. There were still small pockets of rioters running around nearby streets and they would need tackling. The night wasn't over, not for Keith and the rest of the Ealing officers, or any other officer for that matter. There hadn't been enough of them to deal with the level of violence and trouble that had exploded in Hackney, and the police response to it had been lacking. Hackney would be saved but at a cost. Property, shops, cars, and police officers would all be casualties. Keith felt knackered, annoyed and wound-up. This should all have been dealt with far better than it had. There needed to be more discipline, better training among the officers on the streets. And why did it take so long for the senior management to respond? Logistics? He didn't know. He could appreciate that there was a bigger picture but still, it had taken until day three for him to be deployed. For Keith, it just wasn't good enough.

He wouldn't get home until later that day and despite how he felt, at least the job had now been done. And somehow, by some miracle he would never fully understand, no police officer had died.

However, in the Midlands things were bubbling and one group were going to do their best to see that an officer did die, and maybe more than one. As a group of criminals loaded bullets into their guns, they hatched a plan. They were going to set a trap – an ambush – for the police. And then they were going to start shooting.

0800 hrs
Central London
By 8am the Cambridge officers were stood down from Leicester Square and told to return to Central London, where they would be debriefed before being formally released.

Having been on duty since early the previous morning, Mark and the rest of his crew were exhausted. Their sense of humour was already seriously lacking but it was about to be shoved into the abyss. As they returned to their parked carriers they stopped dead in their tracks and stared at them in disbelief. Their carriers were covered in small, round, blue and white 'I'VE MET THE MET' stickers.

These stickers were infamous among police officers all across the UK. The stickers featured an image of a male and female uniformed police officer with the words

'I'VE MET THE MET' emblazoned across the top, and had been around for decades, often handed out to children at fêtes and fairs. There was also a tradition among Met officers to put the stickers in all sorts of unlikely, daring, improbable, and, yes, inappropriate places. They can be found literally all over the world, and there had long been a rumour that there was even a sticker somewhere on the US President's plane, Air Force One. But most of all, the Met had a reputation for plastering them on anything they could get their hands on from other UK forces, whether that was vehicles, stations, property or even individual officers. And sure enough, here were the Cambridgeshire carriers, having been left for only a matter of minutes, now covered in these stickers.

'Wankers,' someone said.

'I don't believe this,' another officer said. 'We come down here, fighting on their cordons for twenty hours and they're stickering our fucking vans!'

Mark walk silently around his carrier, looking at the collection of stickers that now covered it. There was even one placed carefully on the windscreen, over the tax disc. If he remembered nothing else about the riots, he would remember this. Despite all the shit that was going on, all the rioting and all the trouble, these fucking Met officers had still found the time to put their fucking 'I'VE MET THE MET' stickers all over their vans.

The Cambridgeshire carriers weren't the only ones to find themselves at the receiving end of the Met officers' mischief. In retaliation, some forces had made up stickers of their own, especially for the riots. As Mark grumpily peeled away at the blue and white circles with the grinning faces of two London coppers, somewhere out there a Met TSG officer was peeling stickers from his own vehicle, which read: 'SURREY POLICE – SAVING THE MET'.

1100 hrs
Guildford, Surrey
There was a knock at the front door. Richard pulled on his dressing gown and walked lazily down the stairs. When he opened the door, he found his next door neighbour standing there, staring at him and holding a homemade cottage pie.

'Oh, Richard,' she said, sounding surprised. 'What are you doing here?'

'What do you mean, what am I doing here? I live here.'

'Well, I've just been watching the news and there're riots all over London,' she said. 'They're burning the place down.'

'That's right.'

'The commissioner has apparently called everybody in and told them that all leave is cancelled, and everybody is to report to their police stations. But you're still here. I thought you'd be up in London.'

For the first time in nearly three decades as a police officer, Richard felt ashamed. That was his city out there being destroyed, and he wasn't there to protect it. He felt embarrassed that he couldn't help when London needed him the most. Having spoken to other officers the day before, he knew he wasn't alone in feeling like this.

'We weren't been called in,' Richard explained, almost apologetically. 'And not only were we not called in, but I heard from other officers that one of the bosses threatened that if we do just turn up, we will never be allowed to work any overtime ever again.'

'Oh. Well, I made this cottage pie for your family,' she explained. 'I thought your wife and children would be scared to death that you may not be coming back from those terrible riots. I thought she would be stressed so I just wanted to bring this over to say that I hoped everything was all right.'

'Oh, thank you very much,' Richard said, reaching out and taking the pie. 'I'll have that for my tea.'

1500 hrs
Birmingham

Chris had been at home in Wolverhampton with his wife and two kids when he saw the news about Mark Duggan. Things were kicking off in London, but he didn't believe it would affect the Midlands. In his seven years as a police constable in Walsall, close to Birmingham, he had always felt that guns and gangs were more of a London problem, and that the riots were unlikely to spread up to his area.

But Chris was wrong.

He came into work for his late shift – 3pm until midnight. Almost immediately he was told to change into his public order gear. Chris was a Level 2 public order trained officer, but other than policing the odd sporting event, he had never had to 'kit-up' for anything serious and had never been in an actual riot. In fact, Chris had only been trained in public order two months before, having waited for three years for a course.

He and his Level 2 colleagues got ready, pulling on their flame resistant coveralls, leg and arm guards and helmets. The chinstrap on the helmet, and the flameproof balaclava itched against his short, ginger beard – something he liked to believe pointed towards his Viking heritage. They were '1 and 7' one sergeant (who was 'acting up' as an inspector) and seven PCs. Chris had been expecting to sit around the base on standby, but instead they made their way to their headquarters for a briefing. There, he was given hardly any information, and instead checked his Facebook account on his phone; that's when he realised that things had really started to kick off.

Police intelligence units were monitoring BlackBerry messenger and chatter among large groups they believed were looking to gather to start trouble in Birmingham. From what Chris was

246

being told and from what he was finding out, it just seemed people were looking for an opportunity to nick stuff from phone and electrical shops as opposed to anything as serious as the rioting that had been happened in London.

Chris believed that he and his unit would be held in reserve. He had always found that Birmingham officers were usually able to cope with any issues in their city. Birmingham had the most officers of any of the areas of the West Midlands, so Chris felt sure that he and his unit were being drafted in as a precaution.

As the briefing ended, they were told that officers in Birmingham were coming under missile attack. Chris's unit were to go straight to their vans and deploy to the city centre immediately.

After assembling at a nearby police station, the PSUs rolled into Birmingham city centre, to Carrs Lane, a small business street close to the Bullring Shopping Centre. There was looting going on nearby but Chris and his unit remained where they were, acting purely as a 'presence'. They were given no tasks, no orders to move forward; they simply had to stand around.

Then they were told to move location, this time to Corporation Street, the city's busiest area. By now more officers were coming under fire, greater numbers of missiles were being thrown and shops were being attacked. Chris couldn't understand why, with four police serials, they were still being held back. It seemed pointless. Everything seemed to be happening in slow motion. No one was making any quick decisions to get control or to stop things from spiralling out of control. With all the technology, CCTV and radio communications, surely it was possible to organise people better than this? Why weren't they being used? Why weren't they being sent in to stop the rioters and looters?

Chris's serial was told to create cordons across the streets to prevent more people entering the trouble areas so that they could contain it. They stepped down from their carriers and stood in line, fully kitted up but without their protective shields. Everything seemed to be going off and it was all happening extremely close to where they were standing. Somewhere nearby, the sounds of shops being attacked were mixing with the responding sounds of police sirens.

'Okay, listen in,' the sergeant said. 'We need to evacuate the city centre. We have to go in and start clearing out the public. They need to go home for their own safety.'

The officers now collected their riot shields. They were finally going to enter the streets in the centre of the city. Despite the trouble that was already happening, members of the public were still milling around. The officers approached anyone they saw, and told them in no uncertain terms to go home. Nearby, Chris could see groups of youths pulling up hoods and scarves to cover their faces. He continued to do his best to convince people to leave the area but was constantly challenged by disinterested members of the public. Some people purposefully created ways to delay the officers, walking extra slowly or saying that they had to stop and tie their shoelaces and other such nonsense. *Idiots*, Chris thought to himself.

At the end of the streets, the hooded, masked mobs were growing. They hadn't gone unnoticed and the sergeant called out to the officers to form up in their lines.

'We will be taking the next junction,' he instructed. 'On me! GO!'

They ran forward and the mob quickly disappeared, not quite ready to take the police on. Chris held the junction, waiting for the next order, and he smiled as he saw members of the public, who just moments before had been sluggish and leisurely, suddenly clearing out as quickly as they could.

As Chris stood waiting, he watched as a converted prison van pulled up. A police officer opened the back doors and six police Alsatians jumped out eagerly – sniffing the ground, and watching their handlers closely, waiting for a command.

The handlers walked their dogs up to Chris's line, standing a few feet behind them.

'Do you ever wonder if those bloody dogs can tell the difference between a crook and a copper?' The officer standing next to Chris asked.

'I wouldn't want to be the one that finds out,' he replied. But he was pleased that the dogs were there.

The battle for Birmingham had begun.

As well as Birmingham, Manchester and Salford were also experiencing violence. Greater Manchester Police had already sent around one hundred officers to London but then trouble had broken out in their own city. Starting out with just a few youths throwing rocks and bricks at officers, the violence quickly grew until police dressed in riot gear carried out a series of baton charges against the mobs. Gangs of youths then attacked shops, kicking in the glass windows and pulling away metal shutters. Vans and cars were set alight, and a BBC television cameraman was attacked as he filmed in the street. A supermarket and a council building were set on fire. Suddenly the streets of Salford were filled with the high-pitched sound of police sirens, as riot carriers screamed through the area, dashing from one seat of disturbance to the next.

A short time later, Manchester city centre was hit. Buses and fire engines were attacked, and there were reports of gunfire being heard. Someone smashed their way into a small Miss Selfridge store on Market Street and lit a fire. With the shop filled with clothing, the fire soon grew out of control, totally consuming the building. Other shops across the areas were being attacked and looted by hundreds of masked youths. Buses, trams and taxis were prevented from entering the city as police, some on horseback, fought to control the mobs.

Leicester too had seen hundreds of rioters charging through the streets causing damage to shops and setting vehicles alight as they went. But the trouble in these places was nothing in comparison to what had been seen in London, and would be contained quickly.

1600 hrs
London Docklands, Newham
Darin and his TfL crew were on their way to east London, towards the ExCel exhibition centre. Reports were coming in that a bus and a Docklands Light Railway (DLR) station had been attacked.

The three carriers prepared to leave their base and as with the previous day, and as was standard practice, they were expecting to travel in convoy. It was safer that way and it also kept the unit together as one. But as they left Bow Road, one of the carriers turned in a different direction to the other two. Darin wouldn't see that carrier again until they returned to the base later that day. There had been tensions between the supervisors with disagreements over some of the decisions that had been made, and Darin suspected that the sergeant on the carrier didn't want to work with the inspector any more.

As they continued on their way, the inspector was talking over the radio, giving instructions about how to get to the Docklands but Darin was still unsure about which way to go.

He picked up his mobile phone and called the inspector. 'Sir, are you sure that you know the way?'

'Yeah, yeah,' the inspector assured him. 'Stick close. Stick close.'

As they made their way, Darin listened in on the police radio, to the commentary about the rioting that was happening by the ExCel Centre. The main seat of trouble seemed to be on Prince Regent Lane, at the bottom end by Victoria Dock Road, next to Prince Regent DLR.

'Protected vehicles only into the road,' the order was given over the radio.

Darin knew what this meant: only riot carriers with metal grills were to go in. It was a good indication of how dangerous the situation had become. Clearly, missiles were now being hurled at officers and vehicles. It certainly wasn't somewhere that they should be driving into.

Darin continued to pay close attention to the road names. He wanted to be sure that they weren't going anywhere where they weren't wanted or needed, as well as ensuring that they avoided anywhere where they could find themselves trapped or outnumbered. But the closer they got to the area, the more Darin realised that they were going the wrong way. And then, suddenly, ahead of them, there was a crowd of around 200 rioters, who all had their backs to the carriers. Instead of driving to the rendezvous point in front of the rioters, where the other police units were gathering and getting ready to form up, they had driven in *behind* them. They were on Prince Regent Lane. It was a long but regular two-lane road with a low-rise, modern housing estate at one end – the end they were now in.

'Oh shit!' Darin muttered softly.

Hearing the noise of the engines, some of the crowd had spun around. Instantly, word reached the entire mob that there were police carriers behind them. Just like that, the unprotected police carriers were surrounded and overwhelmed.

Rocks, bricks, bottles, wood – they all slammed into the carriers with such force and speed that the noise became deafening to the officers inside the carriers. People started to scream, and Darin knew it was his own officers. Then a man approaching the front of the carrier seized Darin's attention. In his hands he was carrying a huge concrete slab. Time slowed down as Darin watched the man lift and then hurl the slab towards them. The chunk of concrete twisted in the air, flying towards the carrier. Then it hit the windscreen. Smashing, screaming, shouting, and from the crowd, cheering. Thousands of tiny shards of splintered glass flew into the carrier, showering the officers.

There was a moment of shock. Darin turned to look at the driver, sitting next to him. Lines of blood were rolling down his face. Then Darin felt the warm trickles of blood sliding down his own.

The carrier rocked violently, side to side as the mob began pushing it. A couple of female officers at the back of the carrier were crying. The thunderous sounds of the carrier being kicked and hit and struck by dozens of people grew louder as the crowd, stimulated with rage and joy at the smashing of the windscreen, became even more excitable.

Darin knew exactly how serious the situation was: they could all die here. The mob was out of control. They were in a frenzy. It was the sort of delirium that could lead to the murder of police officers. It would only take one in the crowd to start and the rest would follow.

Behind him, officers were holding shields up against the windows, desperately trying to prevent more glass from going in. The carriers were being destroyed, and there was nowhere for the officers to go. They weren't even wearing riot gear, just white cotton shirts and flat caps. Getting out of the carriers would have been suicidal. It didn't matter anyway; they were trapped. The mob would be in the vans soon enough. Either way, they were dead. Literally, dead.

The crowd roared louder. Then a few of them stepped away from the carrier and then more did the same. Some of the crowd started to move further away and the rocking stopped. Darin spun around to see what was going on. There, forcing their way through the crowd, pushing them back with shields and batons, were police riot officers. From their uniform, their protective armour and guards, Darin could see they weren't Met. The riot officers continued with the counter-assault, sliding down, along the sides of the carriers, taking the bricks and the flak from the rioters as they fought them off and protected the TfL unit. They were Humberside Constabulary, and they were saving the Met officers' lives.

With continued baton and shield strikes, the mob was eventually forced back and the Humberside shield units took up position, holding their line around the carriers.

It was now safe enough for Darin and his fellow officers – shaken, bleeding and shocked – to step out of their battered, wrecked carriers. The bloodied driver started to kick the carrier in frustration and anger at being led into the rioting crowd.

'Right, let's get out of here,' the inspector said.

Before they left, another Metropolitan Police inspector, dressed in full riot gear, came over. 'Whatever you do, don't drive down that way,' he warned, pointing to a set of streets ahead of them. 'We've had all kinds of trouble down there.'

The TfL unit boarded there ruined carriers and were promptly led in that very direction.

Mobs ran out from side streets, ambushing the pair of carriers. Bricks and rocks came flying through the air from all sides once more, pounding the already seriously battered minibuses. Officers screamed again, ducking down as the drivers desperately drove the carriers as quickly as they could through the bombardment, before zooming off, away from the trouble and back towards their base.

Back at Bow, the officers got out of the vehicles. They were still seriously shaken by their experiences. The inspector however, was unhappy about something else entirely. At some point, someone had taken a pen and drawn a penis in his flat-cap, on the underside of the crown. It wasn't an unknown occurrence for someone's hat to get 'cocked' but the inspector wasn't impressed. Even so, London was in urgent need for units on the ground, and so the battered, cut, bleeding, angry TfL officers put their differences to one side, found some new carriers to replace their battle-worn vehicles, and set back out to see what they could do; to see where they could help. Everything else could wait.

1700 hrs
Eltham
It had been three days since Inspector Walpole had battled alongside his small unit of officers outside the carpet store in Tottenham. So much had happened since then; so much violence, destruction and anger.

At Hounslow Inspector Walpole met up with his unit once more. Unlike Saturday, when he had only half-a-dozen officers, he now had a full PSU spread across three carriers.

After a briefing at the Met's training establishment at Hendon, they were ordered to Lewisham for mobile patrols. Lewisham had seen a huge amount of trouble and although things finally seemed to have calmed down, no one was taking any chances. There needed to be a strong police presence to ensure that nothing further broke out. As they drove out of the gates at Hendon, the carrier drivers switched on the blue lights and sirens and started to make their way to the other side of London.

Having suffered, like so many other places, with days of violence, Lewisham now seemed relatively calm, and the carriers spent the afternoon driving through the streets without so much as a bottle being thrown at them. They drove down Eltham Hill, a gently sloping A-road lined with respectable looking semi-detached houses. To the east was Eltham itself, where Inspector Walpole's PSU was heading to, and to the west lay Lewisham.

'Jesus!' the driver suddenly said. 'Who are this lot?'

Inspector Walpole peered out of the window, looking closely as the carriers continued down the hill. Ahead of the carriers were more than a hundred middle-aged men, literally marching up the hill towards them. To the officers, they looked like a bunch of hardcore football hooligans and English Defence League (EDL) types.

'Right, stop the carriers. Everyone out,' Inspector Walpole said. 'I want a cordon across this road. We need to hold it until we can figure out exactly what's going on here.'

The carriers stopped and the officers jumped out, quickly creating a line of bodies in front of their carriers and across the hill. The men marched up to meet the line of officers. Many in the group had been drinking, and with that many people bunched together it was easy to smell the beer. Inspector Walpole approached the group. The men claimed that they wanted to help the police and that they wanted to protect their area. Yet they were leaving Eltham and heading directly toward Lewisham.

'We're on your side,' one of the men told Inspector Walpole. 'We're here to help.'

Inspector Walpole realised the potential for trouble, should this group start marching through Lewisham looking for those that they perceived to be responsible for the previous few nights of rioting and looting. He wasn't about to let them continue with their crusade and the Hounslow officers managed to filter the group back towards Eltham. The crowd hadn't been looking to fight the police and their stance of being there to help gave the officers a chance to convince them that going back to Eltham would be best for everyone.

As it happened, the local borough had been monitoring the group. More and more local people were coming out onto the streets and hanging around Eltham town centre. Whereas Lewisham had seen days of trouble and destruction, Eltham had remained untouched, and that was exactly the way the locals wanted it to remain. As the evening went on, the streets became filled with people, reporters, camera crews and police.

The opinion of the locals was that they were looking after their own 'manor'. Rumours had spread that Eltham was on the looters' list of targets, so the locals now roamed the streets determined that they weren't going to allow troublemakers from elsewhere to come to their town and tear the place up. Occasionally someone, for some reason, would start running and huge groups would suddenly run with them, not really knowing why, but following in case there was something going on – in case someone was attacking their town. Emotions were running high and people were getting excitable.

TSG officers soon arrived and the groups were contained in Eltham, never being given a chance to march on Lewisham. For now, the crowd were on side of the police, expressing how they understood that the police were outnumbered and that they needed help. Many of the locals saw themselves as just that – help for the police – and they were prepared to back the police up if needs be. It wouldn't remain that way though. The following evening would see some minor skirmishes. Police units from across the country – from Wales, Lincolnshire and South Yorkshire – already in London to assist the Met would be sent to Eltham. Frustrated, members of the crowd would start to throw beer bottles and lines of police would charge the groups. But other than this, Eltham would remain untouched by the riots.

1800 hrs
Birmingham

In Birmingham, the officers were ordered to start moving again. It was 6pm, and the mobs had become larger and more daring. Missiles began to find their way to the police line. There were only rioters on the streets now; everyone else had cleared off.

'Don't arrest anyone unless you really have to,' the officers were ordered. 'There are Evidence Gatherers and CCTV all over the place. They can mop up the troublemakers afterwards. For now, we need you all on the street.'

This sounded like good sense to Chris. The last thing anyone needed was for officers to be stuck processing prisoners and doing paperwork as Birmingham was burnt to the ground. No, the arrests would come later. For now, they needed to save the city.

The only problem was, by not arresting anyone, Chris quickly realised that all the police serials were really doing was pushing groups of rioters over to the next police serial. Some of the mobs were even being pushed into each other, creating larger groups. No sooner had Chris and his unit cleared a street than he would hear that another police serial was faced with them. It was a frustrating consequence of not making arrests, but what else could they do? Besides, Chris was desperate for the rioting not to spread any further. He thought about his family in Wolverhampton and hoped that by stopping the rioters in 'Brum', 'Wolves' would be spared.

They moved towards Pigeon Park, a local nickname for the green at the very centre of the city, and the location of Birmingham Cathedral. They were ordered to hold the area and try and keep the rioters out. Several shops had already been attacked – the smashed windows and debris being testament to the explosion of violence that had already passed through the area. McDonalds had been targeted, but despite the smashed glass and terrifying violence that the staff had endured, they rushed out with cups of coffee for the weary officers. It would be the first and the last drink that Chris and the rest of his unit would receive, because the rioters were back.

They stood around the park, goading the officers. Chris got back into his line, and the officers charged at the mobs before pulling back and charging again. Back and forth, back and forth.

The youths ran down some side streets and into an alleyway – Needless Alley, it was called, much to Chris's amusement – and Chris chased after them with several other officers. No sooner did they find a group, than they lost them again as they chased them into another alley or side street. The alleys were narrow, dark and hostile. As he turned into another he felt something at his feet. He looked down at the damp, dirty ground and as his eyes adjusted to the darkness, he saw that the entire alley was strewn with the torn packaging of mobile phones. Everywhere he looked were empty boxes and discarded instruction manuals. He kicked some of the boxes out of his way, towards a bin where he saw brand new pairs of trainers – still with the tags on – and other stolen pieces of sports clothing.

As Chris left the alley he walked straight into a hail of bottles and bricks. At every corner, missiles were thrown at their line.

The rioters were throwing anything they could get hold of – sticks, litter; it didn't matter. Everywhere, shops had their windows smashed in and stock looted. Serious rioting had broken out, but at least there were no fires or petrol bombs. From what Chris could gather, things hadn't got as bad as London – not yet anyway – but the city centre was fairly big and the police were being stretched. With little other option, Chris's serial was split up.

'Chris, I need you and four others up on Hill Street,' his sergeant told him. 'Get yourselves up there and make sure no one enters the city through there.'

Hill Street was a long, narrow road leading from Birmingham New Street rail station, before gently sloping upwards into the centre of the city, reaching Victoria Square at the top, by Paradise Street. Victoria Square was a beautiful spot, with fountains and grand, listed Victorian buildings containing council offices and a concert hall in revival Roman architecture. On any normal day it would have been flowing with pedestrians, but now it was deserted.

Chris started to trek towards Hill Street. He looked behind him at the four officers following. The pause in the violence had given them a much needed break but it did little to refresh them. They were all visibly exhausted from the constant chasing around and fighting. To add to this, they hadn't eaten for hours and the air temperature had dropped. It was starting to feel cold.

They reached the top of the narrow street. There was no one else around – just the five of them. They hadn't seen their own carrier for about three hours, having been out on foot since deploying to the city centre. As they stood there, listening to the sounds of their empty stomachs, and slapping their hands against the sides of their bodies to keep warm, Chris watched a teenage boy and a girl about the same age walking calmly towards them.

'You all right there, mate?' Chris asked, unsure as to what the teenaged pair wanted or what they were doing.

'Where's the best place?' the boy asked.

'For what?'

'To watch it.'

'Watch?'

'Yeah, the riots.'

Chris couldn't believe it; this boy had brought his girlfriend out for the evening to watch the rioting, like it was some kind of spectator sport. The other officers, hearing what the boy had asked, looked over in similar disbelief.

After staring at the couple for a moment in weary amazement, Chris said, 'In your bedroom, you idiot. Go home.'

The youth shrugged his shoulders and the romantic pair walked away, arm in arm.

The officers went back to knocking warmth into their bodies and trying not to think about food or water. Having spent hours running around the streets and parks of Birmingham, sweat had soaked into their clothing and as the temperature dropped after the sun went down, the moisture in their suits and on their skin began to get extremely cold. Discomfort was in danger of turning into something far more serious. On top of all that, they were dehydrated. Thirst, hunger, cold and fatigue were laying waste to the five exhausted, isolated officers.

Chris could only hope that no more rioters were going to attack them.

Wednesday 10th August 2011

0100 hrs

Birmingham

As the five officers stood around in silence, the noise of the rioting across the city drifted through the streets and bounced off the stone buildings. Sirens, shouting, screaming, smashing – to Chris it sounded like the noises that come from a distant football ground on match day. It was impossible to tell where the noises originated – which streets, how far away, which direction. Out of all of them, only Chris had any vague idea of where they were, having spent some time studying at the University in the city a few years previously. Even so, he still felt lost. He added this to the list of things you didn't want to be when fighting a riot. Two of the officers with him were from Sandwell. They had somehow ended up with the Walsall PSU even though the Sandwell officers had never worked in Birmingham in their entire careers.

Standing at the top of the lonely hill, Chris and his small band of officers felt isolated and all but forgotten about. At least it was quiet here, he thought. At least they had found a place for some much needed respite, which was in complete contrast to what was happening elsewhere. Other officers were constantly calling up on the radio screaming for help and giving their locations in a desperate bid for assistance. Most of the locations given meant nothing to the officers at the top of Hill Street; they were as unfamiliar with the city as tourists. People could have been around the corner asking for help and they wouldn't have known where they were. The continual shouts over their radios became a depressing soundtrack.

All around the city, trouble was raging. The hundred-year-old Barton Arms pub, to the north of Birmingham, in Aston, was attacked. A gang entered the pub, smashing windows and ransacking the place. Items of furniture were tossed into the street and missiles were thrown at a passing police car. Petrol bombs were lit and thrown and the pub set on fire. But all was not as it seemed. The arson had been committed in order to draw police to the location.

Members of a gang had set an ambush. As officers arrived, hooded men, standing amongst a wild crowd, had drawn their guns, taken aim and pulled the triggers, the sound of gunfire echoing through the streets. A dozen shots were fired at the police from at least four handguns – revolvers and 9mm pistols. The bullets struck a wall above the officers' heads, miraculously missing them. Had the gunmen been better shots and aimed lower, police officers would have almost certainly died.

As a police helicopter hovered above, other gang members took aim and fired at it, twice. The officers on the ground – all unarmed – were ordered to get out of the area immediately. Armed officers then moved in, searching for the gunmen and making a number of arrests at gunpoint.

In a separate assault, the Handsworth West police station on Holyhead Road, which had thankfully been unoccupied, was now ablaze after being attacked. Most distressing of all, though, were the truly tragic events that were unfolding just a couple of miles away. Locals in the Winston Green area of the city, just northwest of Birmingham, had taken to the streets with sticks and bats and bricks to protect their properties and businesses from looters. Tensions had been building in the neighbourhood since the previous night after a group of men had been seen driving around the area and believed to be looking for places to attack and loot.

Now, on this next night, a crowd of up to 150 mostly Asian men, but also some white and black residents, had gathered on the streets. It was a multi-cultural area and although the neighbourhood had one of the highest crime rates in the city, the locals were determined to guard and protect their businesses.

Amongst the jittery crowd were 30-year-old Abdul Musavir and his 31-year-old brother, Shazad Ali (whose wife was four months pregnant), and their 21-year-old friend Haroon Jahan. The three of them stood guard together outside some shops on Dudley Road, and as they chatted, three cars – a Ford Fiesta, an Audi and a Mazda – suddenly sped out of the darkness towards them. A moment later, without warning, the Mazda struck the men – hurling them metres into the air.

Tariq Jahan, a local man, had been standing outside the front of his house with his wife and eldest son when he heard the crash. He and his son rushed over to help in any way that they could. Tariq saw the three men on the ground. He dropped down and checked the first man. It was Shazad Ali and even though he knew Shazad from the local carwash, Tariq didn't immediately recognise him. He checked for a pulse but there was none, so Tariq began to work on Shazad's heart, in a desperate attempt to revive him. Another person approached and took over from Tariq, who then moved onto the next man – Abdul Musavir. Tariq held Abdul's head in his hands and as he lifted his hand away from Abdul's head, he saw that it was covered in blood.

Finally, Tariq reached the third victim. As with the other two, the man was lying on the ground and had his face turned away from Tariq. Tariq reached out and pulled the man over to check his breathing and to place him in the recovery position. As Tariq did so, he noticed blood dripping from the man's nose and running onto his beard. He noticed tiny details such as a small pebble stuck to the man's forehead. He noticed the man's black leather jacket. Then he heard his eldest son scream. In his arms, Tariq Jahan was holding Haroon Jahan, his own son.

Despite Tariq's efforts to save the men, they all died.

The officers on Hill Street were unaware of all of this. On top of that chilly, forgotten hill, there was a sense of loneliness and isolation, but also some peace. One of the officers – the eldest in the small group – slumped down onto the road, sitting on his riot shield in an attempt to keep the cold of the ground away from his body. Chris watched him and said nothing. He knew that the officer suffered from back problems and understood his need to give his body a break. They had been on their feet for hours. It was only surprising that the rest of them hadn't collapsed onto the floor long ago.

As Chris stood looking out across the city, reflecting about what had occurred over the past few hours, thinking about his job, his hunger, the cold, and wondering where the rest of his PSU were and what they were doing, listening to the far off noises of the rioting and fighting, he was suddenly snapped out of his trance. At the bottom of Hill Street, about 40 rioters suddenly appeared. The group wasn't made up of young, excitable kids; most of them looked to be between 18 and 25 years old. They also seemed as though they were looking for a fight – they bristled with aggressive energy. The mob quickly noticed the tiny group of police officers at the top of the hill. They immediately began to pull masks over their faces and hoods over their heads. The five officers were isolated, outnumbered and in serious, serious trouble.

This could be interesting, Chris thought to himself.

The older officer, who was still sitting down, lifted himself off of his shield and stood back up. The five officers drew closer together and stood in a line, facing the group.

A glass bottle shattered on the ground in front of them. Chris looked up at the sky. The group had begun to throw missiles. Now there was no mistaking the group's intent; they were going to attack. Chris lifted his shield in front of his body. More bottles were thrown towards them, smashing on the ground.

The five PCs had no supervisors with them. As well as not seeing their carrier for hours, they also hadn't seen their sergeant, who was himself leading another set of officers in a different part of the city. So someone needed to take charge, and quickly.

'We've got 40 hooding up. What do you what us to do, over?' Chris heard someone saying into their radio.

He looked around, and saw that one of the other officers had called the situation in. But there was no reply, and the bottles continued to rain down on them. The radio traffic was already frantic, with officers all over Birmingham calling for assistance. Their transmission was just one more among dozens. With so much happening across the city and with so many officers outnumbered and needing help, there seemed to be little chance of anyone listening to their urgent call, let alone responding. They were on their own.

But then, seemingly out of nowhere, a tall, well-built inspector – a man Chris had never seen before – appeared and joined this little band of officers. Perhaps their call for help had been heard after all. They looked behind the inspector, expecting to see the rest of his troops following but Chris quickly realised that there were no more; it was just this one, lone police inspector. Now it was six against 40.

The inspector looked down the hill and then turned to the five officers. 'Right, listen in guys,' the inspector said in a broad Scottish accent. 'Here's what we're going to do. I'll give the crowd one warning to desist and move away from the area. If that doesn't work, we'll charge them.'

Chris looked down at the mob, then back at the other officers. They were still lobbing bottles towards the officers, and it was still six against 40. Chris didn't believe there was a chance of the rioters leaving any time soon, so he figured he would be charging towards them in a few moments. It sounded like a crazy plan, but this inspector had an aura about him, a total lack of fear, which was beginning to stir something in Chris.

'MOVE AWAY NOW OR WE WILL USE FORCE!' the inspector shouted at the crowd, who roared back. More bottles smashed on the ground in front of them.

'Draw your batons,' the inspector calmly ordered the five exhausted officers as he pulled out his own.

Chris looked at the inspector. *He's brilliant*, he thought to himself. Here was a boss who wasn't going to stand around and take it. In spite of how badly outnumbered the officers were, this inspector was up for taking on the rioters. He was ready to lead Chris and the rest of his small group into the fight, and to hell with the consequences. This was just what they needed. Adrenaline once again pumped through their cold, tired bodies, giving them warmth and energy.

The inspector stepped forward, baton drawn, staring down at the mob. Then he lifted his baton in the air. Without hesitation, Chris and the others did the same. This was it. They were going in.

'GO! GO! GO!' The inspector shouted.

All six of them surged forward, a tiny band of kamikaze cops charging towards a horde of rioters. Bottles landed hard around them, smashing and splintering. In Chris's vision was a blur of darkness and light from lamp posts. There was shouting and screaming, and Chris didn't know if it was coming from the rioters or the officers around him. Perhaps it was everyone.

The officers were facing odds of seven to one, and Chris knew that they had no chance. This was going to hurt, but what choice did they have? At least they were doing something. Their world had collapsed, there was anarchy on the streets, but they were police officers and that meant they had to fight back. Officers were battling rioters across Birmingham – battling rioters across the country – and this was their battle, here at Hill Street. There was no one else, no more back-up, just them. Chris wasn't even sure if anyone knew where they were and what they were doing.

As the officers charged down the hill, batons in the air, shields held in front of their aching bodies, ready to fight a pitched battle against a violent mob seven times the size of their group, something amazing happened – the rioters started running away. They were actually running away! Chris felt his pace picking up, his heavy boots getting lighter with every stride he made, and the mob continued to scatter. No more bottles were thrown, and the crowd shrunk rapidly. By the time the officers reached New Street Station, at the bottom of Hill Street, it was just the six of them. They had chased the rioters off.

'Right, back to the top,' the inspector told them. 'You need to remain here and hold that hill.'

And with that, the inspector was gone. Chris never saw him again and never found out who he was.

A few minutes later, Chris heard on the radio that the rioters had moved on to the Mailbox shopping area, where they smashed some shop windows. Other officers were now driving around the streets, looking for them.

Chris stood with his thirsty, hungry, exhausted but exhilarated colleagues at the top of Hill Street, guarding the entrance to the city. He listened to the far-off roar of the 'football match'. It was still kicking off but the police operation to retake the city – not to mention the rest of the country – was now well underway. Dozens, perhaps hundreds, of groups of officers of different sizes and in different cities had shown the same attitude as the one the Scottish inspector used to inspire these five officers who now held the hill. No matter how tired, hungry, thirsty, bruised and battered they were, all across the country police officers were now more determined than ever that no one would get past their thin blue line.

Afterwards

On 10th December 2013, following the inquest into the shooting of Mark Duggan, a jury started their deliberations with instructions to deliver a verdict of either 'unlawful killing', 'lawful killing' or an 'open verdict'. On 7th January 2014 (having had to break for Christmas), the jury delivered their verdict. By an 8-to-1 majority the jury concluded that Mark Duggan's death at the hands of the police was a lawful killing.

Almost a year before, on 31st January 2013, Kevin Hutchinson-Foster had been convicted of supplying Mark Duggan with the gun and was sentenced to 11 years imprisonment. Seven of those years were for supplying the gun to Duggan on the day he was shot. Hutchinson-Foster was given an extra four years for possession of the gun with intent to cause fear of violence, and for assault. The day before Duggan collected the gun, Hutchinson-Foster had used it to beat a man almost into unconsciousness.

There was, of course, an inquiry into the rioting of August 2011, and although it was widely acknowledged that the huge scale of the disorder was unprecedented, the police came in for some criticism. For example, rumours had been circulating around Tottenham that the police had executed Mark Duggan – that the police had actually set out to kill him that day. This rumour was allowed to fester and was not publically challenged until *after* the rioting had begun.

The Metropolitan Police were also criticised for responding too slowly to the outbreak of disorder, and then failing to mobilise enough officers when they did finally respond. It was a criticism that the Met itself accepted. Another issue was equipment; some forces ran out of kit, including riot shields, or had inadequate types of vehicles to respond to the disorder. I was told how one inspector at Ealing ran around from one police station to another, desperately searching for and scavenging any pieces of kit he could get his hands on – batons, shields, helmets – to dish out to officers and PCSOs who were about to enter the fray.

Speaking to officers involved in the Brixton and Tottenham riots of the 1980s, many complained about how they had been held back at their stations while rioters went on the rampage. Other officers involved in the 1980s riots complained about a lack of food and water – a basic need – to help keep them going during the long hours of fighting. I heard the exact same complaints from officers fighting on the same streets 30 years later, namely that little thought was given to their welfare during the riots. It seemed that some lessons just hadn't been learnt.

The government report into the 2011 rioting – 'The Rules of Engagement' – found that officers and commanders on the frontline were often found to be 'uncertain about the level of force and tactics that can be used'. The inquiry also stated that 'training had been insufficient; they [the police] therefore erred on the safe side, using less forceful tactics, and standing their ground rather than going forward to tackle disorder.'

In the course of researching this book I spoke to many officers and rather than being 'uncertain about the level of force…that can be used', it seemed to me that their unwillingness to use physical force stemmed from the fact they were worried about being hung out to dry for just doing their job. There was real and widespread concern that individuals' actions could result in them being used as a scapegoat at the first sign of a complaint.

When asked, 83% of the public believed that it was the actions of the police that brought the riots to an end. However, 60% believed that the police could have ended the rioting quicker, and 49% of people believed that the police did not use enough force.

The police themselves estimated that they would need between three and five police officers for every rioter in order to make arrests and deal with the disturbances. But the police were almost always outnumbered, and in the middle of the riots protecting lives and property had to come before arrests, which often meant rioters were moved on from one location to another rather than being taken off the streets.

But after the riots, the response to the criminality was swift and relentless. The police went on the offensive. By September – just four weeks after the riots – almost 4,000 people from all walks of life had been detained across the country, thanks largely to CCTV footage, and more arrests would follow. In fact, so many were arrested so quickly that courts had to be kept open for 24 hours a day to cope with the criminals, and tough sentences were dished out. (At the time of the 2011 riots, there were around 140,000 police officers in England and Wales. Today that number has dropped to around 126,000 and is at its lowest level since 1987.)

During these four days of rioting, over 300 police officers were injured. More than 2,500 commercial premises were attacked, many of which were looted and set alight. Livelihoods and businesses – large corporations as well as small, locally owned shops – were ruined. In all, it was estimated that 48,000 businesses in England suffered financially in one way or another due to the rioting and looting. Financially, the disorder cost the country hundreds of millions of pounds.

Ten police forces recorded crime related to the disturbances, but it was London that suffered most, with 68% of all the offences.

In London, 200 people were displaced due to their homes

being destroyed, damaged or burnt to a point where they were beyond being habitable.

Most tragically of all, five people were killed.

Four years on from the riots, Avon and Somerset Constabulary disbanded their Support Group (their equivalent of the Met's TSG). I was told that some officers had handed in their 'tickets' after the riots, no longer willing to be public order trained.

Nigel has retired from the police and now teaches public order techniques to police forces around the world.

In Birmingham, Chris's short, ginger 'Viking' beard is now 'wizard length'. His rebel streak has extended from his beard to a hipster topknot (he firmly believes that the police are not robots or just a uniform). He didn't receive any commendations for his actions during the riots but used some of the extra money he earned to pay off some debts. He has recently passed his sergeant's exam.

The Cambridgeshire officers never received any commendations for the work they did in London during the riots, 'Not even a thank you.' Although they are quite certain that they have now successfully removed all the 'I'VE MET THE MET' stickers from their carriers (maybe they have, maybe they haven't), Mark still can't figure out how one found its way to the ceiling of his public order training building in Cambridge, 35 feet up.

Richard, the TSG sergeant who had been so incensed at not being called into work, stopped attending his riot training sessions at the Metropolitan Police Public Order Training Centre at Gravesend. Despite remaining a TSG sergeant, he could see no point in having wooden blocks and flaming petrol bombs thrown at him – if they weren't going to use him in an actual riot, what was he training for? He has now retired from the police.

Rachel, from Peckham, who watched through the windows as rioters threw petrol bombs at her police station, left the police in 2015 to start a new career as an airline pilot.

Tom, who had fought so bravely in both Tottenham and Croydon, resigned from the Metropolitan Police a few years later. His experiences during the riots – officers being left to fend for themselves, unfed, and with no water – and other events afterwards left him feeling that the organisation didn't care about its officers. He now runs a personal training and life coaching company.

The small band of Sutton officers, who courageously charged hundreds of rioters and prevented Sutton from being overrun, were all awarded commendations for bravery, either from the Metropolitan Police Commissioner or from their own Borough Commander – Detective Chief Superintendent Guy Ferguson.

Detective Chief Superintendent Guy Ferguson himself, who stood shoulder to shoulder with his officers, has since retired from the police after 32 years service. After the riots he received a Commissioner's Commendation for bravery, professionalism and dedication to duty. It was his second Commissioner's Commendation, having received one in 2002 for his leadership at the Ladbroke Grove rail crash.

The handful of officers who defended the Catford retail park against overwhelming odds all received commendations for bravery.

Sergeant Darin Birmingham, who saw action in Hackney, Ealing and Newham, retired from the police in 2013 having served for 30 years. Never one to 'suffer fools' or tolerate 'poor leadership', Darin continues to be outspoken and holds strong views, particularly around matters involving London gangs, and has appeared on Sky News.

Inspector Walpole continues to serve as a relief inspector at Hounslow. He and the officers he had fought side-by-side with were awarded Commissioner's Commendations for bravery and professionalism for their actions at Tottenham on the first night of the riots.

In Ealing, the borough commander, Detective Chief Superintendent Andy Rowell, who had himself worked throughout the troubles on his own borough, awarded 173 individual commendations to police officers, police staff, and a member of the public. Robin (The Terminator), Sergeant Ashton and Michelle were included in these awards, receiving commendations for bravery. Robin retired reluctantly in 2015, having given the public and the police nearly 37 years of his life.

Keith, who battled against overwhelming numbers in Hackney, was promoted, and is now a sergeant with the Metropolitan Police. He, along with other officers who had fought so bravely in Hackney, never received a commendation.

Other officers have gone on to be promoted in rank and /or moved to different boroughs or departments within the police.

The bus driver from Lewisham, whose bus was commandeered, was 'written up' by the officers he transported around south London, and he received a bravery commendation for his actions from the Lewisham Borough Commander.

As well as police officers, animals were also recognised for their courage during the riots. It is easy to claim that animals have no choice when they enter violent situations, and that they are blindly doing what their handlers are telling them to. However, I do not believe this is the case. Yes, they are trained and they are disciplined, but these animals still have the will and ability to turn away and run, to escape and hide from danger. In a riot, you might think that is what their instincts would tell them to do.

But it didn't happen. Police dogs and horses stayed on the frontline with their handlers and riders because their loyalty to those men and women mattered far more than any danger they might face on the streets, and then they carried on despite the violence and missiles that were aimed at them. Not all dogs and horses make it through their initial training and assessments, and only the best and bravest are used. To claim that they are not courageous is wrong.

After the riots, the charity, PDSA – People's Dispensary for Sick Animals – decided to create an award for animals that had worked bravely during the disturbances. The PDSA Order of Merit – also known as an 'Animal OBE' – was awarded to a number of animals including Obi, the police dog who suffered a fractured skull after being hit in the head with a brick at Tottenham. Obi was also awarded a Special Animal Bravery Award from IFAW – the International Fund for Animal Welfare. Ten police horses received an Order of Merit award from the PDSA for their actions in Tottenham.

In February 2015 – just three and a half years after the riots – the *London Evening Standard* newspaper reported that since the disturbances, London rioters had committed close to another 6,000 criminal offences. These offences included 12 murders, 665 assaults (including 180 woundings and GBHs) 54 sexual offences (including 21 rapes), 719 burglaries, 451 robberies, 1,075 theft offences and 1,819 drug offences.

Darrell Desuze, the youth who punched and killed Richard Mannington Bowes in Ealing, was arrested and charged. He was found guilty of manslaughter and sentenced to eight years imprisonment. He also pleaded guilty to violent disorder and burglary. During the riots, as well as killing a man, Desuze had attacked and looted a number of premises including Tesco Express, Blockbuster Video, Fat Boys Thai restaurant and William Hill bookmakers.

His 31-year-old mother Lavinia was also arrested for perverting the course of justice after she tried to protect her son by cutting up and dumping the clothing he had worn that night. She was sentenced to 18 months imprisonment.

The murder of Trevor Ellis – the man who was shot in the head following a car chase with looters in Croydon – remains unsolved. Although a number of arrests have been made, no one has been charged with his killing. Despite there being three cars of witnesses, a substantial police reward and emotional appeals by his mother, no one has come forward with information.

The handgun used to kill Trevor Ellis was found almost a year later while police were searching a house in Croydon in relation to another inquiry.

Although there is no suggestion that Ellis had been involved in the stealing himself, the two friends that he had been with in the car that night were later jailed for looting at the Cash Converters store in Croydon.

Eight men were arrested and charged with the murders of Abdul Musavir, Shazad Ali and Haroon Jahan, who were run down while protecting businesses in Birmingham. It was claimed by the prosecution that the eight men had set out to deliberately run down and kill pedestrians that night, with the allegation that the Fiesta and the Audi were there to lure people onto the street and then the Mazda would run them down. The eight men were all acquitted of murder and released. Afterwards, the judge described the deaths of the three men as being 'a terrible accident'. The man who had been driving the Mazda, claimed that he had been good friends with brothers Musavir and Ali, and had never intended to run them down.

Tariq Jahan, the father of Haroon Jahan, who came out to help the victims without realising that one of them was his own son, appeared on television just hours after the men's death. With anger growing, talk of a race war and further trouble, he appealed for calm and was later credited with preventing further disturbances and even bringing an end to the rioting. He was praised by many and later received a Pride of Britain award. However, he has since become a critic of the handling of the deaths of the three men and is now appealing for a further inquiry.

A few months after Shazad Ali's death, his wife gave birth to their son.

Five men and one 17-year-old boy were arrested and convicted following the ambush of police in Birmingham. In all, 12 shots were fired from four separate guns at police on the ground as well at the police helicopter that was filming the incident from above. The five men were convicted of riot, arson and firearms offences while the teenager was convicted of riot and firearms offences but not arson. The men – Nicholas Francis, Tyrone Laidley, Jermaine Lewis, Wayne Collins and Renardo Farrell – were given jail sentences of between 18 and 30 years. The 17-year-old, Amirul Rehman, was sentenced to 12 years.

A few months later, two more men were arrested in connection to the shootings and convicted of riot and firearms offences. Wesley Gray was sentenced to 29 years imprisonment and Beniha Laing was given 35 years.

Two women were also arrested and charged with possession of

firearms. Nadeen Banbury was given five years and Janine Francis sentenced to seven-and-a-half years.

Gordon Thompson, the man who set fire to Reeves Corner, was arrested and charged with arson and burglary. At the Old Bailey, after initially denying the claims, he changed his plea to guilty and was sentenced to 11-and-a-half years in jail. Thompson, a father of two, was a career criminal with a violent past. He had been arrested numerous times for offences including armed robbery, domestic assault on his wife, possession of knives and drugs, car theft and shoplifting, and had been jailed a number of times previously.

He originally tried to claim that he was attempting to prevent people from looting the store at Reeves Corner. However, he was caught on camera a number of times looting other stores around Croydon, even posing for a photographer while holding stolen items. His photograph then appeared on the front page of the local newspaper, and Thompson was easily identified.

Monika Konczyk, the Polish lady who had leapt for her life from her burning flat, provided evidence that was used at Thompson's trial. She still lives and works in Croydon.

Reeves furniture store continues to operate out of smaller premises, opposite the original location.

The Carpet Right store in Tottenham was beyond saving. It was knocked down but rebuild to its original 1930s design and reopened two years later.

The media largely ignored Woolwich, which saw the retreat of police officers and the burning down of the Great Harry pub. One news channel had shown video footage of the rioting, although it was described incorrectly as being from Liverpool. A local councillor described Woolwich as being 'airbrushed' out of history. It wasn't even mentioned in the Metropolitan Police's official report into the riots – 'Four Days in August' – other than a line to say that its tube station had been closed. The treatment of Woolwich is perhaps testimony to just how much was happening around the city and the country, all at the same time. On any other day riot police retreating from a violent mob, which then burned down an entire pub would be national news. It makes you wonder how many other places were being bravely fought for by outnumbered police officers, but which no one ever heard about.

A 16-year-old was arrested for the fire at the Great Harry pub and received a four-year sentence for the arson. Fire crews would eventually reach the pub, battling the flames through the night and well into the following morning. The building, though gutted, was saved and the Great Harry pub has since reopened.

Labour MP Heidi Alexander, whose office was attacked and looted in Lee High Road, perhaps echoing the feelings of many, had this to say about the rioters when she spoke about them in Parliament three days later: 'These riots are primarily a result of disaffected, marginalised youths who wanted a ruck. They are the result of mindless idiots who capitalised on an opportunity to nick some trainers from JD Sports or a plasma TV from Argos. Whilst the initial catalyst for the riots in Tottenham may have been anger at the police, I suspect the person who smashed up my constituency office window wouldn't even know who Mark Duggan was.'

Despite the extreme level of violence and destruction, baton gunners were never deployed, and water cannon is still just a political topic. The rioters and the looters were defeated by brave, daring, willing, tenacious officers, who repeatedly put themselves in harm's way, who risked their lives and continued to battle on for hour after hour, day after day, with little thought given to their health or wellbeing. Unfed, thirsty, with just snatches of rest, and many carrying injuries, these men and women stepped up, faced the violent mobs, faced the continual barrage of missiles falling down on them, faced knives, guns and other weapons – all while protected by only a baton, a plastic shield (if they even had that) and a whole lot of guts. They truly were a thin blue line, but in the end they won.

The country, the government and the senior police leadership owe those frontline officers a huge debt.

Police rank structure

All are listed in ascending order:

Constable (Police or Detective – PC / DC)
Sergeant (Police or Detective – PS / DS)
Inspector (Police or Detective – Insp / DI)
Chief Inspector (Police or Detective – Ch Insp / DCI)
Superintendent (Police or Detective – Supt. / D/Supt)
Chief Superintendent (Police or Detective – Ch Supt / DCS)

After this rank, the structure changes according to the force:

London Metropolitan Police Service:
Commander
Deputy Assistant Commissioner (DAC)
Assistant Commissioner (AC)
Deputy Commissioner
Commissioner

City of London Police:
Commander
Assistant Commissioner
Commissioner

County Forces:
Assistant Chief Constable
Deputy Chief Constable
Chief Constable

Glossary

AEP: Attenuating energy projectile. More commonly known as a baton round, or a plastic or rubber bullet, which is fired from a Baton gun. Used in Northern Ireland for decades, it has never been used on mainland Britain. It was a considered tactical option during these riots but went unused.

Area Car: Driven by level 1 or 2 police drivers. A larger and more powerful police response vehicle than an IRV. These cars are often BMWs.

ASP: Extendable friction lock metal baton.

Baton / Shield charge: A tactical option, of coordinating a line or group of officers to charge at rioters.

Baton: Long, police baton. Different styles used by different forces. Some are acrylic, others are metal and have American-style side-handles.

Carrier / Bus: term used for a riot carrier, often adapted Mercedes Sprinter vans.

EAB: Evidence and Actions Book. A small pocket book where officers record incidents and arrests.

GMP: Greater Manchester Police

Gold, Silver, Bronze command structure: A command and control framework created after the murder of PC Keith

Blakelock at Broadwater Farm, where it was found that the usual rank system had failed. The gold (strategic), silver (tactical) and bronze (operational) system is about role rather than rank and should make it clearer as to who is in charge or control.

Guv / Guv'nor: Slang term commonly used for Police Inspectors.

I-Grade / Immediate Response: More urgent incidents and calls for police assistance that require a quicker response, usually involving blue lights and sirens.

Intermediate shield: A shield that is longer and wider than a short, round shield but is not body length. Many county forces use these rather than a combination of long and short shields.

IRV: Immediate Response Vehicle – at the time of the riots these cars were often Vauxhall Astras.

Jankel: Metropolitan police armoured vehicle, primarily used by firearms units.

Level 1 public order officer: TSG officers. Highest level of riot / public order training

Level 2 public order officer: Riot / public order trained. Non-TSG officers volunteer for this level of training.

Level 3 public order officer: Basic level of public order training that all officers receive.

Long shield: Long, body length, clear plastic shields.

Mutual Aid: A provision whereby one force supplies officers to another, usually during a major event or disturbance.

PC: Police Constable – the first rank within the police.

PCSO: Police Community Support Officer – introduced by Home Secretary David Blunkett, PCSOs, sometimes referred to as 'Blunkett's Bobbies', are uniformed officers who work alongside and support police officers but with fewer powers.

PSU: Police Support Unit. A full PSU is a group of Level 2 officers, made of 1 Inspector, 3 Sergeants, 18 Constables, plus 2 medics and 3 drivers (for three carriers that the officers are separated into. These three carriers will patrol and work together as one complete PSU).

Q Car: unmarked robbery patrol cars.

Running Lines: Three rows of short or intermediate shield officers.

Section file: Two rows of officers. Front row would consist of three pairs of long shied officers, with a rear row of short shield officers.

Service / Force mobilisation: All duty Level 2 public order officers are gathered and deployed to scenes of disorder.

Short shield: Small, round, clear plastic shield.

Skipper / 'Skip': slang terms commonly used for Police Sergeant.

SO19 / CO19 (now SC&O19): Specialist Firearms Command. Known as CO19 at the time of Mark Duggan's shooting.

Special Constable / 'Specials': unpaid, uniformed volunteers with the same powers as a regular police officer.

TSG / CO20: Territorial Support Group. Full-time "elite" Level 1 public order trained officers. They are separated across 5 areas of London. Hence, 1TSG (or 1-Area TSG), 2TSG, 3TSG etc.

Acknowledgements

I would like to say a huge thank you to all the officers who spoke to me about their involvements in the policing of the riots. These were very personal experiences and the fact that people took the time to talk to me and tell me about what they went through is very much appreciated. I will refrain from mentioning by name all those I spoke with, firstly because some names and details have been changed – at the officers' requests – or secondly, because they already appear throughout the book. But thank you all.

Many thanks to my agent and publisher Humfrey Hunter, who is always a pleasure to work with and who, once again, has taken one of my ideas and run with it, encouraging and counselling me along the way.

Thank you to my mother, father and brother David, for their continued support. Hello to Jake, Evie, Dexter (another book you are too young to read!) and Nathan. Welcome to the world, Naomi and Bennett – it's an interesting place. 'Salut,' Ethan.

A number of other people have assisted me despite their better instincts probably telling them otherwise. Thank you to Sandie Walpole, Brian, Arron, James, Katy, Kev, Gareth, Janie, Milly, Christine, Paul, Neil, Dick, Ryan, Andy, Graham Wettone, Ellie and Katie's dad (who has actually been helpful for once) and Guy.

Finally, I would like to thank my ever calm, supportive, incredible wife, Lisa. Every day is that much easier, that much more interesting and that much more fantastic because you are in it with me. I love you.

Printed in Great Britain
by Amazon

65174232R00180